D1390341

'The author is surely right on three ___ ___ ___ book. Firstly, that there are no uni ___ fighting world poverty; all problen ___ therefore be local, although internat. ___ the main participants in the debate on world development ___ ___ nomic growth have taken their eyes off the ball of assuring the survival of the poorest and meeting their basic needs. Thirdly, that given the current state of global economy, things will get much worse before they get any better. I know that he speaks with great personal experience and knowledge and commend him for his common-sense approach.' **Timothy T. Thahane,** *Former Vice President and Secretary of the World Bank and now Minister of Finance and Development Planning in Lesotho.*

'It is a really important, engaging and stimulating book; it both needs to be published and debated. I really appreciated the blend of seasoned observation and grasp of macroeconomics. Your clear eyed understanding of what sham government in the poorest countries represent; the single issue and wrong headed charity and NGO activity; the three very basic wants that the truly impoverished require to be met, all these themes come through loud and clear. I was interested in your grassroots level proposals for assisted investment.' **Maggie Brown,** *Media editor of the Guardian.*

'This is an important contribution to the development debate, written by someone who has huge experience as a thinker and practitioner around these issues. His general thesis is that there is a real danger that the significant gains which we have seen in the past decade or two are at risk – from the economic downturn, from climate change and from population growth. You will not agree with everything in it; I hazard a guess that Mr Dembitzer would be disappointed if you did. But it does what a good book should do – it makes you think'. **Myles Wickstead,** *Visiting Professor (International Relations), Open University, and former Head of Secretariat, Commission for Africa.*

'I think the setting out of the problem is masterly. The prose is powerful, concise, clear. The book tackles complicated issues with great simplicity and force... the book outlines some very practical steps that people of good will, and there are millions of them, could take to start improving the situation in the immediate future.' **John M.Lonsdale,** *Emeritus Professor of Modern African History, University of Cambridge.*

'It is difficult to agree with the whole of the book's thesis. Things are getting better in Africa and all change is slow. But at the same time the author does understand poverty at the level where it matters and many of his comments and deductions are correct both in theory and in practice. To me the book raises the basic questions that need urgently to be addressed; how will African leaders confront the growing challenges? how will the leaders of the rich world face up to the harm that has been caused to many fragile economies in the past and continues to this day? I would strongly recommend the book as essential readings for the activists who supported the MAKE POVERTY HISTORY campaign in 2005.' **Dr Adotey Bing-Pappoe,** *former Director of the Africa Centre of London and consultant to NEPAD.*

'A personal inquiry into world poverty by someone of unusually wide experience with stimulating ideas for a less bleak future.' **Johnny Grimond,** *writer-at-large and former Foreign Editor of the Economist.*

Benny Dembitzer has been involved in the field of economic and social development in the South for the last forty years. He studied economics at Cambridge under Amartya Sen, and subsequently followed him briefly in teaching at Trinity College in the mid 1960s. He was on the staff of the Economist Intelligence Unit in London for three and a half years. He directed the work of the Fund for Research and Investment for the Development of Africa (FRIDA) in twenty African countries in the 1970s. At the Commonwealth Secretariat he was for two years adviser on industrial development in the (then) nine Southern Africa

Development Coordination Conference (SADCC) Countries.

Over the years he has worked in 35 countries in Africa and 2 in Asia. They include Pakistan for the Aga Khan; Ethiopia for the United Nations Industrial Development Organization (UNIDO); Lesotho for the International Trade Centre (ITC); Djibouti for the World Bank; Guinea and Indonesia for the United Nations Development Programme (UNDP). He also drafted the UNDP five-year economic development plans for both The Gambia and Liberia. For five years he was economic adviser to the Dutch aid programme in Indonesia. He worked as a consultant for the Department for International Development (DfID) on Fairtrade. He 2003 he worked with UNAIDS in London and Addis Ababa.

He has worked for various voluntary agencies, including OXFAM in Ethiopia; CARE International in Lesotho; International Voluntary Service (IVS; now Skillshare Africa) in Botswana, Cameroun, Lesotho and Swaziland; War on Want in Cameroun. In the early 1970s he undertook undercover missions for Amnesty International in Gabon, Cameroun and Chad. He set up the first shop in London dealing with what is now called Fairtrade in 1973. He was European Director of International Physicians for the Prevention of Nuclear War (IPPNW) when it was awarded the Nobel Peace Prize in 1985. He undertook consultancies for Transparency International, UK, on corruption in the arms trade. In 1985 he became involved with relief operations kick-started by Bob Geldof in Ethiopia.

From 1987 to 2006 he ran the annual GLOBAL PARTNERSHIP, an event bringing together some hundreds of British voluntary agencies working in development. During 2007 and 2008 he was economic adviser to Africa Invest, a fund investing in agriculture in Malawi. Over the last 10 years he has taught economics at various times at Cranfield, London SouthBank, Greenwich and London Metropolitan Universities. He currently runs courses in London on international development for staff of a variety of voluntary agencies and others interested in the problems of the Global South.

BENNY DEMBITZER

THE ATTACK ON WORLD POVERTY

...going back to basics

ETHICAL EVENTS LIMITED
IN ASSOCIATION WITH
GREEN PRINT

Published in the UK 2009 by ETHICAL EVENTS Ltd
in association with Green Print

Green Print is an imprint of The Merlin Press Ltd
6, Crane Street Chambers, Crane Street, Pontypool, Wales NP4 0AA
www.merlinpress.co.uk

Ethical Events Ltd, PO Box 2800, London SE24 9NU
www.ethical-events.org

ISBN 978 1 85425 099 5

2 4 6 8 10 9 7 5 3

Cover design and typesetting by Giles Powell-Smith.

———————————

Ethical Events is a not-for-profit entity established in 2000
to promote a better understanding of the issues confronting
the poor world. Directors; Benny Dembitzer, Bertukan Aberra Dembitzer,
Leah Saba Dembitzer. It organises courses and events related to
this theme that are detailed on the website:
www.ethical-events.org

Join the debate at: **www.attackworldpoverty.blogspot.com**

Contents

PART THREE Living in a Changing World

PART FOUR The Agenda for Change

To Bertukan, Leah, Simone and Sophia

THE ATTACK ON WORLD POVERTY

Thanks

Over the last six years I have submitted drafts of this and earlier versions of the book to many kind friends and former colleagues. I am very grateful to them all. I list some of them because they have tolerated me more than most.

Chris Forssander challenged me over and over again about the logic and clarity of my arguments and helped me redraft many sections of the book. Alastair Bowman looked in great detail at a previous version. Suzanna Blackmore of OXFAM Publishing read a very early version of this book and was most encouraging. Other people who read earlier versions include Dr Ros Hembry of the University of East Anglia; Professor John Lonsdale of Cambridge University; John Burley, formerly director of Finance and Administration at the UN Conference on Trade and Development and before that in various posts in the UN Development Programme and in Uganda; Peter Kellner, President of YouGov; Dr Roger Maconick who was my colleague in Ethiopia; Duncan Parker who worked for the Salvation Army in various parts of the world and currently for cru Investment Management in Malawi; Laurence Cockcroft who is Africa adviser to the Gatsby Trust; Makonnen Wodajeneh who is student mentor at Redbridge College; Laurie Lee who represents the Gates Foundation in the UK. They all read the manuscript in its entirety and made most useful comments. I also must thank Nick Earle for his general encouragement; Lynn Champion, Jules Levin, Bob Hilliard, Terry Brownhill, Julian Filochowski, formerly director of the Catholic Agency for Overseas development (CAFOD), and Nigel Watt for comments on parts of earlier drafts of the manuscript. Dr Tim Thahane, Minister of Development Planning and Finance of Lesotho and Dr Adotey Bing made useful comments to this version.

Charlotte Judet has been an incredibly helpful editor. Kirsty Sanders has done the sub-editing. They both challenged many of my expressions. Giles Powell-Smith has designed an impressive cover and undertook the layout of the book. My daughter Leah produced the index and asked many pertinent questions. My wife Bertukan has patiently supported me throughout and never demurred.

Half of my family is from the South; this has given me an insight into a very different society from my own. Barriers have been eliminated that otherwise would have existed in talking to people of other societies. I have tried to look at development through the eyes of friends and colleagues in the South. Instead of simply taking an academic approach in this book I have relied on experiences that I have gained and that others have gained from working at the grassroots. I have also taken liberally from essays in journals and newspapers because they give a sense of the real lives of people and what is befalling them. I have passed sections of this book to friends from the South whose comments have often been included; the anonymity of some of them has been protected. The conclusions are purely my own.

London, August 2009

A note on the text

Most of the poor people in the world live in the Northern hemisphere as do most of the rich. There are both poor and wealthy countries in the Southern hemisphere as well, such as Zambia and Australia. By convention, however, one tends to refer to the rich North and the poor South. Within this book it has sometimes been necessary to generalise rather than refer to individual countries or specific regions so I have chosen to use the simple geographic division of the North/Northern and the South/Southern to refer to the rich countries and the poor countries respectively.

Both North and South are shorthand expressions for the many actors involved. There are governments, intergovernmental agencies, voluntary organisations, churches, individuals. For most people in the South someone who comes from the North does not wear a badge that automatically identifies him or her and defines them as being different from someone else. For this reason I have simply put everyone together in the book.

I have tried to use the word DEVELOPMENT (in capitals) to indicate the view from the top – the process that occurs on paper, through statistics and in the calculations of policy-making and aid by donors and international organisations – and development (in lower case) as the process that affects (most of the time, does not) people at the bottom of the pyramid. It has not been possible to be totally consistent and I ask for the reader's understanding.

List of abbreviations

BRIC	Brazil, Russia, India, China
BRAC	Bangladesh Rural Advancement Committee
CSR	Corporate Social Responsibility
DfID	Department for International Development
ECOWAS	Economic Community of West African States
FAO	Food and Agricultural Organization of the UN
FDI	Foreign Direct Investment
G8	the seven richest countries in the world plus Russia
G20	the 20 richest countries in the world
GNI	Gross National Income
IFI	International Financial Institutions
IFPRI	International Food Policy Research Institute
IIED	International Institute for Environment and Development
IPCC	International Panel on Climate Change
MDG	the Millennium Development Goals
NGO	Non-governmental organisation
OECD	Organisation for Economic Cooperation and Development
PPP	Purchasing Power Parity
UN	United Nations Organization
UNDP	United Nations Development Programme
UNESCO	United Nations Educational, Scientific and Cultural Organization
WHO	World Health Organization

INTRODUCTION

Why another book on global poverty?

For over 50 years there have been attempts – some not very determined, some more serious – to tackle world poverty. Very little, if anything, has fundamentally changed in most of the poorest countries. What are the reasons? Have policy-makers of the world not tried hard enough? Have they used the wrong tools? Have world events defeated the objectives of those who are concerned? This book tries to look squarely at some of the problems of development that everyone – from the South and from the North – have tried, and are still trying, to address and some that we are all avoiding altogether.

Some societies are resisting change because they have a deeply ingrained resistance to change per se. In India the caste system makes it likely that for many more centuries India's majority will remain extremely poor, indeed the lower castes are likely to remain in virtual slavery to the richer members of society. In other societies global warming will bring gradual, but probably accelerating, catastrophe. This is true for Bangladesh, half of which is predicted to be under water within 30 years, for the Maldives, and most of the island states in the Pacific. Not a single one of the six countries in the Sahel belt of Africa is ever likely to develop, for a very simple geographical reason: the Sahara is advancing. In other societies what the North thinks is necessary to underpin development, such as basic democracy and working institutions, is unlikely ever to emerge. Sudan, Somalia and the Democratic Republic of Congo are among these. There are forces and interests of such magnitude that the flows of funds escaping the

1

poor world are far greater than the total aid the North gives to the South. The arms trade, the flight of international capital to offshore locations, the repayment of interest on capital borrowed and the payments of dues to patent owners primarily based in rich countries under international licence and copyright agreements – each of these is larger than the total amount of aid the North gives to the South.

The tools the North has been using in the pursuit of its own development, and has thus urged others to use, are not adequate to solve the current challenges of world poverty. Good institutions are based on a sense of shared responsibility for the common good – a range of attitudes that include loyalty to the nation to which you belong, a sense of common aims and mutual trust and an obligation towards others. These are Northern ideas and, by and large, not common across the globe. Not because other people are not good or kind or do not care about their fellow human beings, but because the channels through which such obligations and duties can be manifested vary from society to society. In the North people are kind (sometimes) to others they do not know. In other societies extended family and clan loyalties are the recipients of generosity. The North has reached a stage of economic development through a series of particular events and accidents but there is no reason to believe that the accidents that have led countries in the North to be where they are will necessarily occur or be recreated in other societies. Globalisation has been a tool of economic development that has suited the North. But this very globalisation that has benefited the North and some other countries, including China, Malaysia, Indonesia and South Korea, has led to global food shortage as an unintended consequence. Those who have nothing to trade with cannot buy food. They have to grow it on land that is becoming more difficult to till and fertilise. The rich world gives food to those who are starving – food purchased in the North. This process has underpinned the production of farmers in the North and destroyed farming in the South.

The world has been trying to solve the wrong problems. There are three sets of issues that should be top of the agenda if we all want to help the poorest pull themselves out of poverty. Firstly, population growth is out of control. Ethiopia has an estimated six million people going hungry in 'normal' years. By 2050 the country will have a population of around 140 million, twice the current population. How many millions will regularly starve in 'bad' years? The funds from the Gates or Clinton Foundations to combat HIV/AIDS and malaria keep more people alive only for them to die of starvation later on in life. Secondly, for most of the poor world, governments do not work – they work only for those who are in government. 'Government' in those countries works by default against the interest of the poorest. For most people of the South governments are a nightmare, a Kafkaesque construction, a form of organisation that has been created by the North that suits cultures that have managed to create or maintain a sense of national homogeneity. Thirdly, most policy-makers think that economics is a self-correcting system and that a balance between demand and supply of basic goods needed by the poorest will be achieved through the mechanisms now in existence in societies of the North. They won't: the economies of the poorer countries need specific targets and management to ensure equitable economic development. Free economic activity will not lead to progress.

The world needs to revert to the key target that was set in the 1950s and early 1960s. The clear target then was the end of world poverty. Over the last 45 years or so, policy-makers and politicians in the North and in the South, but above all in the World Bank, IMF and other institutions dominated by the North, have moved away from that clear and focused aim. The world has become a much more complex place. We have witnessed the coming of independence to poor countries, the emergence and then disappearance of the Cold War, the explosive growth in the price of oil, a doubling of the world's population in the last 50 years, the phenomenon of globalisation, the decreasing importance of the West in international affairs, the emergence of global terrorism. Trying to cope with these issues has made the focus less clear and caused the main actors to move away from the central issue of addressing world poverty. This has resulted in policy changes across the board detrimental to the poor, for example, the dismantling of the structures that would have led to more agricultural development and support for poor farmers. The World Bank and the IMF have been caught in this maelstrom of forces and, in trying to maintain their roles, have marginalised other institutions that, given more power, could have achieved more – including, for example, the Food and Agriculture Organization of the UN (FAO). Preoccupations with financial rectitude, with industrialisation, with finance for international trade, with globalisation, and so on, have all led to the abandonment of the priority of ensuring that the poorest people can enjoy the first human right – the right to survive. Most international agencies work fundamentally to build their own empires and protect their territories.

Policy-makers need to move away from the blind acceptance that economics, as the North understands it, should dominate the analysis of development needs, problems, issues and solutions. A holistic approach to society is needed. Yes, we need economic development, for the poorest in particular; 'It's economics, stupid' was the catch phrase of President Clinton's first bid for the White House in 1992. But not everyone is in the world of economic growth; almost one third of global population is in the world of hand-to-mouth survival. The process of democratisation is something that Northern intelligentsia love, but it has failed even in societies that everyone believed were on their way to becoming more successful, such as Kenya or Pakistan. It has fragmented those societies; the very process of liberalisation in the terms that the North has defined that process has set back the ultimate aims of that same process. The North loves human rights. But such human rights (individual rights would be a better expression) militate against the interests of society at large. The one-child policy of China is unpalatable to many Westerners, but it has been one of the key elements in raising living standards across China and has liberated women by enabling them to enter the labour force and earn their own money. (Britain had the parallel experience of the entry of women into the labour force during the First World War.) With a few exceptions there is very little effective democracy across Africa; it is skin deep. There is certainly more apparent democracy but also more corruption because political parties can only survive by squeezing any source of income – be it from the state, foreign aid donors, their own business people or their own citizens.

Why has the North not understood what is happening and found the right remedies? The main reason is that it has applied its understanding of what works in the North to other societies as if the world were ruled by one economic system. But the world is made up of four major economic groups that move at different speeds and are propelled by different engines. The OECD economies benefit from growth and integration and thus globalisation. The BRIC countries (Brazil, Russia, India and China) are large and fast-moving with little effective democracy and strong interventionist governments. The resource-rich world is buying into the first world because it is generating more revenue than it can use and consume sensibly. The fourth world is the poor world and is in danger of remaining on the outside forever. The first world's priorities are very different from those of the fourth world; the North is not starving.

The war on world poverty is currently not succeeding because it needs to be fought at three different levels, but is being fought at only two, those that are least relevant. The first of these is the grand opera – the United Nations and international gatherings where important people talk to other important people. The second is the quicksand of bureaucracy, where people who think they are important use up all the available resources to convince one another of what they should be doing and how they should be doing whatever they do. They fly from one meeting to the next and produce endless new papers and logical frameworks. Voluntary organisations from the West are part of this quicksand; their (head office) staffs often add to the problems and not to the solutions. They are not encouraging self-sufficiency but ongoing dependence instead. Then there is the third level: the village – where everything should happen and nothing does. There the attack on poverty fails; the village remains deeply isolated, deeply conservative and in the throes of feudal forces.

The current recipe is 'more of the same' and that will lead to continuing failure. Different tools are required to cope with the real challenges; they would include local democracy (it is opposed by the elites because it would work against their interests), more local participation in local and regional policy-making, and reshaping the mandate of international institutions. Most importantly, in order to attack world poverty, the world needs to concentrate its efforts at the village level. The focus should be on education, which will enable people to understand the confines of the societies in which they live and will be the first step towards liberty and human rights. Introducing universal primary education would cost approximately the same as Europeans spend annually on ice cream[1]. Policy-makers need to encourage social organisations such as mutual societies, savings institutions, cooperatives and other social mechanisms that enabled groups of individuals to stand up to their rulers. The North has abandoned such organisations because it has moved on. Yet, most societies in the poor world need to rediscover them. Then the world needs to concentrate on generating economic growth because that is the engine of development of society. As people become less poor, they become freer. Activists need to change their approach. They should not be fascinated by 'development at the global level' that raises issues that few theoreticians, let alone those pop stars who become UN goodwill ambassadors, understand at all. They should deal with the local needs of different target groups. The poor are not a homogeneous group – they are collections, sometime very large, of individuals with very different needs. Refugees, the handicapped, nomads, minority castes and tribes, the very young and the very old, and women in most parts of the world need to be helped in terms specific to their needs. There is no universal solution to the problems of world poverty. The poor world needs 'smart aid'.

Both very large and very small changes in domestic policy in the rich world are needed; for example, on the one hand, changes in EU import rules and subsidies to agriculture and, on the other, changes in the way Britain recruits staff from abroad for the NHS and schools. Global trade rules are shaped by much more powerful interests than goodwill of well-intentioned people. Good people will not be able to change the operations of the World Trade Organization (WTO), even with President Obama in the White House. So, let activists give up attempting change at the grand opera level; they should instead concentrate on being more efficient midwifes of economic development at the grassroots. Let rich people give up little bits of charity and create more economic opportunities. Aid has become an extension of welfare, and that does not create long-term empowerment. 'Smart' investment might just do it. Above all, the North and powerful new-comers like China, should allow communities in the poor South develop in ways of their own choosing and back them in their efforts. They need 'development' at the right level and not 'DEVELOPMENT" as an evaluation of progress through statistical and political estimates that do not reflect change at the base. Human rights do matter, but in the first phase of confronting survival, the world should spend more effort on ensuring collective social organisations. Individual rights will emerge when individuals have escaped the deepest level of poverty.

PART ONE

Poverty
The Intractable Problem

Because the primary intermediaries between poor people in the South and richer people in the North are the media and the voluntary organisations, both of which are hardly unbiased vehicles of information, most people do not properly understand the challenges of development and the reality of poverty and underdevelopment. Poverty becomes almost a romantic state of affairs.

Let us go back and look at some of the realities. If the physical environment in which you live is inimical to long-term growth, if the structures of your society limit personal development, and if rules of international trade (by omission or commission) work against your needs, things look pretty hopeless. There are many parts of the world that may never develop; the base on which any economic prosperity can happen is totally absent. The real challenge is still to find ways in which the problems that exist can be tackled in the context in which they arise.

Let us start by looking briefly at what the real challenges are in the physical, human and global domains.

THE POOREST TWENTY COUNTRIES (data for 2006) From the World Bank Annual report 2008						
	A	B	C	D	E	F	G
Country	Population (million)	% growth 2000-06	$ per capita	% Pop below $1 @ day	% Pop below $2 @ day	$ PPP GNI per capita	% of children under 5 malnourished
Burkina Faso	14	3.1	460	27.2	71.8	1330	38
Burundi	8	3.1	100	54.6	87.6	710	45
Central African Rep	4	1.3	360	66.6	84.2	1280	24
Congo Dem Rep	59	2.8	130			720	31
Eritrea	5	4.1	200			1090	40
Ethiopia	73	2	180	23	77.8	1190	38
Guinea	9	1.9	410			2410	38
Madagascar	19	2.7	280	61	85.1	960	42
Malawi	13	1.9	170	20.8	62.9	720	22
Mali	14	3	440	36.1	72.1	1130	33
Mozambique	20	2	340	36.2	74.1	220	24
Nepal	28	2.1	290	24.1	68.5	1630	45
Niger	14	3.4	260	60.6	85.8	830	40
Rwanda	9	2.4	250	60.3	87.8	1270	23
Sierra Leone	6	3.7	240	57	74.5	850	27
Tajikistan	7	1.2	390	7.4	42.8	1410	
Tanzania	39	2.6	350	57.8	89.9	740	29
Togo	6	2.7	350			1490	
Uganda	30	3.4	300			1490	23
Zimbabwe	13	0.6	340	56.1	83	1950	16

CHAPTER ONE

What is poverty?

One would think that poverty is a pretty clear reality; if you do not have enough to eat, to clothe yourself, or to afford decent housing you are poor. But some of those elements are subjective; does one need three meals a day or would two be enough? How much housing is necessary in order to live a decent life? How much more in order to have some privacy? Defining poverty is much more difficult than just relying on the immediate evidence of lack of goods and services. One needs to look at poverty from the outside to find a way to understand it for the purposes of policy-making and indeed of addressing it in full. In philosophical terms the best way by far is to use Amartya Sen's[2] definition: it is the lack of freedom of opportunity. If you have the opportunity to do your own thing, to develop yourself, to make choice, you become free. But then we need to consider what prevents people from being free, and of course the reasons for the lack of freedom are quite different according to the particular circumstances. I would submit that it is the lack of depth in appreciating and understanding those varied circumstances that leads to the muddle international policy-makers are currently experiencing. In thinking about poverty the North has moved away from thinking of immediate deprivation to the wider concept of Amartya Sen. However, even Sen's approach – even if it might be blasphemous to say it – depends on the way the rich look at poverty, which is not necessarily the way the poorest would look at it.

Let us start with the World Bank's definition of mid-2008 that absolute poverty is someone who lives on less than $1.25 per day. This means that there are around 1.25 billion people in poverty across the world[3]. The International Centre for Poverty, based in Brazil, estimates that there are considerably more poor people in the world than that – close to 1.75 billion in 2008[4]. According to FAO, more than two billion people are affected by 'hidden hunger'. This is defined as survival on a very limited diet, eating the same food almost every day, without sufficient vitamins and minerals[5]. Two dollars per day was the daily subsidy given by the European Union in 2003 to each cow within the EU[6]. The Chronic Poverty Research Centre in mid 2008 estimated the number of people living on less than half a US dollar per day, in other words the poorest of the poor, at between 320 and 443 million, and the numbers are increasing[7]. All the estimates of numbers were made before the drastic rise in prices of foodstuff in 2007 and 2008; the numbers are thus likely to be much greater. But, let us be frank; these figures are abstract quantities they do not convey the millions of personal tragedies that poverty really is.

Poverty is usually defined as a relative state of affairs. If your neighbours are rich and you have much less than them, you are poor. The continuing challenge is that an increase in wealth of certain parts of society leads to more comparative poverty, because others are not benefiting in the same way and thus becoming poor relative to the new rich – they have less freedom. But there is another level of poverty, one at which there is no improvement at all in absolute terms. If you are ill you should be able to see a doctor and buy medicines; for those living in rural poverty there is no hope of this. There are certain clear indicators of the reality of absolute poverty and this is where all effort should be concentrated. These are the people who are lacking in everything that makes human life bearable. None of the policies or research projects that are pursued now by governments, international organisations, international congresses and conferences, research bodies and academic institutions can solve the problems of long-term survival of the poorest on earth.

Who are the poor?

There is an important point to be made about world poverty. There are hundreds of millions of poor people but they do not form a homogeneous group. Instead there are many different groups of poor people in many different parts of the world. They include the pastoralists of Northern Kenya and Southern Ethiopia whose pastures have dried up; the slum dwellers of all the large cities of Africa and Latin America, and most of Asia (e.g. Cairo, Lagos, Rio de Janeiro, and Mumbai); the low status tribes of the Sahelian belt who have been historical victims of the endogenous slave trade; the Untouchables of India who are denied any economic opportunities; the people who suffer from chronic mental health problems in northern Bengal because their wells have been poisoned by chemicals; the delta inhabitants of the Eastern States of Nigeria whose fish have been poisoned by the leakages from the oil wells; the people who have become refugees in camps in the Eastern part of the Democratic Republic of Congo because of ethnic fighting in Rwanda and Burundi; the child soldiers of Burma who are kept in slavery by the military junta. They would include probably all those with physical handicaps everywhere in the Southern world, people with a mental disability and people with debilitating diseases. There is no universal solution to tackling the very different problems of the different groups. Some groups listed above are poor because they are trapped by racial prejudices, others by customs and religion, others by the geography of the areas in which they live. This range of issues leads to some incredibly difficult targets in trying to tackle 'development'. It will take more than a bit of money or more investment or a few volunteers to solve some of these real issues – and the outsider will have only a very limited role to play in achieving long-lasting change. The only long-lasting change will come from within, with possibly a bit of help from the outside.

What do the poor do?

Let us take an isolated village in up-country Gambia. The typical village inland, about an hour north from Serekunda, lies inside the Sahel. It comprises eight to ten huts. Each hut will have walls made of dried mud, cemented together by cow dung, a roof made of straw which will be propped up by a few bamboo poles or, if the owner is relatively well off, by wooden poles. The hut will have a small stove in one corner to heat food. There will be a few large pots, somewhere to sit, perhaps a bedstead on which the oldest member of the family might rest, perhaps the elderly mother of either the man of the house or his wife. It is likely that there will be a container, possibly an enamel or plastic basin filled with water, in which dishes will be washed. There will be another receptacle, a large jug or perhaps a plastic barrel, in which the drinking water, or what passes for drinking water, will be kept and this will be used first thing in the morning to fetch water. It will require an enormous physical effort to transport water up to three times a day. It is as if a Northerner were to carry his/her air luggage allowance on his/her head for four to five hours a day. There are a few communal water pumps in the region provided by the Government or one of the international voluntary or official aid agencies but they tend to be in the larger villages.

The hut will be surrounded by a small garden where the family will try to grow some vegetables, perhaps tomatoes or greens. There might be some chickens and there will almost certainly be a dog lazing about. In a poor society such as The Gambia a young girl will wake up around five in the morning, as the sun rises. She will go to collect water on foot from the river or at a borehole at least 30 minutes or more away and will carry it back on her head. The previous day she will have collected bits of wood from the bushes around the hut, bark dropped by the goats, dry leaves to start the fire. She will cook porridge, cassava, sweet potatoes or whatever breakfast is usual for the family. Then perhaps she will walk an hour or so to go to school, together with her male siblings. If she is the eldest child of the family, she might have to stay behind to look after older male and female relatives. School will be for the boys and the younger sisters. At some stage during the day she will go out to collect wood for the next day.

In those areas where there is land to be cultivated, the women of the family and children over 12-14 years, will go out to work it. In most of West Africa as in other parts of Africa men will go out to do paid work, if there is any. If there is no paid work, the men will stay at home and do nothing. You need some form of oil to cook the meal and the women will be grinding any nut that can be found to produce a bit of liquid; it takes hours on end.

There is smoke permanently in the hut. The number of children and adults with chronic bronchial problems is enormous; smoke inhalation is estimated to cause around 300,000 deaths a year in Africa alone, with an estimated 1.6 million worldwide[8].

It is difficult to keep oneself clean. Often cow dung, if there is any, will be collected for this purpose. It is reputed to contain a small amount of caustic substances and thus can be used as soap. Cow dung will also be used for fuel and for keeping in place the mud with which the hut is built and regularly rebuilt after a heavy rain. Human waste is kept to fertilise the land. But, in spite of much hard work, the land is often infertile; it might take 10,000 years to form one inch of humus on the land and in one night the whole can be washed away in a downpour.

Living in the slums

When life in the countryside becomes impossible – because you have been dispossessed, or your breadwinner is seriously ill or has died, or your village has been submerged – people move to the city. The best bits of terrain have already been taken by those who came a long time ago so families will move to whatever space there is left. The only water available is from a communal pump. Children will play in canals full of human excreta, rubbish and rats. Whenever there is a major downpour of rain, huts in the more unstable positions will be washed away and families may be swept away with them. People have to forage all day to manage to get a bit of food, by doing services for others, by going through piles of rubbish to extract a few bottles of plastic to resell to some dealer. In Brazil alone out of a population of close to 190 million people, it is estimated there are 20 million homeless and another 40 millions in slums without safe water or sanitation. Gangs tend to dominate life in the slums. The police are incredibly corrupt in most parts of the world; they are instruments of oppression, not of justice. They should of course protect the most vulnerable members of these communities, but that is the scenario of dreams.

The village in Senegal

M'bour, about two hours down the coast of Senegal from the capital, Dakar, is a small town squeezed between the Atlantic and the Sahel, that zone of Africa that forms the southern end of the Sahara. This area of land, while not yet desert, is nearly barren. There has been an increasing concentration of salt caused by water evaporation. In addition, the little agriculture that there is has relied on increasing inputs of fertilisers, which use yet more water, and the land produces less. The price of food brought to the market from those areas of the country that still have a surplus has gone up steadily. This is a worldwide phenomenon which we shall explore later in the book.

More people are growing desperate; young men and women in the villages cannot make a living – the patches of land available for tilling are decreasing in size, so fewer people are needed to work on them. They try to find jobs in the cities, but these are scarce and if you do not have a decent education and know the right people, it can be impossible. They have to attempt to migrate to Europe almost as a rite of passage. At nightfall, a boat, possibly with someone at the front who will be given a compass, will be pointed in the direction of the Canary Islands. Those who don't die of heat, exhaustion or dehydration during the crossing will land on the coast of one of the Canary Islands where they will be whisked away into the interior, to one of the processing centres. There they will be shepherded to one of the airfields and will be taken to mainland Spain, about three hours away by a small plane. With a bit of luck they might eventually find some way to earn a bit of a living in Spain. If not they will be repatriated. Back in the villages of Senegal the elderly now look after the little ones, because the in-between generation has disappeared to go to seek work in Europe (or have succumbed to the ravages of AIDS).

The nomad in East Africa

In Northern Kenya the main ethnic group is the Samburu. They have lived for hundreds of years as nomadic cattlemen, moving large numbers of animals from one part of the country to another, often crossing into Ethiopia, because the land has never been sufficiently rich to grow enough grass in any one place and water has always been scarce. However, the gradual worsening of the climate over the last 20 years or so has meant that there is now almost no grass anywhere, and water is no longer replenishing the natural waterholes for the animals, and the animals are dying. The Samburu do not understand that they have to become sedentary, start to develop agriculture and dig for water.

Their physique is adapted to long-distance walking, not to digging. They certainly do not have the capital required to become sedentary farmers. They have no tools to achieve this – for them and other nomadic groups – cataclysmic change of life. The nomadic population of Ethiopia is around 12 per cent of the total population of the country – about eight million people – while in Kenya there are approximately four million nomads. They are all dying silently. A similar pattern is being repeated across most of the Sahelian countries; Mauritania, Mali, Burkina Faso, Niger and Chad.

The factory worker in Shanghai

In 2007 the National Labour committee, an American labour organisation, investigated Wal-Mart for its labour practices. Factories all over China, including some that supply international companies such as Dell Computers, the Wal-Mart Corporation and Disney, were found to be employing children, forcing workers to work for up to 16 hours per day and paying below the minimum wage (which was as low as $0.55 per hour). It discovered that in one case a company had forcibly recruited some 500 school children aged 16 to work for up to 15 hours per day seven days per week to fulfil the peak production periods in the early summer to meet the quota of goods demanded by the company at Christmas time for the US. There are, from time to time, appeals by NGOs to the companies and indeed there have been improvements. But at the same time lives of the young Chinese workers seem to be cheap. According to the Shanghai Academy of Social Sciences some 40,000 fingers are lost or broken on production lines every year in China[9].

The woman in Afghanistan

Seven years after the West started to fight the Taliban little seems to have changed for the women in Afghanistan. Despite the existence of a law that bans the practice of women marrying below the age of 16, almost 60 per cent of brides are below this age. Some 60 per cent of marriages are forced. The illiteracy rate among women is 88 per cent. Little girls as young as six years are sold by their desperately poor families into slavery or marriage (the two seem to be interchangeable) in many villages, either to pay for debts or to settle family feuds. The little girls are then subject to sexual exploitation, many of them by more than one member of their new families. The girl becomes a commodity[10]. In July 2009 the Afghan Parliament passed a law that allows the husband of a woman who refuses his sexual advances to be starved of food and water until she submits.

The economics of need

One could give many examples of abject poverty and its implications, of what it means to have to fight to survive day after day, to go to sleep hungry every night of your life. Very few people reading this book have experienced anything like it. This means that they will not really appreciate the pain of being poor, desperately poor. Yet the numbers of the poor are enormous. In India the Dalit, the Untouchables, those who do not belong to any caste, number around 170 million, more than two-and-a-half times the population of the UK, and most of them live in poverty. Very few will be able to get on the ladder of economic advancement at all, they will remain at the bottom of the social and economic order all their lives and their children will inherit their poverty. In India alone there are more people who live below the $1.25 per day indicator than in the whole of Africa, yet India is a relatively successful country and one whose economy is expected to grow significantly in the next decade. The same cannot be said of sub-Saharan Africa. There are about 600 million people in China alone living on between $1 and $2 per day in 2009.

The economic system the North understands does not touch the lives of the really poor. In a village in Malawi to which I am linked through a project, a young woman in her early 20s was recently given a note in kwacha, the local currency, for some work she had done. She had never seen a currency note in her life. It was a sum of unimaginable wealth in her eyes. Her experience is not unique; in most poor societies there is no cash. Barter is wonderful but it keeps you at the lowest level of economic life. You can barter mangoes for tomatoes and a few bags of sorghum for bags of maize and other basic foodstuff, but try to buy a cheap mattress for your sick grandmother with a large amount of mangoes and you will fail.

Economics works in different ways in different societies. In Northern societies the main motivation of the manufacturer is to introduce labour-saving devices. There are however many other manufacturers and, if you cannot find a job in one industry, there are jobs in other sectors and there is even a social safety net. Trying to save labour in a Southern context would lead to a disastrous result; it would increase the number of people unemployed without any protection. This is the sort of policy fact that one needs to accept; the economies of poor countries have to meet different requirements and thus require different approaches to those of rich countries.

Reaching the monetary economy

People in a pre-monetised economy might indeed from time to time have handled coins and even notes, but the economic systems within which they live are not able to generate the constant flow of income that could at all be likened to a modern economic system. To that extent the poor who live in the cities are better off than the poor who live in the rural areas; in the cities more people will have come across some form of monetary reward. The things on which they spend their money though will not be different from the items of those who live off barter in the countryside. But I doubt if more than a handful of people in the rural parts of Africa, which is where the overwhelming majority (60–80 per cent) of the population live, will be part of an economic system that can be evaluated or controlled or directed in any way. The economy is entirely dependent on seasons and on the most basic demands. The people who live in rural areas will have their lives dictated by the demands to fill their stomachs and those of their children and elderly parents. They will need shelter and apparel of some kind and the economic system does not provide any of that, because they live outside any economic system.

What do the poor want?

Just as for women or slaves there are very few recorded and documented histories of the poor. Those who write are the privileged few; they inevitably see life from their own vantage point and their capacity to imagine the poverty of the members of their societies tends to be skewed by their own values and experiences[11]. Thus the rich do not really understand the challenges that face the wretched of the earth. The fundamental issue is that generally the rich are guessing what the poor want. They think that they are in a position to develop, and that the poor could achieve that undefined goal with a little of help from the outside – and the rich are often willing to give that help. The poor might want to develop, but there is a much more important challenge to overcome first, that of survival. We all confuse the issues. If you are a refugee, if you live in constant fear for your life, if you are a child soldier or a member of a community that is threatened by violence, if your physical environment has worsened so much that your animals have died and you are forced to move to pastures new, how can you think of anything else except survival on a day-to-day basis? There cannot be any development under those conditions. The misunderstanding is to some extent perpetuated by the misuse of commonly used words; the Northern world refers to the poorer countries of the world as 'developing'. Most of them are not developing – they are dirt poor and will probably remain dirt poor as things stand. The bottom billion do not have any economy – they have to fight for survival. They live within the economy of need.

Those who work in the field of economic development have many suggestions as to how to reduce poverty. Not often, however, are they able to determine what the poor want – apart from being less poor! Go to any small town, any village, any city in Africa and try to find out what people want. It is not that difficult to gauge their desires and their needs. It is not the issues that seem to dominate Northern agendas – mortgages, climate change, globalisation, privacy, civil rights, pornography, narcotics, inflation – that interest them. They need to cope with the daily challenges of hunger, insufficient income, permanent ill-health, dirty water, children's diarrhoea, lack of housing and a worsening physical environment. They need to survive today and tomorrow. Their agenda is very pressing and their time is immediate.

Voices of the poor

In 2000 the World Bank[12] undertook probably the most important study to date to gauge the priorities of the poor. The study was entitled 'Voices of the Poor from Many Lands'. It makes a remarkable document. The researchers interviewed some 40,000 people in 60 countries. It will not surprise the reader who has any knowledge of the South that the priority was the need for physical security. In most parts of the world the very poor are at constant physical risk. It might seem blindingly obvious to say that those who have become refugees, that the nomads who have lost their grazing land, that the people caught in civil war and the slum dwellers are desperate for some sort of physical security and stability in their environment, but it is worth stating nonetheless. The second need given was the desire to work their own plot of land; they are actually saying 'just give us the opportunity and we will do our own thing'. The third need was to be offered access to some sort of healthcare and education. The study was undertaken with a view to finding out what poor people actually thought about their own condition and to give them a voice. What is most interesting, and by-and-large has been ignored by the World Bank, as well as other international organisations and most politicians in both the North and the South, is the desire of poor people to have a voice and be empowered. They very seldom have a voice that anyone wants to hear and therefore they have little empowerment. To people who live in democracies in the North that call means they want a political voice, expressed through political parties – which is the North's way of doing things. But this is not what the poor are really asking for. They just want basic justice. The world is not really answering that desperate call.

Specific problems need specific solutions

Most problems are specific to peoples and situations, therefore solutions in the field of economic and social development need to be well-targeted. For example, if you are a nomad and your waterholes are disappearing and your animals cannot eat and drink in the places that you and your ancestors have used for the last millennia, you need a solution that is different from that of the low-caste Indian who will only be given the task to clean toilets because he or she is not deemed worthy to perform any other job. The first issue clearly relates to the physical environment while the second is a problem created by the culture and traditions of India. The fact that Bangladeshi textile workers are losing their jobs because Chinese workers are taking over the manufacture of cheap textiles is neither of the above – rather it has to do with the globalisation of production and marketing.

There are thus three different groups of issues that we shall address in the following three chapters. The first are the physical constraints – the problems of basic geography and climate. Some countries, such as Mali, Burkina Faso, Mauritania, Niger, Bangladesh, the Maldives, and most of the Pacific Island States are facing physical situations that will clearly prevent them from ever developing. Some pockets of each of those countries might 'develop', but it is very unlikely that the entire country will. The second group of issues concerns human constraints. Rural exodus, migration, unchecked population growth and the spread of disease all mean that the countries of the South have to meet challenges that the rich cannot even start to comprehend. The third group of issues relates to the global context in which societies operate. For example, the export of subsidised food from the EU leads to the destruction of agriculture in Africa. In each of these cases there might be solutions, but they are fundamentally different one from the other. Not accepting that specific problems need specific solutions means that we all are obsessed by theories, and there is no one-size-fits-all theory or solution.

The measurement of poverty

One of the key problems in the entire way in which politicians in both North and South, as well as the international financial institutions (World Bank, International Monetary Fund, Regional Development Banks, European Development Fund), and bilateral aid mechanisms view DEVELOPMENT is that they rely on data that are the product of statistical tools they have developed. You measure what can be measured and the World Bank is excellent at that. This is why everyone always quotes them; the Bank has the resources to employ some very clever people and they go on happily researching their subjects. But there is a catch – a serious catch – and it is this. A great deal of what can be measured relies on the monetary economy and not on what affects the poor. This is why so often one talks about serious improvements and even impressive DEVELOPMENT in some countries, for example, in Zambia and Mozambique (one of the darlings of the international aid community) in the last 10-15 years. But is it really development as it affects the poorest? Probably not at all, because most of their lives are lived outside the parameters of the monetary economy. One very interesting approach and critique of the whole approach of the methods of analysis of the monetary institutions came out in mid 2008 in a book on Mozambique – *Do Bicycles Equal Development in Mozambique?* Joseph Hanlon and Teresa Smart analyse the way in which, with an annual growth of 7 percent, substantial foreign investment, and rapid expansion of education, that country is often billed by donors as a DEVELOPMENT success. However, poverty is increasing. There is greater class divide and the local elites have more in common with the foreign investor and donor than with their own people. The authors argue that the model that is being imposed by the international community on Mozambique and its own elites is simply not working. In their view the DEVELOPMENT model based on neo-liberalism and the Millennium Development Goals has failed[13].

CHAPTER TWO

The physical constraints

The 2007 Report of the International Panel on Climate Change (IPCC) predicted that by 2030 the average temperature across the African continent will have risen by a minimum of 2.5°C. This process will not occur at an even rate across the globe; countries round the equator will suffer more because they are closer to the sun, therefore a proportional increase means a larger increase in absolute terms in temperature rise in some of the poorest countries in the world. That will mean a decrease in water levels and rainfall, an increase in deser-tification and a rise in sea levels. These will affect the Nile area and the Mediterranean coast of Egypt particularly, as well as large parts of West Africa. There will be a loss of some 600,000sq km of arable land. In Asia, in the seven mega-deltas, from the Ganges in India to the Yangtze in China, there will be enormous damage due to flooding. There will be the increased risk of waterborne diseases. Crop yields in Central and South East Asia are predicted to fall by around 30 per cent. In the southern hemisphere, the warming of the Antarctic and the disappearance of the glaciers in the Andes will lead to reduced rainfall. Parts of the Amazon forest will become semi-arid savannah. In late 2008 the temperature in the Arctic reached levels that had been predicted to arise only 10 to 15 years hence[14]. So, is it too late? Some respected authorities say that it already is; that is certainly the view of James Lovelock who considers we have passed the point of no return[15]. He argues that changes might be continuous, but not necessarily in an even way – there could be unpredictable acceleration of events. Others give the world a few more years to act before we reach that point[16]. Either way, we should not bank on any solutions being implemented any day soon and it is worth remembering that while the North might be able to take measures to protect itself, the poor cannot. A study undertaken in 2006 by Lord Stern for the British Government estimated that a small investment of perhaps 1 to 1.5 per cent of GDP now would save at least 5 percent the costs of GDP that ignoring such consequences would represent by 2050[17]. It urged governments of the world to start acting now, before it is too late, and to include some help to the South to cope with climate change. Governments and international organisations have failed to take any notice.

The availability of food

The world is losing enormous tracts of arable land every year. The amount of food produced in the world is decreasing. The price of most basic foodstuffs – cereals and rice in particular – is rising. Poor countries are becoming ever more dependent on imported food; their lands are becoming less fertile, the seeds cannot resist the droughts, artificial fertilisers are beyond reach and there is no investment. UNICEF calculated that an additional 40 million children will go hungry because of the rise in food prices; their health and therefore personal development will suffer and this poverty will become multigenerational[18]. More and more land in the world is being used to grow ethanol-producing crops and palm oil for the North and feed for animals for the better off of the world[19]. The World Bank estimated that an additional 200 million people are in danger of going hungry as a result of the recent (mid 2007 onwards) rise in prices.

In a study published in May 2009 that was produced in collaboration with FAO and IFAD, the International Institute for Environment and Development (IIED) estimated that in a five-year period to March 2009 some 2.5 million hectares of land deals had been signed in just 5 countries in Africa. The study covered only deals including over 1,000 hectares – which is already an enormous size in most of Africa. In all such deals inevitably the poorest would lose out; they have no power and no voice[20]. Saudi Arabia and Gulf countries are buying farming land in Africa, not to produce more food for Africans, but to export it back to their own countries. We need to look no further than China to estimate need; it has 20 percent of the world's population but only 7 percent of the world's arable land. China has lost 8.67 million hectares of farmland between 1996 and 2006 due to urbanisation, migration, climate change and other factors. The policy-makers estimate that the country needs a minimum of 120 million hectares of farmland to feed its own people[21]. At the end of 2008 it was estimated that some 10,000 farmers from Hebei Province alone had moved from China to 18 African countries to teach African farmers Chinese methods of cultivation[22]. It is also likely that most of these farmers from China will all try to become businessmen and to export that food back to China; it would make very good commercial sense to do so because selling locally would not generate foreign currency. Local farmers will be marginalised.

In many parts of the world, including enormous tracts of Brazil, rainforest is being cut down to provide land on which animal feed is grown, which is needed to provide for the increasing demands of the North as well as of the slightly better off people of the South. These feeds include soya beans and barley. Animals, however, are bad converters of food; it takes about nine tons of vegetable feed to provide one ton of pork.

Water and sanitation

Around one billion people live without clean water and approximately 2.5 billion have no adequate sanitation[23]. About half of the population of the world has to collect water from distant sources and about one-third of rural households in the world lack even a simple latrine. As people move into urban areas there is the added demand for indoor toilets and water from taps. The average Londoner consumes 163 litres of water per day and the demand is increasing. Increased prosperity leads to an increase in industrial activity, which requires an increase in water consumption, yet everywhere in the world the availability of fresh water is decreasing. The search for water is the central daily activity for the people of most of the poor world. It dominates the life of women of all ages and particularly of the younger women in the community. Salinity of the land is increasing in many places, usually due to the overuse and mismanagement of the few regular sources of water. Salt accumulates in the water and when the water evaporates the salt residues are left on the land, causing it to become permanently barren. Where there is little water it should be better managed, but that becomes less possible where social structures are weak.

There is an increasing demand for water as population increases; during the 20th century the population of the world increased more than thrice, but the demand for water rose six times. The rapid advance of deserts is just one result; Lake Chad, a vital water supply for six countries in West Africa, has shrunk by 95 per cent in the past 40 years. There are now areas of the world that will suffer permanent and increasing shortages of water, such as North Africa and the Middle East. These two regions, with approximately 5 per cent of the population of the globe, have just 1 per cent of the world's available resources of fresh water. However, fortunately these countries have enough wealth to allow them to set up desalination plants to supply their domestic needs.

The issue of water supply is complicated by the fact that so many different players are involved. In many parts of Africa water is controlled by the village chief. He will probably charge a levy for people to collect water. This by itself is probably unavoidable because the well has to be maintained, but there is clearly injustice all along the line. In villages in Niger for example, the Chief will employ someone to collect money on his behalf, but the man will not charge the village chief or his family or his friends or other important people for water. That means that those who have no connections will pay for those who are already better off. There is no clarity in the work that has to be carried out, for example, in the construction of the well, in the pump, in the maintenance of the structures. There is, in short, no overall management of the water system. There are over 50,000 water points in Africa that have in effect died. If the well does not function, there is no clean water. The villagers will have to wait for a donor who might be interested in their plight. Without proper water management the situation will persist[24].

At present it is estimated that approximately 40 per cent of the world's population lives with shortages of water, but this figure is likely to increase over the next 25 years to as much as 66 per cent by 2035. By 2013 the population of China will have increased from the current 1.3 billion to about 1.5 billion and the demand for water for irrigation is likely to rise from 400 billion to around 665 billion cubic metres[25]. That amount of water simply is not available within China. Even in Europe the problems are increasing; in countries such as Portugal, Spain and Greece land is becoming more arid and needs more water for irrigation. It is becoming desperately urgent that there should be a global strategy for more and more investment in water management and better coordination of efforts. In Africa only 3 per cent of renewable water resources are managed compared with 80 per cent in the US. The melting of the glaciers in the Himalayas, which feed the Ganges in India, is threatening the survival of some 360 million people in India and Bangladesh and 388 million who live by the Yangtze in China[26].

The Food and Agricultural Organization of the UN (FAO) estimates that by 2050 more than four billion people will live in countries that are chronically short of water. One of the Millennium Development Goals is to halve the number of people without access to clean water by 2025. To achieve this goal water would have to be made available to an additional 440,000 people every day of every week of every year for the next ten years, at a cost of approximately $25 billion per year. But the funds do not exist and the question as to what mechanisms of implementation are most effective on the ground goes unanswered.

Transport and physical communications

The Report of Commission for Africa that was established by the British Government in 2004[27] reminded the world of some of the realities of life across the African continent. There are few rivers that enable people to move across the continent and there is only a limited road network. Where there is anything it is the remnant of the system that enabled the colonial power to take minerals and raw materials from the interior of the country to the nearest port for export to the 'mother' country. There are airports in the capital cities but air transport is limited to too few people – it is not a viable method of transporting produce. People in remote areas often do not bother to produce beyond basic subsistence needs because the roads are so awful and transport is so rare, expensive and dangerous that taking crops to sell in town makes no commercial sense at all. African produce still moves on the heads of its women as it has for the last few millennia. The cost of building roads across the continent is prohibitive; Africa will never have the physical structure it needs in spite of all the promises of jam tomorrow. South Asia benefits from an enormous network of rivers; Africa has very few. Roads cannot withstand the downpours that occur in very short bursts in many of parts of Africa; they would sweep away any of the roads in Europe and would require to be built to standards higher than those of the North.

The need for energy

All societies need energy and any sort of economic development requires an increasing input of energy. Most of the North's energy comes from oil, while most of the poor depend on wood and coal. The world might run out of oil in the next five years or ten years or fifty years, depending on whom you believe; the whole field is subject to unreliable estimates of supplies, reserves, and consumption. During 2007, 2008 and early 2009 consumer prices across most of Africa have not gone down[28]. More and more energy is needed but for the wrong uses; it is estimated that more power is now used in the US for cooling and for air conditioning than for heating. In the UK people now heat their homes to 20°C; it was 17°C in 1970[29]. The introduction of alternative sources of energy is urgent. The introduction of biofuels will lead to less food being available in case of emergencies, more destruction of tropical forests and intrusion on land required for growing food. The price of oil is not decreasing for many of the items for which it is main feedstock; there will be no decrease in the price of fertilisers and pesticides, as well as daily items of consumption, such as plastic buckets and shoes, photovoltaic cells and medicines. For the richer members of the poorest countries this will be a serious setback; daily tasks such as transport and cooking are becoming extremely expensive. Paraffin will go up in price as it is an oil derivative. For the poorest in the poor countries access to wood or charcoal or coal will become even more expensive. This is an area of need of the South that the North seems to have totally ignored, yet the absence of forest cover will inevitably lead to greater poverty in many rural areas across the whole of the poor world.

Biofuels

The North's need for energy has now spilled over into alternative fuel needs. One of the most important ones, because it can be obtained with little investment and can produce short-term results, is biofuel. To create biofuel, ethanol is extracted from sugar cane and other plants; this can then be used as fuel for an increasing variety of vehicles. This is likely to be at the expense of food being grown for local people, who do not have the income with which to purchase the food they require. Land needed for the growth of these plants is already a major cause of destruction of the virgin forest in Brazil and Indonesia. Likewise, biofuel crops are grown on good arable land in certain parts of Africa. It is not bad news for everyone of course. Since 2002 farmers in the central belt of the US have had some of the best years ever; the price of their corn, which can be transformed into biofuel, has doubled[30]. Some countries, including Mozambique, are already devoting considerable parts of their arable land to the growth of biofuel crops, both for their own needs but primarily for export. There is a similar growth in demand for palm oil, which is used for cooking and for many prepared foods. This demand has resulted in millions of acres of virgin forest being decimated in order to make space for palm plantations. In the long term the consequences of the reduction of the forest are inestimable, even if in the short term a few more people are being paid to do the basic work. The phenomenon is especially acute in Malaysia and Indonesia where the habitat of the orang-utan is threatened. Additionally, such activities, as is the case with all cash crops, are volatile, as they respond to the demands of the North. In the present economic recession the South will suffer far more than the North.

Properly managed, the demand for biofuel crops could be one of the main sources of income for the poor farmer in the South. It could pump cash in the economy and would meet some of their own demands for energy, but it is currently grown primarily as an export crop by international entities. Moreover, too much biofuel is grown on land that could be used for edible crops. The international community and national governments have not done enough to ensure that biofuel crops are grown on marginal land. The need to obtain cash from the outside world overrides all other priorities.

CHAPTER THREE
The human constraints

The priorities of societies vary according to their level of economic development. In the North they include ensuring food and energy supplies, the push to export, the need to cope with labour surpluses or shortages, the preservation of national autonomy. These economic priorities translate into political priorities. In poorer societies there are different priorities that hardly appear on our horizon. They include the growth of population, rural exodus and urbanisation, untreated diseases, poor health and sanitation, migration of skilled people. Tackling these should be the core priorities of the poorest societies and they would lead to totally different aims and tools from those of the North. But the North does not seem willing or able to accept the enormous differences in approach that these political and economic priorities would require. Let us start by looking at some of the enormous and very different challenges that the South faces.

Population increase
Population growth is without doubt the first challenge of the poor world. Population is increasing rapidly throughout the poorest parts of the world. Sexual activity is a natural force in humans, but the North has both social forces that restrict population growth and access to contraceptives with which to control the number of children it brings into the world. It is becoming more and more expensive to rear children; this is the primary reason why people in the North no longer have large families. There is plenty of evidence that as people become richer anywhere they automatically reduce the size of their

families. There are examples of this among black middle classes in South Africa and in Indian middle classes in the States of Tamil Nadu and Kerala. There is a close correlation between the level of education of the mother and family size; even after five years of education the mother is better able to protect herself from unwanted pregnancies. The very serious challenge is to make all classes of people understand that their wealth will increase if they reduce the size of their families.

Why do populations grow in the South? One reason for having children is because children are the only form of security for someone in old age – children will look after their parents once they are no longer able to look after themselves. Another reason is that people lack the knowledge or the means to limit the number of children produced. Historically population levels controlled themselves as more children died in the first year or so of life than lived (this is still the case in some countries). In economic terms there is a negative side to having children – they are expensive to have and to rear – but this issue only arises later on in the development of an economy, usually when people start to reach a slightly more prosperous level. Individuals need to be very confident of their economic survival before they start deliberately restricting the number of children per family.

Population growth places an enormous strain on some societies. In Kenya, for example, the increase of school-age children means that the country needs to build two new schools every single week simply to maintain the same percentage of children at school. Even the spread of HIV/AIDS is not slowing down the net rate of population increase. The North gives very little priority to this fundamental issue. If it ever decided seriously to tackle child mortality in the South, for example by introducing the measures of mass child immunisation that were undertaken in Western Europe around the first decade of the 20th century, there will be an even greater surge in population resulting in an even greater number of starving people. Instead of excoriating China for its one-child policy, the world should welcome it for slowing down population growth. Many people would argue that the fact that China has introduced the one-child policy, in spite of all the exceptions and corruption, is fundamental to its economic advancement. More women have achieved status because they are now independent economic agents. Fewer children mean fewer people in poverty, fewer people looking for jobs and the possibility of raising living standards. The state, through coercion, has liberated women by forcing men to take their responsibility more seriously.

It is quite obvious, but it needs restating, that if population grows at the same rate, or faster than economic progress, there is no net development[31]. This is the classic Malthusian trap that affected Europe as much as it does the poor world now. It is unpleasant to state, but the fact is that all efforts to save lives, particularly of newborn babies, are likely to result only in more people dying of starvation later on as long as we do not attack the core issue – ensuring self-sustaining economic development.

Societal context

Economic development must have a societal base on which it can grow. If you have structures that are fundamentally inimical to development, for example a religious structure that makes it impossible to own property or to borrow money, economic development along lines that the North understands and fosters will not be possible, unless those structures change or adapt very substantially. Assumptions are made that Northern economic systems – primarily based on the principles of economic self-interest and individualism – can be applied to other societies governed by very different rules. This ignores the reality that we all live in societies that are not developing through some harmonious across-the-board equality but through competing interest groups. These groups are increasingly blind to the concept of the 'common good', the very principle Northern policy-makers are trying to convince poor countries to adopt in their policies. The consequences of the war in Iraq should have taught the Northern world that there is more to nation-building than the export of the concept of democracy (whatever that might be). The caste system in India is one structure that makes it impossible for the whole of society to develop. Development in India involves primarily the higher castes; the people at the base, the Untouchables or Dalits, have seen very few improvements in their standards of living. The richest 36 Indian individuals in

2007 had a combined wealth of $191 billion, far outweighing the top 36 Chinese who had a combined wealth of approximately half that amount[32]. The Government of India might claim that the caste of gravediggers might now benefit from the right to dig trenches for cable television in the cities, but that is hardly a serious improvement. In Mauritania in West Africa slavery was formally abolished only in 2004. The reality is that there are many tribes whose status is so low that, to this day, they will not be granted rights to economic development or personal freedom by the higher tribes. To pretend otherwise is unrealistic, yet most international decision-makers ignore this sort of unpleasant reality and the governments of that country (and neighbouring ones) pretend the issue does not exist. Government there remains feudal.

Rural exodus and urbanisation

There has been a massive rural exodus across the globe in the last 30 years, and at some point during this current decade the number of people in the world who live in cities will exceed the number of people who live in rural areas. This exodus has been caused by a combination of factors. Devaluation of the land has made the people who live in the rural areas much worse off. The lack of incentives for the farmers to stay on the land and produce food that they can sell at a decent price has accelerated the process. Subsidies to EU and US farmers to create and then export their surplus food have similarly reduced the value of produce on the land in the South. The average age of farmers in Africa is increasing, a clear sign that young people do not wish to stay on the farm[33]. The cities are more attractive; if a country begins electrification or builds new roads, that process is likely to start in, or possibly be entirely limited to, the major centres of population and there are likely to be more facilities in the cities than in rural areas. The flight from village to city will continue to increase for the foreseeable future. It is a phenomenon that is affecting Asia particularly; much less noticeably Africa, but it will in the future.

Urbanisation is one of the great forces sweeping across most parts of the poor world; this has the inevitable consequence of greater squalor. According to the UN Millennium indicators, some 837 million people in the world lived in urban slums in October 2006. This is not just a question of not having a decent roof over your head, but a complete set of indicators of incredible poverty and deprivation. Urban dwellers in the slums do not have any property rights. Their home is at the whim and mercy of the authorities or of people who simply have more brute force. There will certainly be no easy access to clean water and no hygienic facilities of any type. In most slums diseases, including measles, meningitis and cholera, are rife. Slum housing highlights the weakness of governance and the lack of responsibility of governments towards their poor.

There is an economic as well as a social logic in the move to urbanisation; most of the world's largest and fastest-growing cities are in the countries with the largest national economies. Asia hosts most of the world's largest cities while North America and sub-Saharan Africa have the most 'new' large cities. In 2005 the largest city in the world was Tokyo, with approximately 34 million people in the metropolitan area as a whole and 12.5 million in the city itself. São Paolo followed with 20 million and Mexico City with 19 million. Mumbai currently has over 13 million inhabitants and Dhaka in Bangladesh will soon join 15 other cities with over 10 million inhabitants. In Africa the largest cities are Lagos, Kinshasa and Cairo. There has been a steady growth; in 1950 the only city in the world with a population of over 10 million was New York. By 1975 five cities had risen to that number. By 2000 Asia alone had 10 cities over the 10 million mark. Some data provided by the World Bank are quite frightening: 16 out of the 20 most polluted cities in the world are located in China and 90 per cent of urban groundwater in China is contaminated. The World Health Organization (WHO) states that 2.4 million people die each year from causes directly attributable to air pollution alone[34].

Urbanisation and the pressure on large cities is not a problem restricted to the South. All major cities in the world are affected by similar problems. To solve them a totally new approach is required. A report published in April 2007 estimated that some $40 billion will be needed to improve infrastructure in the big cities of the developed world. It gives as examples of the need for improvements the drought in London in mid 2006 and the blackout in the Queens District of

New York for nine days in the same year[35]. The first was, in part, due to the leaking pipes in London, some of which were the original wooden (sic!) type from the Victorian era. In New York some of the electric cables were over 60 years old. The report urges a much more coordinated approach across all the different agencies in each city involved in providing electricity, water, transport and other essential services. By 2050, the vast majority of the world will be living in enormous urban expansions, with extremely poor facilities, wide open to illnesses and dissent. The rich world cannot cope with these problems; how can the poor world begin to organise and finance solutions to their problems?

Health

Africa is scourged by diseases that the North no longer knows or rarely sees, such as malaria, leprosy, river blindness, dengue fever, sleeping sickness and tuberculosis. They attract little or no medical research or investment because the people affected cannot afford to pay for the medicines that would result from that research. Other illnesses that maim or kill approximately half a million people every year include ascariasis, the most common worm infection that affects around 175 million people; schistosomiasis (also called bilharzias), a flatworm infection (166 million); elephantiasis, a worm infection of the lymph system (46 million); and trachoma, the most common cause of preventable blindness (33 million). These diseases are not treated by international organisations or bilateral donors, who all concentrate on the three major killers – HIV/AIDS, malaria and tuberculosis. Yet, it is claimed that a cocktail of four common drugs, costing less than $0.50 per person would cure most of these other diseases. The problem is that these forgotten diseases are less attractive to the international aid fraternity and the UN agencies such as the WHO. These organisations work with prestigious laboratories and world-famous scientists who concentrate on areas of research that will bring enormous dollops of money to pharmaceutical companies and possibly a Nobel Prize in medicine to the researchers. Finding a vaccine for HIV/AIDS will achieve this aim, curing leprosy may not. Yet treating these 'minor' illnesses would substantially reduce the incapacity of around 750 million people and allow them to become more active members of their communities[36].

Approximately three million people contract malaria each year around the world and it is estimated that at least 300 million people suffer from it. Malaria kills as many as 3,000 children per day in Africa – well over a million per year. In much of sub-Saharan Africa malaria deaths have doubled in the past decade and the numbers continue to rise. Only in the last couple of years there seems to have been a bottoming out of the numbers of new cases, primarily as a result of the successful introduction of bednets impregnated with anti-malaria substances in many parts of rural Africa. One of the reasons for the spread is because mutations of the plasmodium micro-organism causing the illness have made it more and more difficult to develop effective vaccines. While the malaria parasite was making a quiet comeback in the 1970s, research and development on a vaccine had run dry. The Global Fund to fight HIV/AIDS, Tuberculosis and Malaria came into being in January 2002. The near absence of anti-malarial drugs research may be understandable, with the pharmaceutical industry seeing limited commercial sense to invest in the development of drugs for a disease that largely affects people making less than $1 a day, but it is hardly commendable. The present need is straightforward: to invest in research and development for anti-malarial drugs. The cost of investment is very small compared with the cost of the catastrophe when the medicine cabinet is dry. The human toll will be immense as mortality and morbidity rates soar. Here again there is an interesting example of the link between the action of the North and consequences in the South. Some people would argue that the pesticide DDT could have eradicated malaria but a change in emphasis in the North occurred after Rachel Clarkson wrote her book *Silent Spring* in 1964[37]. There is no doubt that the book had an honourable aim – including warning consumers in the North of the danger of increasing cancer, but the result has led to unanticipated consequences for millions of people in the South. This is a clear conflict of interests – one of many that one meets in the field of development. Perhaps one should welcome the fact that the Bill and Melinda Gates Foundation put $287 million into the Malaria Eradication Campaign. But is it really a good idea to work on malaria prevention rather than on decreasing birth rates? What will happen to the millions who survive? Here thus is the wider challenge; education to prevent the spread of the disease; researching the possibility of a vaccine; and ensuring economic development that would increase prosperity for all.

Tuberculosis is still a major world disease that affects up to three million people a year. Approximately half a million people die from TB every year in Africa alone. More than 300,000 people around the world are infected each year by a form of TB that is resistant to at least two of the most commonly used drugs, which means that they become twice as expensive to cure as those suffering from the non-resistant form of tuberculosis. Some 500,000 people a year die from diseases that are caused by diarrhoea, most of them caused by E.coli. In March 2004 scientists announced that they had discovered a vaccine against Bombay Belly or Montezuma's Revenge, which could save up to 85 per cent of the peoples of the world who are affected by it every year. More importantly, from the pharmaceutical companies' perspective at least, there could be a market for this medicine for up to $400 million a year from the travelling public. Here is a very good example of how efficient the market can be; the disease is the major killer of infants in the poor world, but their parents cannot afford the medicines. However, as soon as a market can be seen, the pharmaceutical companies can develop a remedy.

The scourge of HIV/AIDS

After cancer and malaria, the biggest killer, and one that is still spreading at an alarming rate, is HIV/AIDS. Approximately 22 million people across the African continent were infected at the end of 2007[38]. The consequences are becoming more and more visible and the health budgets of the countries of sub-Saharan Africa are unable to cope. It is now accepted in the North that it is possible to retard the onset of full-blown AIDS through expensive treatment. But, because it is expensive, in parts of the world where the public is not able to pay, the situation is now out of control. There are already entire villages in countries such as Malawi and Zambia that are bereft of able-bodied people; more than 11 million children have been orphaned by AIDS.

Thousands of households are headed by either grandparents or pre-teen children. The profound social changes that the spread of HIV/AIDS is causing will be felt for many generations. There is only one positive aspect; because the disease affects both the poor and the rich countries of the world research is being undertaken in the North that otherwise would not be undertaken at all.

HIV/AIDS is a particularly difficult issue for the poorest countries of the world to cope with. Those who are affected tend to be the more mobile or the more educated members of the community. They include people who move to the cities to get employment and therefore receive a regular income – including teachers, nurses, truck drivers, miners, and migrant workers. HIV/AIDS is therefore killing the productive sector across most of Africa. To take a single example: two teachers per day are dying of AIDS in Tunisia alone. If treatment is initiated, experience points toward two certainties: first, drug resistance will inevitably set in among a certain percentage each year – even in the best of medical environments – and, second, medical care costs increase over time. Contrast it with cancer, which is estimated to still be the main cause of death worldwide. Many cancers can be treated cheaply if caught in time: that kind of investment could provide cures for millions. PACT, a coalition of NGOs, estimates that cervical cancer can be cured with 30 radiotherapy treatments at an average price of a few dollars per treatment. The battle against the spread of HIV/AIDS will require more engagement by men, but will be spearheaded by women. Women have very little economic force and social status and often no legal status at all, thus they are much more exposed to contagion than men. If HIV/AIDS prevention is to work more aid must be provided directly to women as a way to fight its spread.

In August 2003 it was announced that the US Government was cutting funds to HIV/AIDS programmes for refugees undertaken by seven international agencies because it objected to the activities of one of them, Marie Stopes International. The US Department of State indicated that Congress prohibited them from contributing to organisations that supported the policy of the Chinese government to repress population growth and limit the size of families to one child

per family. Marie Stopes International was found to be guilty by association. In reality this is a demonstration that the government of the
US was bowing down to the pressures of the right-wing Christian
Coalition to enforce its views on the entire world. The Christian
Coalition believes that the best way to prevent the spread of
HIV/AIDS is to prevent and discourage people from having sex outside marriage. In June 2003 Mr Bush had promised a total of $15 bil-
lion to combat HIV/AIDS; Congress a few weeks later cut this down
to $2 billion. The refusal of the US under President Bush (who did
more to help Africa through trade initiatives rather than Clinton ever
did) to continue supporting organisations that offer education in safe
sex has condemned millions of people to death. Now, under the latest
edicts of President Obama, things will change.

Over the last 20 years HIV/AIDS has generated its own endless
spin-offs. Many millions of dollars have been invested to discover the
cure for the disease and the first pharmaceutical company to come out
with the right cure will be able to mint billions of dollars. There are
entire university departments undertaking research on all sorts of
issues relating to it across the world and several voluntary agencies
have sprung up to work on some aspect or other of the disease. But for
Africa, where people will not be able to pay, the real answer has to be
a vaccine. There is a UN agency, UNAIDS, set up in 1995. It is difficult to judge what this agency has achieved – probably very little – but
it has added to the number of better-off people from better-off circles
in both poor and rich countries who lead comfortable lives endlessly
jetting from one part of the world to the other on UNAIDS' behalf.
Clearly that sort of enormous challenge has to be met, but one must
question whether the establishment of another UN Agency is the real
way to tackle it. An enormous range of good work is being carried out
by WHO – the parent body of UNAIDS – for example in identifying
diseases, introducing equivalence certificates, commissioning
research on avian flu, ensuring the maintenance of standards of education of medical personnel across the world. But that is done through
delegation of functions to existing bodies. In addition there is the endless number of meetings to attend. It was estimated that around
10,000 people attended the 2004 World Aids Congress in Thailand.

Even at a modest estimate of $3,000 per person (to cover travel, hotel and related costs, as well as the salary costs of those involved), that would have totalled around $30 million, a very considerable sum that could have gone towards fighting HIV/AIDS itself. Policy-making must be tackled in different ways.

Migration, refugees and displaced persons

The most visible sign that we live in a globalised world is the phenomenon of migration. There has been human migration forever, but it is only since the advent of strict national frontiers that movement has been controlled and monitored, and often viewed as a major challenge. The problem is considerably graver for the South than it is for the North – one of the key problems facing the poor world is the fact that their best people migrate. Many of the ablest people from the South, who have been educated at the expense of everyone – the poorest as well as the richest – are granted visas to the promised lands once they achieve qualifications that the North will accept (teachers, doctors, midwifes, nurses and computer engineers, for example). Others will try to migrate illegally and join the unseen masses toiling in restaurants, cleaning streets, picking agricultural produce in the fields and working as security guards in supermarkets in rich countries. It is the ablest and most enterprising youngsters who escape, not the illiterate. You need considerable courage and personal resourcefulness or sheer fear and desperation to cross country after country to reach some distant haven.

Migration is an unstoppable force; no country can transform itself into a fortress. The UK suffers from brain drain when its ablest scientists join university research departments in the US that are better equipped. But the brain drain of the South affects the daily lives of the poorest; they lose doctors, nurses, dentists, teachers who migrate to Northern countries. In addition there are groups of people the North urges to migrate and it will grant them visas. These include young people with qualifications the North needs; few of the countries in the North are producing enough doctors and nurses or teachers. There is a young and productive population in some parts of the world but an ageing population in most of Western Europe. Western Europe has job vacancies to fill, so it becomes an attractive destination. Africa is the best example of this migration, but India and Mexico also offer examples, as well as China, where it is more difficult to assess the problem as the government is unwilling to publish figures.

Two separate phenomena are those of refugees and internally displaced persons. In 2000 an estimated 50 million people were refugees and perhaps as many as half among them were environmental refugees: people who have had to leave their countries because they could no longer live off the land. They are victims of civil wars and often just local militias. There are millions of desperately poor people living as refugees in camps across the world – from the DRC to South Africa (for refugees from Zimbabwe), from Thailand to Jordan, from Chad to Palestine. The worsening physical environment will add to these 'political' refugees. The International Institute for Environment and Development (IIED) estimated that some five million people from Burkina Faso and Mali have migrated to the Ivory Coast since the 1960s simply due to environmental reasons[39].

Deforestation, soil erosion, drought, desertification and other physical problems force people to move, and many of them move to other parts of their own countries. Internal migration, particularly within the poorest nations, will increase because people will not be able to live where they have settled; they will become internally displaced people. This in turn causes other problems, leading to clashes with the existing population. That is the situation in most of Central/West Africa and has contributed to the fighting in Darfur. In China some six million people are probably environmental migrants within their own country out of a total of some 120 million people who have become internal migrants. Much of the tension and fighting that have occurred in both Tibet and Xinjiang is due to the influx of much poorer Han Chinese who have moved to the South West to escape much poorer conditions in their own parts of the country.

The practical realities of dealing with population and migration affect the North and the South so differently that they are effectively not facing with the same issues. As an example let us look at the migration of health-care staff.

The brain drain of health-care professionals

Figures published by the Home Office in Britain in 2005 showed that in 2003 some 44,500 people with qualifications in health-care from outside the EU were issued with work permits to work in the UK, an increase of ten times the figure a decade earlier. Most of them were prepared to work where British people are not prepared to go, such as hospitals, clinics and doctors' surgeries in the inner cities. The majority were nurses – over 27,000 were recruited in 2003. The Philippines topped the list with some 8,700, followed by India with 7,300, and South Africa with 4,400. The British Government struck deals with some of the countries in the poor world where there is a shortage of qualified health-care professionals not to recruit for the National Health Service, but agreed to continue recruiting in some other countries, including the Philippines and India, where there does not appear to be a problem. But private recruitment agencies are not subject to the ban; of the top 25 countries from which the UK recruited personnel in 2003, some 15 are on the list from which the British Government (in the shape of the Department for International Development) agreed there should be no recruitment. This migration results also in severe financial distortions.

In 2005 there were an estimated 400 doctors and 1,000 nurses trained in Ghana working in the NHS in the UK. In the UK it costs £250,000 to train a doctor and £10,000 to train a nurse. Ghana thus had absorbed costs of £140 million on behalf of the UK[40].

In 2005 around 12,500 doctors and 16,000 nurses were 'poached' from poor African countries to work in the National Health Service in the UK. From Kenya 386 nurses reached the UK, from Ghana 660, from Malawi 192, from Botswana 226, from Nigeria 1,496, from Zambia 444 and from Zimbabwe 1,561. The BBC estimated that the cost to African countries of training key medical staff who then migrated to the UK was £270 million in 2003 alone. The WHO estimated that only 750,000 health workers were available to care for 682 million people in sub-Saharan Africa, which had more than 20 million people infected with HIV/AIDS, or 60 per cent of the global total. 'It is estimated that 20,000 highly qualified Africans are now emigrating every year,' the WHO report added[41].

Poor national governance

Several states in the world, for a variety of reasons, suffer from the most appalling level of national governance and there are more of them in Africa than anywhere else. The whole concept of the state as a viable entity has collapsed in places such as Somalia, Afghanistan and the Democratic Republic of Congo – all countries where the state is just little more than a geographical demarcation. But there are many other states that simply do not function properly. In the Central African Republic the government runs the capital and nothing else. Zimbabwe is run by a vicious tyrant. Equatorial Guinea, Eritrea and The Gambia are under the thumb of capricious dictatorships. There are other states where governance is a very vague concept; it might involve a few thousand people but it is not a serious engine for the development and the running of nations. Nigeria is riven apart from a continuing rivalry between the elites that run the Federal Government and the elites that run State Governments.

Corruption

Corruption is unfortunately present in most societies and at most levels. It can be nothing more sinister than the invitation to lunch by a potential supplier to a potential client to discuss mutual benefits. At the other end of the scale can be the massive pay-offs made by Northern arms companies which supply foreign countries, such as the Swedish company, Bofors, to Indian middlemen. Corruption is endemic in some societies; in India you need to pay the receptionist to be admitted to a hospital, the nurse to be given a bed, the doctor to be operated on, the pharmacist to be given the medicines, and so on down the line. In Uganda the teacher will have to pay the person who delivers their salaries, meagre enough as they are to start with. In Mexico City the policeman is allocated a quota of money that has to be collected from motorists; if he does not collect that quota he will have his pay docked. In most African states you will come across armed soldiers at roadblocks demanding bribes for letting you through. Their salaries are paid irregularly if at all, so they are corrupt but they are also victims of a rotten system – this is very much 'corruption for need'. Across the whole of the poor world teachers and hospital staff are often not paid by their superiors, who will pocket their wages. The most vulnerable members of communities are left to suffer.

There is also systematic corruption that occurs when government business is conducted. In Kenya, for example, the Government set up a special DEVELOPMENT fund of almost $100 million to build or improve schools, health facilities and roads. Unfortunately it was also a source of cash to which a lot of people were able to help themselves because there was no management or supervision capacity, nor any transparency in the system[42]. Richard Dowden, the Director of the Royal African Society, gives a wonderful example of how deeply corruption is entrenched in Nigeria. A recently returned senior adviser to the President found that an order for action by the President himself had not been implemented by the person who had received it because there was no banknote attached to it. The International Tribunal on Rwanda, established in Arusha in Tanzania, was attacked from within by corruption by some of its senior staff: the people at the top were expropriating the Tribunal's funds. Meanwhile the perpetrators of the genocide were in gaols in Rwanda receiving three meals a day and good medical attention whilst thousands and thousands of their surviving victims – mainly women who had been raped – were dying slow painful deaths as a result of HIV/AIDS inflicted upon them. Even within international organisations it is impossible to devise systems that are corruption-free.

Corruption is so commonplace that it is doubtful that it will ever be eradicated. There is no tradition of applying transparency and openness in most countries and international donors do not seem to insist on it. Corruption is almost inevitable when one government gives aid to another government because governments cannot ask awkward questions from their peers in other governments. Therefore, by working through governments, donors do seem to condone corruption – this is 'corruption for greed'. But let us remember that corruption pervades Northern societies as well. No fewer than three of the top advisers President Obama had invited in January 2009 to become members of his Cabinet were found to have 'tax troubles'. That is a euphemism for having fiddled their tax returns. Because of the publicity, the President had to withdraw their names from nomination. In a similar vein, Jonathan Aitken, a former member of the British Cabinet, went to jail for corruption in June 1999. The EU in 2007 suspended all transition aid to Bulgaria because the bulk of it goes to local mafias and the Government is either unwilling or unable to rein it in. The most egregious examples of enormous, consistent, ongoing corruption ever will probably surface in a few years' time; it is likely to have been in the ripping off by US companies of their own Government's funds devoted to the reconstruction of Iraq.

In a few countries there is a clear and consistent drive towards transparency and determination at the top of government to eradicate corruption and move towards genuine popular accountability, but this is not the general picture across Africa. Nigeria pushed out its Finance Minister, Mrs Ngozi Okonjo-Iweala, in 2006, after three years during which she had introduced reforms and things clearly improved. The person appointed to head the Economic and Financial Crimes Commission had to fee to Britain fearing for his life. In 2009 South Africa, Kenya, Zambia, Sierra Leone, Malawi, all showed increasing reluctance to tackle the cancer of corruption at the highest level of national government[43].

CHAPTER FOUR

The global constraints

In addition to the physical and human constraints that some societies experience from within, in a globalised world there are external forces that are increasingly becoming more powerful than domestic ones. The weaker the country the more open it is to some of these external drivers. Such forces do not affect every society to the same extent; some are buffeted by global systems to a much greater extent than others. The smaller and the weaker they are, the more exposed they become. China can to a large extent control capital flows, but the Central African Republic cannot.

The weakness of international governance

Most of the international institutions that exist today were designed in different times to perform functions that probably made sense then, but no longer do in the same way. International organisations at best are reflections and extensions of Northern policies and intentions; at worst their very existence is working against the interests of the people they should be helping, the poorest of the world. Northern governments will never give the United Nations and its agencies the power and authority they require to achieve the tasks they were mandated to perform. We only need the example of Iraq to remind us that the most powerful nations in the North did not allow their actions to be scrutinised and possibly condemned by the Security Council. None of the key global issues – the environment, water shortages, disease control, the arms trade, international migration, increase salinity of the land, terrorism, international crime, corruption – will ever be controllable unless we have a working and powerful international system of governance. The same nations that call for the strengthening of the international system are unwilling to give the United Nations the tools with which to achieve it. Under Paul Wolfowitz (the President of the World Bank who had to resign over cronyism), lending to most countries that appeared to allow corruption was stopped, yet World Bank lending to Iraq and Afghanistan, two countries where virtually no governance existed at the time, increased. Presumably the fact that they were both countries of strategic interest to the US was of some relevance.

In the last few years there has been call after call from governments and various groups within civil society for the international institutions to be strengthened and reformed. The problem of course is that such calls for reform achieve very little because the same national governments that join the clamour for change retain power over key issues and are in reality unwilling to cede any such power. The major countries might call for rationalisation and system-wide coherence but that is resented by the smaller nations, who see that opportunities for influencing decision-making (but also opportunities for patronage) would quickly evaporate.

There are several UN agencies that have a specific, highly targeted mandate (weather watch, telecommunication, postal services, air travel, etc) that work extremly well exactly because of that.

Arms

According to Saferworld, a British NGO, wars and conflicts of all types cost the African continent approximately $18 billion per year between 1990 and 2005 – approximately $300 billion in total[44]. This is roughly equal to the aid sub-Saharan countries received in that period from all sources. The countries of the world are not prepared to, and perhaps no longer even able to, halt the increase in weapons. One rogue Pakistani nuclear scientist became single-handedly responsible for the spread of nuclear technology to both North Korea and Iran. He is fêted in his own country. Russia and the Ukraine, the two major exporters of small arms to illicit regimes, strongly resist any attempt to reduce or control their arms exports. They claim that small arms are some of the few export items in which they can actually compete with the North on an equal footing. China is unwilling to stop exporting fighter aircraft and anti-personnel mines to its own client states, including Sudan. It is one of the few ways in which it can ensure that they pay back some of the money that China has to pay them for its oil.

Unjust trade

Perhaps the most blatant example of the hypocrisy of the North is the way in which it impedes and restricts trade from the South. There are a number of separate yet related issues and we need to look at them in turn. The theoretical foundation of international trade is the doctrine of comparative advantages, first enunciated by David Ricardo some 150 years ago. This theory suggests that individuals and countries should concentrate on producing what they are comparatively better at producing, meaning at a lower opportunity cost, than another person or country. But this comparison hides two fundamental assumptions; the first is that everyone starts at the same level of ability and with the same amount of investment behind them and the second is that the costs of moving goods from one part of the world to another are negligible and do not cancel out the comparative advantages that arise from the production process. We do accept that sunny countries in the South are better at attracting holidaymakers and they should indeed specialise in tourism, but the doctrine fails when we come to any activity in which skills and capital investment are crucial. How can one say that Dutch workers are better at roasting coffee than Ethiopian workers? They are not, they have no greater innate capacity, but they have the machinery that represents many years of investment (physical capital) and they have thus trained their workers (human capital). At that stage the whole doctrine of comparative advantages is vitiated by the capacity to attract investment, which the Dutch have and the Ethiopians have not. Furthermore, the setting up of tariffs and quotas, which restrict the ability of a country to export to other countries, makes it impossible for the advantages of specialisation to take effect. Even if Ethiopia were able to invest in coffee roasting and blending, because value has been added to the primary product, its processed coffee would be taxed to a degree that would make it financially unviable to sell in the EU. The result is that Ethiopia and any other country that exports primary commodities are simply punished for trying to improve their products.

The final nail in the coffin is that the North gives huge subsidies to industries that should not be subsidised (except perhaps for short terms) but have to be for political reasons. This is true for the whole of agriculture within the EU. The prices paid under the Common Agricultural Policy (CAP) in Europe to allow small farmers to stay in business mean that the average prices of agricultural goods are about twice as high within the EU as world prices. It also means that each European family has to subsidise the food that it buys to the tune of approximately \$50 per month[45]. Perhaps that would be justified if the benefits really went to the poorest farmers, but they do not. In both the UK and France, for example, the beneficiaries are large-scale landowners and agribusinesses. The subsidies mean that the farmer can produce surpluses, which are then purchased by donor agencies to be given to poor countries in the South. Donating food to the poor, rather than investing in local food production, permanently ensures their poverty. The OECD countries together give their farmers around \$350 billion in subsidies per year[46]. This sum exceeds the annual GDP of all the sub-Saharan countries put together and is more than three times higher than all the official aid given to the South. The US gives \$3 billion in annual subsidy to its 25,000 cotton farmers. This lowers the price of US cotton on world markets to such an extent that some 10 million people in West Africa are not able to make a livelihood from their cotton production.

Globalisation

Poor countries have always welcomed the establishment of an international framework which would codify the way in which international trade is conducted, ensuring rights of appeal, preventing unfair subsidies, and so on. But they have been marginalised in the establishment of the framework to regulate such international trade. The creation of the WTO was the result of discussions held among the participants at the World Economic Forum at Davos, a small, fashionable and extremely expensive skiing resort in Switzerland. It was the result of discussions among people who probably had never, between all of them, missed a meal in their lives, unless it was as part of a slimming diet. There were probably some good people among them, but that is not the point. The world agenda set through the WTO is not one that would in any way reflect the needs of the poorest on earth and there is no getting away from that crucial point, in spite of all the paeans that have been sung in praise of the globalisation that has resulted from the setting up of the WTO. The key problem is that it deals just with trade, and not, for example, with access to raw materials or expertise or capital. Furthermore, it is probably a phenomenon that will work well in good times, when there is an expansion in world demand and thus of world trade, but might be far more problematic in periods of economic contraction.

In a study undertaken for the World Bank in 1999 its then Chief Economist, Joseph Stiglitz, discovered that the 48 poorest countries in the world, which included all the sub-Saharan countries with the exception of South Africa, had fared worse under globalisation than before[47]. A few countries that have discovered oil and possess other minerals have done well or could do well, but the overall picture has not changed dramatically. That is one of the crucial lessons policy-makers ignore. The Northern world has become so mesmerised by globalisation that it often seems not to know what it is about. It operates at so many levels that the very word is confusing. It is like asking 'is religion good or bad?' It depends on what you mean by it. Among the very early globalisers were some of the Northern non-governmental organisations, such as Amnesty International and Greenpeace. At the level of human concern everyone clearly should welcome globalisation, but whilst globalisation has increased the volume of trade and therefore the number of jobs in a few countries, worldwide it has negatively affected the economies of the weakest countries. And who within the poorest world loses out even more? The women and those they look after – the old, the handicapped, the sick, the children – as the markets for what they produce or could produce if they were on a level playing field disappear. The more transient members of communities, the poorest ethnic groups, refugees and internally displaced people similarly lose out. In other words, the poorest are the worst affected. Because of EU subsidies, tomatoes in tins exported from Italy are cheaper in Accra than local tomatoes. Onions from the Netherlands are cheaper in Dakar than locally produced onions. Frozen chickens from France are cheaper in Nigeria than locally reared fresh chickens. All this is happening because, although the rules of the WTO demand that all barriers to imports from other signatory countries should be dismantled, in fact all food exported from rich countries is subsidised.

To enable us to judge whether globalisation has been a useful tool in reducing poverty one needs to compare growth in one period before globalisation with one afterwards. One such study was undertaken by Dr Ha-Joon Chang using World Bank World Development Report figures[48]. Only for China do the figures clearly correlate with the creation of new jobs and therefore the direct reduction in poverty. In the 1960s and 1970s in Latin America, under the imprecise and ill-defined policies for developing their own industries, the rate of growth of real per capita income was around 3.1 per cent per year. In the era of globalisation, since the beginning of the 90s, the rate of growth has been around 1.7 per cent per year over 15 years. In Africa the figures were much lower. In the 20 years to 1980 the growth rate was 1-2 per cent per year and since then they have actually declined. If one excludes China, the rate of economic growth of all regions in the world has been slower since the advent of globalisation than it had been before. Now, as the world is entering a period of global recession, the countries that benefitted from being able to export their raw materials to the North or China, are likely to be those that will suffer most acutely from the downturn in the world economy.

The sad reality is that markets are only as good as the policies that have been devised not to encourage them but to control them. Of their own accord markets do not provide a fair balance; the interests of the producers always exceed the interest of the consumers. The reason is very clear; the producers are well organised and the consumers, by definition, operate as an unorganised body[49]. This is the field of asymmetric economics so ably studied by Stiglitz (for which he got the Nobel Prize in economics). It is the result of a world of supply-side economics.

The 'Third World' debt

Poor countries have been borrowing to finance projects and meet the costs of various needs in their own countries since their independence in the 1950s and 1960s. They were borrowing cautiously and staying within tight financial constraints – the lenders saw to that. Then they started to borrow on a massive scale in the mid 1970s. Substantial debts started to arise because from about 1973, at the time of the first rise in the price of oil, two phenomena occurred at the same time. There was a lot of money (the so-called petrodollars) sloshing about in the capital markets (primarily in London) that needed to be recycled; banks were thus very liquid and keen to lend[50]. At the same time an illusion had started to emerge about economic growth; it was believed that if you had a good project, in fact lots of good projects, each would grow and the economy as a whole would blossom and there would be enough money generated by each profitable project to repay the loans. According to this approach, the more projects one devised, the more likely it would be that one project would bolster the next one and altogether they would lead to a vibrant economy. Several governments found it easy to borrow for virtually any projects they wanted to start. By the late 1970s lending by the World Bank and other development banks started to balloon. Sadly the borrowing did not go primarily into creating lasting infrastructures; most debts were incurred by governments to purchase arms and many projects were developed for the satisfaction of urban elites. A significant amount of money disappeared altogether. As with personal debts, once you fail to keep up your repayments, interest is added and the debt escalates beyond control. Colossal debts have been accumulating across most of the developing world and the results have been catastrophic. Round the turn of the century, several countries had incurred debts that greatly exceeded their GDP.

In the 1980's many Northern governments encouraged the national institutions they had created to expand their lending to finance the exports of their own manufacturers. The system is quite simple and attractive (if you are an exporter). For example, a French company that wishes to export textile machinery to a country in the Middle East needs to establish a financial bridge until the purchaser has repaid the

entire cost of the machinery. The repayment might extend over perhaps a 10-year period. In fact companies compete in offering the
longest repayment period to their customers to ensure that the order
comes to them and does not go to a competitor in another country.
The conditions of the loan become more important than the quality of
the product itself. The customer, however, might not be particularly
well-known to the supplier and there may be a political risk in supplying goods to that customer's country. Therefore the exporter is more
than happy to take out insurance cover against not being repaid. The
insurance consists of a small premium, perhaps two to three per cent
on top of what the supplier needs to repay its bank until the capital
repayment has been completed. A government-backed export financ-
ing body covers that insurance risk. The result is that firstly, the company makes the sale, and jobs are created in the UK (or France or the
US or Germany). Secondly, it most likely means repeat orders and
payments to the supplier for spare parts for years to come. Thirdly,
and most important of all, if the purchaser defaults, the bill is picked
up by the taxpayer at large, because the body that has provided insurance is usually publicly funded. This neat trick has been used particularly in the arms industry, ensuring that countries often purchase
unnecessary weapons, whilst enriching the intermediaries in both the
North and the South in the process.

The result is that governments of poor countries, who are often
the purchasers of those products, become indebted to the exporter for
years and years to come. The debts of some of the countries involved
are simply enormous; in Zambia or Malawi the interest on the debt
alone – not including the repayment of any capital – was greater than
the amount of money those Governments were able to put in their
budgets for either health or education. An estimated $14.2 billion
leaves Africa every year in the payment of their international debt, and
this is more than twice the total amount of new money it receives in
aid. There has been a long history of campaigning to resolve this issue
and in the last couple of years the North has started to cancel parts of
the debts. The campaign began with the work of Susan George[51] who
alerted the world to the challenges in the 1980s; the cudgels were then
taken up by campaigners all over the world, particularly in the UK. For

example, after seven years, The Gambia just completed in 2008 the international debt cancellation process. This small West African country, where 60 per cent of the population lives on less than $1 per day, will initially see around $140 million of its debts wiped out, with $374 million to follow, meaning that over three-quarters of its debt burden will have been cancelled. In 2005, at Gleneagles, the G8 had promised to double the amount of aid to $50 billion by 2010. OECD estimated in mid 2009 that its members would miss the target of aid by $23 billion[52].

Capital flight and offshore banking

Another force of significant importance of which the world does not yet seem fully aware is that of tax avoidance. The issues and problems that it causes are only slowly coming to the fore and it will be a battle-ground for many years to come. A common form of tax avoidance is for a company or a rich individual to pretend to have its headquarters or home in a part of the world where the level of taxation is very low or non-existent. This sort of place typically would be one of the former British colonies or British protected territories, such as the Bahamas, the Cayman Islands or the British Virgin Islands, but also Guernsey, Jersey, the Isle of Man. The company or individual pays a small fee, or perhaps a small percentage of its capital, to set up 'domicile' there. The laws of that land do not require the submission of comprehensive or detailed annual accounts and the company or individual in question can transfer all their worldwide profits to that country.

While this may sound like a minor activity, it is a grave threat to the international community and to developing countries in particular. It means that individuals and companies can transfer profits that they make in one part of the world to another. The international system and governments in both the North and the South allow multinational corporations to do this quite legally, and yet both sets of governments lose out. The US Internal Revenue Service estimates that the US loses $75 billion a year because US corporations and wealthy people set up shell headquarters or residences in offshore tax havens. It is estimated that the total placed in such offshore funds is around

$11.5 trillion, a figure around 10 times the size of the UK GDP and almost as much as the US GDP. About $250 billion is lost to developing countries in tax revenues through such loopholes; the World Bank estimated back in 2002 that this sum was approximately five times what it would have cost to achieve all the Millennium Development Goals by 2015[53]. The Bank also estimated that the total cost of corruption, criminal activities and tax evasion to poor countries as well as countries in transition (the former Soviet Republics in particular) together amounted to between $1 trillion and $1.6 trillion[54]. The issues have been studied at length by the Global Integrity Financial Program. In early 2009 it was estimated that the amount of illegal financial flows from poor country was about 10 times as much as all official development assistance[55].

The fight against terrorism: the new cold war

Since the attack on the Twin Towers in New York on 11 September 2001 (9/11), the world has seen the emergence of a new phenomenon – global terrorism. It is not that terrorism did not exist before 9/11, but previously terrorists had not profited from the globalised world. Some of the 9/11 plotters had studied in Germany and the US; some had taken flying lessons in the US; some had purchased weapons on the internet. They had attacked innocent civilians in their determination to bring down the ultimate target of global power. The fact that terrorists had already struck US targets in both Tanzania and Kenya some five years earlier had not been seen as a global threat; after all both are poor African countries and did not appear on the international radar. The real significance, however, is not the terrorism itself, bad as it is, but that the mobilisation of forces required to fight it have become international. At one level this means that the world is increasingly divided between the good people (those who are on the side of the North in the sense that they fight the terrorists exactly the way the North tells them to) and the bad ones (those who do not). Uzbekistan, which by all definitions must be one of the worst states in the world in terms of repression of human rights, corruption and torture – all the things that make life insufferable to individual citizens – is a country which one cannot criticise now because it fights terrorism[56]. The same has happened across many African countries; strong heads of state are being made stronger so that they can stand up to insurgents within their own borders. Personal rights and democratic dissent do not carry much weight. The 'war against terror' has resurrected the controlling polarity of the old cold war.

The globalisation of crime

Crime pays and big crime pays big. Over the last two decades there has been a phenomenal increase in the level of international criminality. International gangs concentrate on three main types of activities; drugs, people and wildlife. In 2009 the UN Office on Drugs and Crime estimated the global trade in illegal drugs at about $320 billion[57]. In 1999 the UN calculated that trafficking in human beings was worth around $5 billion a year. David Batstone estimated that it was around $31 billion in 2005 and involved 27 million people worlwide[58]. Most criminals operate outside their own borders and can thus avoid the attention of their own police forces. In the UK there is evidence of the operations of the Chinese triads. In the US there is evidence that the Sicilian mafia participates in the heroin trade. The Japanese Yakuza are financing pornography in the Netherlands. It is now also apparent that a number of the criminal cartels are operating strategic alliances across the world to export their own particular crimes. Globalisation has made possible the theft of a high-value car on the streets of Mexico City and its reappearance at a later stage on the streets of Moscow. But even more worrying is the way in which international crime has become an integral part of the structures of some states in Eastern Europe and Central Asia. Misha Glenny, in his book on international crime (McMafia; *Crime Without Frontiers*), showed how the international crime networks have insinuated themselves into the very fabric of some of the newly independent countries[59]. The globalisation of money transfers took place too fast, before there had been a proper system for checking the export of currencies and this has been exploited by these networks. It made it easy to slip laundered money through very lax (or sometime non-existent) tax systems.

One of the least pleasant aspects of the globalisation of trade in narcotics has been the way in which some of the South American cartels have moved into countries in West Africa and destabilised them. Guinea Bissau is now very much of a haven for narcotics from Colombia on their way to Europe; Guinea (Conakry) is not far behind. There is a serious danger that Ghana could also move that way, as well as some of the much weaker countries in the region. Certainly Nigerian gangs have become very adept at using their fellow citizens as 'mules' transporting drugs illegally into Western Europe. In November 2007 the Home Office calculated that the amount of illegal drugs imported in the UK was worth £8 billion per year[60].

Intellectual property rights

The principle of protecting intellectual property is simple and possibly fair enough; if you have spent years of work and millions of pounds to discover the best way to cure the common cold, you should have some protection for that work and for that investment. If you have devoted years of your life to performing excellent music and you want to produce a record of that music, your hard work should be rewarded in some way or other. This is why patents and copyright agreements came into being: to protect those who have a legitimate claim to ownership of that product or artwork. In general the granting of a patent for the manufacturing or marketing of a product entails two different agreements. One is that the contents of the patent should be better known so that the whole world would then have the information available and indeed benefit from the product or process by obtaining a licence to manufacture it, while at the same time protecting the patent owner. The other is that as a result of legitimately acquiring such rights, other people and companies or institutions could perhaps get more out of that initial patented product than perhaps even the initial owner could (for example, by using that process in a totally different domain). The poor world however is at a considerable disadvantage in this transaction. It does not possess private corporate entities that could invest in research and therefore benefit from patent applications. At the same time, because poor governments are not able to afford to put public funds into supporting basic research, they are likely to be excluded forever from the production benefits of this system.

Intellectual property rights of genetically modified seeds is a very specific area of work where the power of the larger companies is in direct opposition to the interest of the public good in the rich countries as well as in the poor countries. Private companies move into the public domain to monopolise what was free and make it private; the patenting of the DNA of rice is one such case. Northern companies have been trying to register the patent for basmati rice, a variety of rice that Indian farmers have grown for thousands of years. The two companies that took out the patent, Syngenta and Novartis, announced in January 2001 that they had completed the process of the crop gene sequence for rice. It will help the development of genetically modified varieties of rice; this is therefore a way to privatise the entire production of rice. Objectors view this as a way in which wheat and corn (the last one has a similar structure to rice) will be next in line. Syngenta pledged that it would not charge for technology fees or royalties on the patents for subsistence farmers. But ActionAid, one of the most vocal opponents of the company, claimed that at that stage already some 229 patents on rice had been taken out by the big five GM companies. The Indian Government is protecting its farmers from the incursion of the Northern companies, but under international patent laws, the first company that manages to register the full sequencing of the genes of any plant would have the right to issue licences to others who may wish to use it. In Ethiopia the main staple food is teff, a form of grass cereal, which grows well in the rarefied air of the region. If patents were obtained by foreign companies for teff, farmers in Ethiopia would have to pay the multinational companies to use those genes and to sow their land. As a result the price of their food would have to go up.

The consequences of these patenting and copyright issues will be disastrous for the poor world. Poor countries will have to pay a licence to develop, or use, or adopt virtually anything on which there is a patent in the rich world. This is as true for the components of a car as it is for the drugs for malaria and for the rice or corn they have grown for centuries. The figures for the best estimate of net aid in 40-50 years time are around the $50-60 billion mark, but the expected increase in rights that the South will have to pay to the North is likely to be around $60 billion. The result will be that the North will take from the South more or less the same amount that it will give in aid[61].

A brief comment

It is impossible to calculate with any degree of certainty how much money reaches the poor world and how much leaves it. A considerable amount of guesswork is involved in calculating the amount of money that leaves poor countries illegally. Conversely, some aid given by the North is in the form of goods whose monetary value is difficult to estimate. It is, however, clear that far more money leaves Africa all the time than reaches it. We have seen above some of the ways in which the North bleeds the South. There is in addition the cost of consultants, which is estimated at around $12 billion per year, most of it flowing back to the countries that have 'given' aid. All in all, it is estimated that about $5 leaves the African continent for every $1 that reaches it[62].

CHAPTER FIVE

Issues below the radar

There is an assumption in the North that the life of people at the bottom of the pyramid is improving and that they becoming less poor. This is incorrect. The divide between the rich and poor, if anything, is growing. There are simple reasons for his. If we put two people in the same society, one with a capital of £50,000 and one with a capital of £10,000, and assume the same rate of growth of income or investments, say at 3 per cent per year, the one with the higher capital will grow in absolute terms ever further apart from the one with lower capital. If we have someone with a capital of £10,000 and the other with none at all, the gap will carry on growing at an even faster rate. This is happening between the richer and poorer members of in the communities of the North and between members of rich countries and those of the poorest of the earth. But there is another reason, and it is much more complex; through the process of DEVELOPMENT – that is the trickle down approach – only those who are touched, directly or indirectly, profit from the process. This would not involve just the intermediaries, but, for example, any manufacturer of sports shoes in any country in South Asia. Those at the top of the pyramid (even those who are employed at miserable wages) benefit disproportionately more from the DEVELOPMENT of society than those at the bottom. This leads to an expansion of a middle class that is the natural ally of the North. This process is 'corrupting' their 'development'. The process skews development by 'selecting' the beneficiary. This greatly unsettles society; all evidence is that the more egalitarian societies are also the most stable.

The increasing social divide

Social mobility has come to a halt in most societies for which data exists. It is like an hourglass with a very narrow neck, with the neck narrowing further all the time. An example of this divide is the expansion of university education in the UK, which has resulted not in more people from a poor socio-economic background being able to access university education, but in the dimmer children of the middle classes attending university. In India certainly there is a very evident growing divide between the richer members of society and the poorest. The arrival of international marketing chains such as Tesco and Wal-Mart has also heralded the arrival of methods of greater exploitation of small-scale suppliers of products to these chains and the disappearance of petty traders. The middle classes can buy standardised merchandise at low prices and can shop in air-conditioned malls. It is good for those who work in those shops whose conditions are improving, but the balance has moved further in favour of owners, shareholders and management of these chains and not of their suppliers. There is more poverty in the UK than in many other parts of Europe, although in global terms average wealth (the per capita Gross Domestic Product) is the fourth highest in the world. This masks the fact that over the past few years there has been growing inequality in many parts of the country. In March 2007, in a report published by the government, Households below Average Income (HBAI) showed that 51 per cent of children in inner London live in poverty.

This phenomenon is happening in other parts of the world at a worse rate than in the UK. In Nigeria the percentage of the population living on less than a dollar per day has increased from 32 per cent in 1997 to 71 per cent in 2007. In India a similar situation exists. The Government of India does not have the resources required to provide schooling to all children therefore the children of the poor will not go to school, they will remain poor, and they will become poorer than the children of the richer families who can afford to go to school and then move up the ladder. Most economic DEVELOPMENT in the South results in the expansion of the middle classes[63]. The provision of more international scholarships, the growth of manufacturing industries, the new opportunities that have been thrown up by international trade have all resulted in a disproportionate increase in the middle economic stratum of society. The greatest beneficiaries of any DEVELOPMENT of a free capitalistic society must be those who own or are close to capital itself. This will include certainly those in the professions since they are the key people in transforming society, but also government officials, people in banking, teaching, clerks in ministerial offices and local authorities, anyone who has the power to grant a permit of some kind. These people are the human capital of any society. The growth of civil society and aid from the North in many poor countries has provided an expansion of jobs for the middle classes. The beneficiaries will not be the poorest, such as the peasant farmers, who are the largest single group in any poor society, or the migrants in a shanty town on the outskirts of the city. For example, indigenous and tribal people represent approximately 5 per cent of the world's population, but over 15 per cent of the world's poor[64]. The newly employed worker in manufacturing will certainly be one of the new beneficiaries of this expansion – even if exploited (by any of the North's definitions) at the same time. He/she will be the one who will be able to gain a little increase in purchasing power. Current forms of economic DEVELOPMENT are not very good at improving the lot of the poorest. This phenomenon should worry everyone; inequality breeds instability[65].

The state and ethnicity

The state is such a dominant and powerful institution in Northern societies because it is so ubiquitous. It permeates all Northern thinking so extensively that few people in the North can envisage any system that does not encompass it. The richer nations have developed over generations certainties about the role of the state, the institutions within it and the division of powers that achieve a balance between players within the state. In most Northern societies there is at least the concept of the head of state, the church, the government, parliament in some form or other, the army, the police and so on, each functioning as independent entities. The emergence of the state in the particular forms found in the North has happened through historical evolution or sometimes accident. By developing in roughly similar ways the countries of Europe managed to avoid being gobbled up by each other. The North evaluates societies and their achievements by the degree of effectiveness in which governments operate, dovetailing and balancing one institution with another. But the functions and role of the state in the North is gradually and radically changing. There are changes in the attitude to sovereignty with the expansion of the EU at one end and the emergence of smaller units of government, such as parliaments in Scotland and in Wales. Yugoslavia broke up into six different statelets, Czechoslovakia into its two component nations (which coincidentally applied to join the EU in the same month). At the same time, for most countries of the South, the North seems to insist on the need for a strong centralised state, with all the problems that this implies.

There is no doubt that the democratic processes within the older states in Europe have managed to keep some sort of balance of different ethnic interests. One of the virtues of democracy is blind acceptance of the equality of all members of society. At the same time, the emergence of the EU, an economic giant although a political pigmy, has become a powerful force in eliminating different ethnic interests within Europe. The loosening of the centralised structured in some of the older nation states has both enabled and encouraged the emergence of smaller states and smaller entities. To that extent Europe has become much more like the US; more power in the economic and legal fields at the top layer of government decision-making and more democracy on most other issues at a lower level, that of the individual state. There are thus fundamental reasons why the state is becoming an ever-decreasingly important tool that determines the essential framework of society. The key factor in this evolution has been growing prosperity across Europe; everyone depends less on the state and all are growing more alike in their needs and wants and in the ways in which they try to satisfy them. The growing economic recession of 2009 and 2010 will, as one would expect, make governments again the mainstay of the economic systems and reverse this trend. The power of the market will be reduced to some extent.

In the South most societies are vastly heterogeneous. The isolation of many of them has often made it impossible to reconcile different forces and interests. Few societies in the South – and in Africa and Asia in particular – have any degree of social cohesion. There are some, such as Lesotho and Swaziland, which are made up of one ethnic group; they are very small and will never be able to survive economically on their own – no more than Luxembourg or the Netherlands could. Mauritius and the Seychelles are also small and homogeneous and have been among the best-governed countries in Africa[66]. Central authority tends to be very weak in all poor heterogeneous societies.

In many parts of the South ethnic identity is a serious issue. In several countries one ethnic group gains power over another by force or dominates by sheer numbers. Power is not shared equally. The use of one language over another implies the acceptance of the power of a particular group of people who will try to dominate and ease out those who belong to a different ethnic group and speak a different language. Having control over the state means gaining control over the spoils of power that go with it. It is a particular concern for the intelligentsia and the ambitious potential politician from a minority group who will resent not having access to the benefits and privileges that go with running the state[67]. There is therefore a delicate and complex demarcation line to be drawn between local power and central power.

Most countries in Africa operate at three 'political' levels. The first is the local ethnic group, the second is the state, and the third is the nation. Nigeria comprises over 300 different ethnic groups, 25 States, and is one federation and one sovereign nation. Ethiopia has over 80 ethnic groups, seven states and one federation. The prognosis for successful nation building is not good. Sub-Saharan Africa has more than 2,500 languages[68], but the ability of people to use their language in education and in dealing with the state is particularly limited. You cannot have access to education, enter political life, or benefit from the system of justice if you are not fluent in the majority language. In more than 30 countries in sub-Saharan Africa the official language is different from the one used most commonly. Only 13 per cent of the children in primary school are taught in their native language. By definition millions of people are excluded from the system. This intense isolation is not a phenomenon that the North has not experienced as well. By the end of the 18th century (just before the Revolution) in France there were 4 distinct language groups; Romanic, Germanic, Celtic and Basque. They were subdivided in 55 major dialects and hundreds of sub-dialects. There were many more that were unknown or unrecognised. Many villages across the country were totally isolated and in practice independent tribes and independent states. It took a bloody Revolution and the Napoleonic empire to create a nation[69].

When devolved power has been achieved, as in the case of Nigeria or Ethiopia, an increasing amount of state resources is spent on running the regional or state governments. Perhaps the most extreme form of this division of spoils is what is happening in Iraq just now: there the Shia's run some ministries, the Sunni's some others, and the Kurds a few others. That in turn means more corruption and patronage; more money flows about the system and more people need to be appointed to serve local bureaucracies. The North understands this system because it has imposed it. But in the present circumstances that state of affairs cannot mean efficient government. An example of the opposite is that of Tanzania, which has benefited to some extent by having one lingua franca, Swahili, which is a made-up language. Additionally, the country does not have any numerically overwhelming ethnic group that can dominate the others. These two factors have contributed to a great deal of continuity and peace. An efficient government implies and demands a system in which the bureaucracy that serves the elected government is impartial and efficient. And yet how can you develop an impartial government bureaucracy if access to education is limited to one section of the population?

In the conditions described above we can see why so many attempts by Africans and others to organise any continent-wide initiatives with African leaders amount to so little. There is nothing at the base that is meaningful. India, on a much smaller surface, has roughly the same population as the whole of Africa. It has a system of Federal Government that works because some components are strong and many have been built or adapted from older structures. In Africa, on the other hand, because of the weakness of the base, all institutions such as the New Economic Partnership for Africa (NEPAD) based in Johannesburg, or the Africa Union, based in Addis Ababa, or the various regional banks (such as the West African Regional Bank) amount to little more than jobs for the boys. But they are institutions that the North likes because they parallel the ones that exist in the North and create more people who speak the international languages. The fact that they represent virtually nothing on the ground seems to matter very little.

The need for jobs

As the worldwide economic recession starts to bite in late 2008 and early 2009, more people are losing their jobs in Northern societies; by the end of 2009 as many as 3 million people might be out of work in the UK, perhaps 13-14 percent of the working population. It is bad for a society in which unemployment for the best part of the last 50 years has been very low. In the South the situation is infinitely worse; there is no country in Africa, except for South Africa, where paid employment reaches even half of the population. A decreasing demand for goods by the North or raw materials from China will add to the numbers of the unemployed. The persistent increase in population will add to the demand for more jobs, as well as opportunities for personal advancement and social mobility. The flight to the cities will increase and, in the absence of any improvement to their lifestyle, people will be more and more susceptible to extreme messages. The exclusion of people from the few jobs available – because they belong to the wrong ethnic group or come from the wrong part of the country – means that there are lots of capable people without jobs. All these factors are contributing to a bomb with a long fuse. Few countries will be able to absorb such large numbers into the labour force. It is a range of challenges that the North no longer experiences and does not comprehend. Policy-makers forget that about half of Africa is under 15 years of age and inevitably will get younger for a few more years before the age level starts to stabilise.

Growth is not development

A key event in the world's economy took place in the late 1950s and early 1960s, when the natural resources of the world began to be consumed by humans at a faster rate than they could be replenished. Fish stocks could not keep pace with the rate of consumption. Forest cover was being eroded at a faster rate than could be recovered – particularly the slow-growing species of wood that took more time to grow. It took approximately 20 years before people in the North first realised that the rate at which they were exploiting the environment was accelerating beyond replenishment – this was the beginning of a growing awareness that there is a sophisticated and complicated set of arguments between growth and development. Growth is obviously linked intrinsically with the pressure on resources; if by growing more we make life worse for everyone, the net benefits can range from nil (when the economy is doing well) to negative (when the economy is progressing at an average pace). The most important proponent of this approach in the UK is the New Economics Foundation (NEF), which has shown through its studies that growth is not working. At its simplest, the argument is along the following lines: if a child suffers from asthma because the emission from cars and lorries is making it more difficult to breathe clean air, there are two different solutions. You can either try to create additional wealth to treat that child or you can reduce the amount of emission through legislation, good leadership and improved engines. NEF calculated that 'between 1990 and 2001, just 60 cents of every $100 of extra income generated by global growth contributed to poverty reduction'. In other words, it took an extra $166 of production and consumption, with all the associated environmental damage, to generate each $1 of poverty reduction[70].

Externalities

Before we all started to become aware of the negative influences of our economic activities on the physical environment, most development was extremely expensive in terms of wastage of resources. This meant not only that mines were depleted through wasteful extraction, but also that fish were harvested without any concern for restocking and that water in rivers and lakes was viewed as a raw material that had no owner and could thus be used without much concern as to the consequences. Someone else will pay for the consequences of any industrial or economic action – someone other than those directly involved in the activity. Economists call these costs 'externalities'. The world is suffering enormously because of the waste that have been discharged in the oceans; whales and dolphins are dying in increasingly large numbers because they have ingested plastic waste or industrial oils discharged from ocean-going ships. Large inland seas such as the Aral Sea and Lake Chad are dying because of over-usage. Acid rain generated by industrial pollution in the North of the UK was killing forests in Scandinavia, and so on. The consequences of not taking into account the real costs of industrial and economic activities are now being paid for by the world as a whole. China and India, by following the same path as the countries of the West, are becoming some of the worst polluters and creating externalities. Their own people are suffering more than most – more and more people are dying of pollution in the big cities in China than ever before. If the world really wanted to do something about reducing global externalities the rich countries should be prepared to pay the price, rather than asking the poorest to meet the remedial costs on their own. This would mean, for example, paying Brazil for not cutting down large expanses of the Mato Grosso every year[71].

The wrong people go into development

One of the most severe problems with the whole field of economic and social development is that it is dominated by the wrong people. There are too many macroeconomists responsible for policy-making and planning and not enough people with practical and relevant experience. The senior and powerful people in international financial and economic organisations have had very little relevant experience and are very unlikely to have ever worked at the bottom of the pyramid. They probably have never had to deal with unworkable policies, vile and rotten bureaucracies and unresponsive systems. Most of the brightest people in the World Bank, the IMF and other international organisations tend to be graduates of prestigious American business schools, where their defining influences have not been the needs of the people whose problems they are charged to solve, but some professor who is bent on an arcane solution to non-existing problems. They are full of zeal and only look at some irrelevant bottom line. A diminishing number of people who have current or recent experience in the field, who have had to cope with practical problems to make agriculture work or small-scale industries develop or a social financial system take-off, end up working out policies in those fields. Yet this, the bottom of the pyramid, is where development happens or does not happen.

It is interesting to note that for most of the last 20 years the Politburo of the Peoples' Republic of China was dominated by engineers. It could be argued that the approach that China has taken, of attacking DEVELOPMENT priorities at a purely technocratic level, with total insensitivity to human rights issues, has been a plus in its economic development strategy. The norms of the international financial institutions have paralleled this approach. They have told the world to care about financial rectitude – often again at the expense of the poorest. The leadership of international financial bodies has thus been found wanting. The World Bank has no greater claim to moral standing than the Chinese Government. The appointment of Paul Wolfowitz as its President in 2005 crowned its role as a tool of US power; he had no obvious qualification for the post (although he had been US Ambassador to Indonesia) and was appointed because he was close to President Bush. The appointment of Paul Zoelick who, when US trade negotiator had worked against the interests of the South, as his successor again denotes top-level decisions that have nothing to do with needs at the grass-roots.

Keynes was reticent about regarding economics as a precise science because it demanded a mechanistic approach to human behaviour, which he did not think could be used as a yardstick. Yet most of the principles that have been at the base of the establishment of financial and economic institutions across the world – from the IMF and the World Bank to the regional development banks, and assumptions regarding project delivery and implementation – have ignored the more diverse anthropological dimensions of the development paradigm. The World Bank until the early 1990s apparently had only one anthropologist. Its personnel are made up overwhelmingly of bright people from all over the world who have very limited exposure to the wider problems and issues of development and very few of them come from poor backgrounds. This is why, for example, there has been very little encouragement of social organisations in projects that involve the Bank. It took a grass-roots initiative in the South – the Grameen Bank in Bangladesh and its countless imitators across the world – to develop a Southern response, a response from the poorest themselves, to their needs for finance. The conclusion that we need to draw from this is that, while economists might have appropriated the debate on economic DEVELOPMENT, the key to development does not lie within economic thinking. It is to be found in social forces, political priorities, international relations and above all, it is a matter for local solutions to local problems.

Why are general macroeconomic theories not generally relevant to the needs on the ground? There are both various theoretical and practical reasons. First of all it is that the best policies are irrelevant in the absence of a mechanism of implementation and transmission. You may want to pump money into the system, but the little entrepreneur will not get the money at a rate of interest she can afford or under conditions that she can understand and respect because the local bank does not function properly. You have a great Minister of Education, but the system of building village schools does not exist. It goes down all along the chain; too many institutions that are simply not fit for purpose are set up to help the small-scale entrepreneurs or pupils in rural schools or expectant mothers in the slums. Throughout Africa there are Chambers of Commerce where no one has any commercial experience. There are small-scale industrial organisations that have no-one who can guide the small entrepreneur because the issues are beyond their competence. The genuine initiator and courageous entrepreneur is highly determined and individualistic and is often much more aware of what she needs than her mentor. It takes a long time to generate a class of entrepreneurs and risk takers. In the North this development at the base arose from a very slow evolution of the apprenticeship system. No one can develop in the abstract the range of skills that are needed. You need to have the knowledge, the determination and the stamina. If you run the smallest workshop making furniture you need to be there all day, every day. You need to be able to supervise the delivery of wood, or to ensure that the apprentices do not take some of the raw materials or products out the back door. You need to talk to the visitor who has come to buy the bed she ordered and she needs to be told what progress has been made or to check that the nails that are being delivered are right ones. This is all knowledge that the individual needs to develop through experience.

Here we encounter a problem that is common to the people in the field of governance in the North as well as in the South. There are too many people who in total innocence spend years thinking of ways of getting poor people out of poverty. There are many voluntary organisations in the UK and elsewhere that have become fascinated by the mirage of being able to influence Western governments. Many intelligent people have been seduced by the intellectual brilliance of arguments and have obtained PhDs in recondite fields within 'DEVELOP-MENT' only to tell us, for example, that wars are not very good for poor people. Most of us, whether we have worked in the Third World or not, could have told them that for free. There are some extremely brilliant people in universities, in the Department for International Development in the UK and in the voluntary organisations. These are the people who end up in the World Bank or regional development banks or as advisers to governments. DEVELOPMENT becomes a series of interconnected abstract concepts. Whenever there is a new DEVELOPMENT initiative, the first part of the fund will be set aside for the research and policy-making departments. There is very seldom any attempt at using existing mechanisms for disbursement or implementation on the ground. The problem of course is one that affects the intellectual and academic communities everywhere; intelligent people need to establish their credentials by working on new theories. That is good for your CV, for your eventual senior appointment or professorship and will make or break careers.

New development thinking needed

Over the last 50 years or so while poverty might have been reduced in a number of countries across the world particularly in South East Asia, the absolute number of poor people is still growing. Policy-makers should have learnt a number of lessons, and the lessons should have put into action. The first lesson is that whether one likes it or not the official attitude to development still concentrates far too much on the top-down approach. The North seems to believe that a functioning government will translate into a functioning society and a functioning economy. There is little evidence in fact that this is happening. In a framework in which service to society and a sense of personal obligation to people to whom we are not related is weak and where central government is deficient, the concept of belonging to a common society is non-existent, and where there is very little physical security, government cannot function properly and the rest therefore does not work. New approaches to the challenges of poverty and development need to be pursued. It is not that development cannot be achieved – let us be clear that it can. Rather it is that in all rich and poor countries alike, the approaches have too often been blind to solutions that local people would prefer. If you are poor, you do want to become less poor and you will have many ideas of your own as to how to achieve this. You need opportunities not constraints, and non-functioning governments are constraints.

One fundamental problem is that policy-makers have failed to understand the essential mechanism for the transmission of decision-making and policy-making. There are economists who study how countries should concentrate on poverty reduction strategies, but who will implement the poverty reduction strategies? In the UK if the politicians instruct the planners that money is to be allocated to the eradication of illiteracy, that will be translated into actions that will have to be undertaken by those people who train teachers and it is they who will work out how many additional teachers might be needed. There will be builders or architects who will work out how many new buildings that will require. There will be countless retired heads of schools or perhaps consultants in the field of education who will be more than happy to be involved and will make things happen. These people do not exist in a poor economy. The cascade of available expertise required at each different level of implementation of the decision is not available, therefore the entire castle collapses. While international consultants can often fill a gap, the use of such people raises other issues. Too many of them have no relevant experience. Many are appointed for reasons other than their expertise. Many more cannot find or train local counterparts to work with. They thus leave things as they are, usually after producing a big, thick, some-times intelligent report that will help to stabilise the wobbly desk of some official in the Ministry that commissioned the study or perhaps did not commission it, but was forced by one of the donor agencies into accepting that they needed this particular study. These foreign experts – the providers of what is called technical assistance – were found by Robert Cassen in 1986[72] to be of limited value in the devel-opment of Africa and 21 years later were found by Roger Riddell[73] to be still only of limited value. Yet they eat up to $12 billion a year of the aid that the rich world disburses to the poor world annually. In other words it is money that in theory the rich world gives to the poor world but in practice keep for itself.

Another major problem is that in our type of economic structure the key tool for development has become the private corporate body. Private companies function well in many ways, although the credit crunch has shown the world that bankers are more interested in the pursuit of their own happiness than that of their shareholders. The theory is an extension of Adam Smith's approach; if shareholders get the right returns, management will keep their jobs. If management are happy, they will devote their energies to the development of the com-pany and collectively those efforts will develop the economy. But stim-uli that work well in Northern societies do not necessarily work well in others. For most of the first half of the 20th century the greatest challenge facing the economies of the North was the lack of demand and the incapacity of politicians to understand the role of demand in the economy as a whole. Keynes showed how the management of demand is central to the management of the economy. In the 1920's and 1930's the unacceptable level of unemployment became the plat-form on which both nazism and communism were built. The North applied the relevant lessons from the end of the Second World War for some 35 years. The period of pre-war rearmament and the demands of the war machines ensured full employment in the countries that became involved. The huge demands that an army of almost two million people placed on the economy of the US laid the true founda-tions of that country's economic success, which has continued ever since. In the same way in Western Europe the period of post-war reconstruction meant that for most of the 1950s and 1960s there was no serious unemployment. London Transport opened a recruitment office in the West Indies because there were not enough workers at home. Similarly in West Germany there were enough jobs to employ all people of working age, plus all those who managed to escape from East Germany and other former German-occupied lands in the East, as well as thousands of Turkish workers. In France the vacuum was filled by Algerians and Moroccans. The key role of labour in the process of economic development was well explored by Sir Arthur Lewis, winner of the Nobel Prize for Economics in 1979.

The arrival of Mrs Thatcher in Britain and President Reagan in the US heralded a fundamental change in the approach to economic management in the North. Those societies moved, in a brief period of time, from concentrating on demand management to supply-side economics. It was no longer a question of generating jobs and protecting them, but of concentrating on what could be produced in the most efficient way. The success of this policy of course was the result of various factors happening more or less at the same time. The privatisation of strategic industries that had been managed by central government (telephones, postal services, railways, gas, electricity, water, air transport and so on) meant that the workers were subject to a discipline fundamentally different from that which they had previously been used to. It reduced government controls and increased the profits of private companies, enabling some of them to invest at levels significantly beyond what they had previously been used to – to everyone's benefit. At the same time it enriched some individuals beyond their wildest dreams of avarice. The lifting of restrictions on capital movement encouraged firms to move to countries where production costs enabled ever-cheaper production and greater profits and greater reinvestment.

Most of the changes that have been described above relate to the North, to the economic development and advancement of the richer parts of the world. The North is generally doing well; even if its economies fluctuate and there is a temporary increase of unemployment from perhaps 3 or 4 per cent to even 15 per cent, the vast majority of its people will still have jobs and an income. There is furthermore a safety net provided in most states in the North that will not let people starve. This book is being written as the world is entering what looks like the worst economic recession for perhaps 80 years, but still the rich world will have resources because governments have tools to raise finance, even if that means indebting everyone for years to come. The poorest in the richest societies will suffer, but most of them will still receive some social protection and have some income. The economic stimuli and priorities of the richer parts of the world are very different from those of the poorest on earth. They are literally at the margins of world economy.

CHAPTER SIX
When different worlds collide

One could argue that the very system the West operates militates in its favour against those who, for a variety of circumstances, are poorer or weaker. The relationship between the North and the South has been, and continues to be, one of powerful nations on the one side and far weaker nations on the other; powerful corporations versus very weak national entities. The only global forum where poor countries have the same rights and the same power as the rich countries is the United Nations but the UN has been marginalised whenever it suited the more powerful nations and groups. In this chapter I want to look at a few specific sectors in which the North has interacted with poorer nations of the world, and to evaluate the outcomes. Let us start with one of the best-known cases, that of Nestlé and the baby milk scandal. We will then look at the more complex relationship between the pharmaceutical companies and South Africa, and then at a number of commodities.

The baby milk scandal
The case of the baby milk companies in the 'Third World' is a small example of a large problem, but it provides a clear case of the continuing clash of interests. There had been accusations from time to time throughout the 1960s that children in countries such as Zambia and Malawi had died because they had been fed milk in powder form. The British charity War on Want wrote a report in 1974 in which it detailed the issue[74]. The result was conclusive and very simple. Many parents in poor countries had been convinced that milk in powdered

form would be better for their children than mothers' milk. They had bought the tins, diluted the powder to make it last longer, and fed it to their children. Many children had died. The problems of course are multiple. Powdered milk in tins does eventually expire and people who are illiterate do not necessarily notice the dates. You need clean water, the implements you use must be washed, the teat and bottle must be sterilised and the dosage and dilution religiously observed. Of course such elementary rules of caution and hygiene cannot be observed in most circumstances in poor environments. Very often the water will be unclean and it is often extremely difficult to observe the requirements to have clean implements. Furthermore, mothers would often dilute the milk more than stipulated simply to make it last longer because it is so expensive. Nestlé was singled out as the largest company in the field selling powdered milk in sub-Saharan Africa.

There was an international outcry and eventually the WHO began to take notice. The major companies in the field agreed to a joint code of practice under which they would not sell such products where there was no way of ensuring safe usage. This code has been in existence for three decades, but the companies do not seem to have learnt the intended lessons. In spite of having been regularly censured by the WHO for overselling the benefits of powdered milk, Nestlé, for example, has continued to do so. In a number of countries it has continued to organise the establishment of mother and baby clubs. The company says that these are for education and health promotion, but organisations such as the Baby Milk Action Group state that they have plenty of evidence that these clubs are a means of marketing Nestlé products.

It would be simplistic to accuse Nestlé alone of sheer greed. However, the company could control much more seriously where the tins of powdered milk end up than it seems to do now. But the company is in the business of making money and like in any other market, be it cigarettes or beer, it will move where it can find people willing to purchase its products. If that means encouraging purchases through marketing, publicity or providing inducements to buy the products, it will do it.

The pharmaceutical drugs issue

One of the best examples of why the whole issue of the role, power and functions of international companies cannot be the solution for the South is the area of pharmaceutical drugs. What are the real costs of drugs? For many years the major international pharmaceutical companies were resisting any call to reduce the prices of drugs to combat HIV/AIDS in poor countries. In Thailand one tablet of a drug known as Biozole, manufactured by Pfizer, cost $0.20 while in South Africa over the counter it cost around $13. In Thailand there were companies, supported by the Government, which produced generic substitutes, but none in South Africa, and thus the manufacturer could set its own price. The South African Government decided in 1997 to take on the companies. Firstly it decided to buy large quantities of drugs from India and distribute them to people suffering from the disease. Secondly it decided that it would offer licences to manufacture, distribute and market the drugs within South Africa. The issue was due to come to a head in the courts in South Africa in March 2001. The 39 major pharmaceutical companies that were opposed to the Government's decisions argued that this could affect their fundamental right to manufacture the drug in any part of the world and to control the price. The fact that just 1 per cent of total drug sales was accounted for by the entire continent of Africa did not seem very relevant to them. At the end of the day the pharmaceutical companies do not feel that they have any responsibility to help the poorest countries. Their raison d'être is to make money for their shareholders. Eventually a combination of Southern governments and the general public in the North forced the companies to change their approach; they abandoned the court case just a few weeks before it was due to be heard. Many groups, including OXFAM, Médecins sans Frontières, and others, particularly a coalition of smaller NGOs within South Africa itself, united to support the action of the South African Minister of Health. In a joint statement they claimed that this decision by the companies marked a decisive shift in the balance of power from large multinationals to the governments of the poor countries themselves. The groups calculated that the five biggest companies involved in the unheard week-long appeal to the High Court would have sold $2.2 billion worth of medicines and made a $560 million profit on these sales in that week. The Secretary General of the UN had been one of the key intermediaries involved in trying to draw some sort of balance between the various parties. The result is not only that drugs are now available, but also that poor countries are much freer to buy drugs where they wish to if they can afford to.

But the real reason why the companies decided not to proceed with the case emerged in January 2001: the companies, apparently for the first time, had seen the position papers of the Government's defence. In those documents it was shown that the Government of South Africa would have argued in court that, contrary to the argument of the companies that they needed the money to protect their research programmes, the governments of the countries in which their headquarters were located had already funded the basic research to the tune of several hundreds of millions of dollars. The companies simply could not argue that the profit would be reinvested and was thus essential to the future of the drugs themselves.

The general lesson to be learnt is that pure commercialism simply cannot work. The forces that make our pharmaceutical companies produce Viagra and other similar drugs are the same that neglect the production of anti-malaria pills that would make it possible for millions of people in the South to survive one of the greatest killers of all. Now there are new funds that have been generated through the Global Initiative to combat malaria and the economics of research and production are changing.

Oil

Arms, oil and tourism are the three largest industries in the world. Oil companies are among the most important of the multinationals; their power is truly enormous and their spread is worldwide. They are also often accused of being complicit in serious crimes. The availability of oil and other raw materials has led to the shorthand definition of the 'resource curse' – the fact that in poor countries that have been shown to be rich in minerals, oil and gas, there has been a very mixed bag of consequences from their exploitation.

The discovery of oil in Equatorial Guinea in the last 10 years has been a disaster for the country. There are around 500,000 people in this poor former Spanish colony and the average per capita income is less than $2 per day. The Head of State is Theodoro Obiang who came to power in 1979 by overthrowing and killing his uncle. In 1995 US oil companies discovered massive reserves of oil just offshore. Large companies, led by Exxon, have invested around $6 billion in the country and around 300,000 barrels of oil now flow daily from the area. There are more than 3,000 expatriates working in Equatorial Guinea and there is even a direct daily flight from Houston in Texas to the capital. In 2004 the country was estimated to have received up to $700 million in oil revenues but most of it seems to have disappeared into the private bank accounts at Riggs Bank in Washington of the family of the dictator. The US reopened its Embassy in October 2003 after closing it for eight years because of human rights abuses. More than 70 political opponents were jailed in 2002; some of them were held in such physical positions that they sustained broken bones, which eventually killed them. The overarching aim of the US Administration is to see the present supply of oil from that part of Africa rise from the present 15 per cent of US demand to around 25 per cent, which will lead to a substantial decrease in the need for Saudi supplies. But the benefits of the massive investment have not gone to local people; there has been no visible increase in physical infrastructure, roads or bridges for example. One new hospital has been built and a couple of schools in the capital. The rest of the country has not benefited at all from the massive investment in their single, non-renewable resource.

BP Amoco is the main investor in PetroChina that in turn is the largest investor in the Greater Nile Petroleum Operating Company. BP Amoco is not a direct operator in Sudan, but it has invested some $578 million in PetroChina. This enables PetroChina to invest more in Sudan. The money generated by the oil means that the Sudanese Government is able to buy weapons, wage war and ultimately kill its own people. Sudan is not the only country in which BP has an interest via PetroChina.

The damage that Shell's subsidiary has caused to the south-eastern states of Nigeria has been well documented over the years. The company used the army to force local people to accept installation and refinery facilities that have polluted their rivers and killed the wildlife. In the process villages were looted and villagers raped by soldiers. In 1998 the local Ogoni people, led by Ken Sera-Wiwa, began to protest against the company's behaviour and attack oil installations in their area. Sera-Wiwa was eventually tried (the majority of the court members were military men as the court case was heard during the military dictatorship), found guilty and executed. As a result of the oil exploration in the Ogoni Delta, oysters and crabs are now too poisonous to eat. Thousands of people have lost their livelihood and have become environmental refugees in their own country. In mid 2003 the President of the Nigerian Labour Congress complained that civil servants in the Ministry of Oil were perpetrating an elaborate scam. In spite of the fact that some $700 million had been spent on repairs to the oil facilities at the time, the oil refineries were working below capacity. In this way they were able to justify the reimportation of refined oil and benefit personally from the imports. This scam had in fact been started by General Abacha when he became President at the time of military rule and had not been abrogated.

Diamonds

The diamond trade is one of the forces that perpetuate bonded labour and slavery in the mines. Global Witness, a small UK NGO, researched the role that diamonds played in the Angolan conflict. It found that it was the main source of income for the various warring factions during the 1980s and 1990s. Diamonds fuelled the war that kept Jonas Savimbi fighting in Angola, using weapons bought from NATO countries and with the support of the South African Government (which at the time was governed by apartheid laws). Most governments in the world flouted the United Nations Security Council embargo on unofficial Angolan diamonds. Over the last three years the poor image of the gems has affected profits; companies claimed that the sale of diamonds had dropped by approximately 20 per cent in Europe. In both Europe and the US the various participants in the diamond business established the Kimberley Code – a voluntary agreement not to deal with diamonds that do not certify that they are not the product of wars and that they have been legally exported from the producing countries. In 2004 Global Witness conducted an exhaustive survey of the marketing of diamonds in the US, where approximately 50 per cent of all diamonds are sold. The survey aimed to find out how well the Kimberley Code was adhered to. It was shown that the trade did not respect the principles of the Code, but, as happened with the fur companies that became the target of many people concerned with cruelty to animals, the campaigning did eventually start to make people aware of the situation.

The trade in illegal diamonds undertaken by Charles Taylor and his followers was the driving force behind a war in Liberia in which an estimated 200,000 people were killed during the first half of the 1990s. This was probably the first war in which the majority of the fighters were young children, stolen from their families and forced to do the bidding of their seniors. The children were brutalised from the start; most of them were initiated into the fighting by having to execute a close member of their family in front of their community, thus ensuring that they could not go back to their own villages. The Economic Community of West African States (ECOWAS) sent a military force to the area, predominantly comprised of Nigerian troops. The officers stole the soldiers' pay and used it to purchase diamonds on the black market. Meanwhile the ordinary Nigerian soldiers, unable to survive without pay, in turn started to pillage the villages they had been sent to defend.

There have been close to an estimated two million deaths in the Democratic Republic of Congo (DRC) since 2003, most of them in the eastern part of the country and a large proportion of them linked to the trade in diamonds and other valuable minerals that can be found in that part of the world. Young men and women have been coerced by local militiamen to work as porters or soldiers and the girls have been used as sex slaves. The industry claims that it does not know of such exploitation, but this seems impossible. In 1998 the government of President Kabila of the DRC approached the President of Zimbabwe to ask for help as he was besieged from all sides. An agreement was reached under which the diamond mine at Mbuji-Mayi, which had been valued at around $1 billion, was handed over to Mr Mugabe in exchange for the use of the Zimbabwean army. Because there are currently such enormous difficulties in getting diamonds out of Zimbabwe, the mine is using its operations as a cover for the smuggling of diamonds that come from Angola and Sierra Leone. It was also mentioned in a UN report that the operators were regularly withdrawing large amounts of money (as much as $500,000 at a time) from its Hambros Bank account in London to be taken to Kinshasa; in other words laundering it[75].

Coffee

The fluctuation in the world price of coffee is a very good example of what happens in the international arena for primary products. It is not difficult to grow coffee and some 80 countries round the world produce the two main types of coffee – Robusta (low quality) and Arabica (high quality) – with more and more countries producing the Robusta variety which is easier to cultivate and therefore cheaper. Production prices fluctuate and competition is intense because of elements that are totally outside the control of the farmers. Encouraging more producers to enter the international arena and to start exporting simply reduces the income of everyone already involved in coffee production. If coffee is affected by blight in one part of the world, the farmers in that part of the world lose out. Producers in other parts of the world might then be able to repay their debts, but this climate of uncertainty is not conducive to long-term planning. It is not surprising that in areas that could grow coca – the base for cocaine – such as Colombia and Peru, the temptation for the farmers is to move out of coffee into more lucrative products. At the international level the International Coffee Organisation was hoping that there could be a return to Arabica, rather than to Robusta varieties that in the long run do not make coffee attractive to consumers. If the quality of the product could be maintained, there would be better returns to the farmers who have spent generations producing coffee. In 2006 the world coffee market was worth about $70 billion worldwide, but the coffee-producing countries were making only $5.5 billion.

Coffee was discovered as a wild bean in Ethiopia probably at around the 9th century. It still grows wild in the forests of some parts of the country. It grows best in the South Western part of Ethiopia, close to the Sudanese border. The Kaffa region of the country is renowned for its coffee and the region has given the name to the plant. Ethiopia grows mainly the Arabica variety, but the four multinationals that control the price of coffee on world markets (Nestlé, Kraft, Procter & Gamble, and Sara Lee) and together buy about half of the total coffee produced in the world, have flooded the world coffee market with other varieties, mainly Robusta. Multinationals make enormous profits and have been able to establish a range of world brands, such as Nescafé and Maxwell House. Through heavy advertising they are able to sell these brands at a high profit. There is no relationship with either the world price of coffee or the price they pay to producers. In fact they pay less and less to the farmers. People who do not grow any coffee but have the facilities for roasting, packaging, and marketing will take the overwhelming share of the wealth that is generated by the growth of coffee. In the UK it is not unusual to pay as much over £2 in Starbucks for a cup of coffee; the farmer will probably get around 1.5p of that cup.

The coffee plant takes three years to mature and thus there is great uncertainty that the profit made in the first year of production will begin to pay for the long gestation period. One of the problems with coffee is that the berries ripen at different times and thus have to be hand-picked; mechanical collection mixes ripe and unripe berries and thus the coffee is of poor quality. As long as the main way of collecting coffee berries is by hand, millions of jobs will be saved in some of the poorest countries in the world. The situation is now likely to change in those countries wherever GM beans are being introduced. GM coffee berries all ripen at the same time, therefore they can be harvested at the same time, by machine. Several countries will be affected by this technology and millions more poor people will be thrown into poverty because their only source of income will disappear.

At the moment about 70 per cent of all coffee is grown by some seven million poor farmers in a range of countries from Central and South America to Uganda, Kenya and Ethiopia. These smallholders sometimes use a space no larger than a backyard in which to grow their crop. Approximately 125 million people depend on the income from coffee for their primary source of cash income[76]. Most of the producers are periodically not able to recoup the inputs (in terms of seeds and fertilisers) and certainly not the value of their labour in any way. They continue to work in the hope that from time to time the market will change in their favour. They need to get hold of cash, at any cost, and thus the economic value of their time and labour does not come into the equation. The total production that is purchased by organisations that belong to the Fair Trade mark is about 500,000 bags and for the producers that supply these beans the prices have been maintained, but clearly it is very small beer as a percentage of world production and consumption. Ordinary farmers will not be able to afford the expensive GM seeds or the machinery, which will thus remain the prerogative of the larger companies because once they incur debts they have to sell their land. Forcing them off the land will mean that they have to work for the large coffee producers, such as Nestlé, at miserable wages without any security of employment.

The most important coffee producer in the world is Brazil, which accounts for about 25 per cent of world production, followed by Vietnam, which now accounts for around 10 per cent. The case of Vietnam is very interesting. Probably the single most important factor in determining the world price for coffee has been that for the first time ever there has been enormous production (as much as 60 million 60kg bags in a good year) from that country. Ten years ago Vietnam was a small-scale producer of coffee, but with aid from USAID (the official US aid agency) and the World Bank, it started to increase and export its production. As a result it is decreasing the value of coffee exports of other producers. World production has thus increased. That in turn reduces prices and means that consumers get cheaper coffee, but at the same time the producers are being reduced to greater poverty, except those from Vietnam, who now have a bit of income. The price of coffee to the consumers in the shops had not changed in the five years to 2002, but income to the producers had actually decreased considerably. In 2006 they received, on average, approximately 9p for a 1kg of unprocessed beans, a decrease over two years of about 20 percent. At the end of the chain in the UK the same item will sell for perhaps an average of £17. Supply is growing at approximately 2 per cent per annum, while demand is increasing at about 1.5 per cent.

Coffee is the second largest internationally traded commodity; it is only surpassed by oil in its world scale and in importance (but oil is much more important in volume and in quantity, let's be clear!). Coffee prices are at present at an abysmally low level. In Guatemala farmers are losing their livelihoods because landowners find that the cost of harvesting the coffee beans is greater than the value of the coffee they sell to the usual intermediaries. The same is occurring in Ethiopia, another desperately poor country that has tried for years to improve its crop but finds that things are getting worse by the day. Here as well the cost of producing the coffee is greater than the price it will fetch on both their domestic and international markets. Some conspiracy theorists would say that the US deliberately encouraged the development of coffee in Vietnam in order to bring down the price. The truth is probably that both the World Bank and USAID wanted to help that country and coffee presented itself as a wonderful commodity for a poor country that has gone through hell. No one was thinking about the wider picture. It is an unfortunate consequence that the livelihoods of millions of people all over the world are threatened as a result. But it is also an example of why globalisation is not the simple solution; it is just a way of encouraging the poorest people on earth to produce more so that the North has cheaper primary products. There have to be more powerful regulatory mechanisms to ensure fairness.

There are 11 countries in Africa that rely on one single item for more than 50 per cent in value of their exports. Each of these commodities is highly reliant on movements in world demand or supply for that export. There is a long gestation period; coffee and tea need three years, cocoa three to five years. If in any of the years of growth there is an excess of supply in one part of the world some of producers will be discouraged from growing their crop. If a fungus attacks the product in any part of the world, there will be greater demand for that very product grown elsewhere. There is inevitably a mechanism through which the companies, needing a constant supply, can even out the ups and downs in the market of the primary product. This has led to a world market through the process of auctions. But the present system, under WTO rule, does not allow the producers to organise themselves so that they can build up stocks to protect themselves from price fluctuations. The World Bank at the same time actively discourages individual countries from using public funds to cushion local producers through local stockpiling. Yet the same market allows the intervention of speculators – people who are not in the market for real coffee, but only to acquire 'phantom' quantities that they can resell, hopefully at a vast profit.

Cotton

The US Government spends between $3 billion and $4 billion a year subsidising some 25,000 American cotton farmers, more than the annual amount it gives to Africa in aid[77]. In West Africa approximately one million farmers, that is some 10 million people when one includes their families, rely on cotton as their main export. A typical small farm in Africa will make perhaps $300 per year from the production of cotton. But as a result of the American subsidy the world price of cotton is highly depressed and the subsidy to the US producers is distorting world production; US cotton prices are about one third of world price. In June 2004 the US lost a major case before the WTO concerning the billions of dollars of annual subsidies it gives to its cotton farmers. The WTO ruled that such subsidies to farmers are illegal, but the US ignored the ruling. President Bush was courting the cotton farmers who he saw as crucial in his 2004 re-election. (Normally the farmers are Democrat voters and their support was therefore vital.) The US continues to subsidise its cotton farmers.

Some eight million hectares of cotton are cultivated in India, requiring some 50 per cent of the country's total consumption of pesticides. This adds up to a serious threat to the well-being of the country's people, to the environment and to biodiversity. Yet there are ways to improve the crop and to reduce the harm that the pesticides cause. Field trials by Professor Swaminathan (the father of the Green Revolution in India) at his research Institute in Madras of cotton that had been bioengineered with a bacterial protein that protects against insect invaders, raises yields by 40-70 per cent, and needs fewer pesticides. But it is unlikely that India and some of the other poorest countries will ever be able to afford the new seeds.

A brief comment

There are examples of this kind of totally unequal relationship in all fields of primary commodities. Sugar is one commodity that WHO is encouraging countries to consider more closely. Too much sugar is bad for people's health. More and more people everywhere die because of obesity that causes heart problems, diabetes, and circulatory problems. The US sugar lobby and parallel organisations in other Western countries are fighting the WHO by claiming that there is no evidence that sugar is bad for you. Likewise, the tobacco companies are clearly selling a product that is harmful to people and to the health services of the North and the South, yet they are allowed to sell cigarettes to people in countries other than their own without health warnings. In most countries in Africa and Asia the sale of all tobacco products is in the hands of state monopolies, which are more interested in the revenue potential than the health of their citizens.

PART TWO

Poverty
A Vicious Circle

In Part One we saw how most poor nations are caught in a vice. They are restricted by geography, by their internal structures, by their rulers, by the behaviour of their more powerful partners or by the buffeting of global forces. They are, in most cases, boxed-in.

In Part Two we examine the major sectors of human activity that can either serve or impede development, depending on the wider environment.

First we need to define what we mean by 'development' and how it might happen. Some societies might simply not be motivated to develop at all; one can imagine a highly feudal situation which will not budge. This is true for Mauritania or Niger. In other societies, such as South Korea or Singapore, governments have become the champions of their own people in the process of economic development.

There have to be the tools through which this 'development' can take place; there are only so many tools at the disposal of societies. Societies in the North might be primarily dominated by commercial and industrial entities that create employment, offer motivation and opportunities to individuals to advance, and to governments to obtain the income – through taxation – needed to provide the 'common goods'. In the South the state plays a very different role; it is not a neutral backdrop that all can enjoy. It is a powerful negative force on most members of society, for all those who do not belong to the group in power. Apart from specific cases, we tend to assume that governments across the world behave decently towards their citizens.

Then there is the business community, which across most of Africa is extremely weak and generally seen at best as an extension of the governing classes.

Civil society in the North has a powerful role to play in sustaining the wider society, and complementing and challenging both the commercial world and state services, but in the South it often assumes a role of opposition to government.

Lastly there is aid, which is one of the major determinants of the North's relationship with the poor world, because it is the key telescope through which it has come to look at most of the South. The North does not look at poor countries in terms of their own dynamics or needs; it looks in terms of their dependence on the North. But aid is not the powerful tool for lifting people out of poverty that most people across the world would like it to be. Firstly it is a very poor force in counteracting the much greater forces that attack the poorest, the forces that we looked at in Part One. But much of the time aid – both the aid disbursed by governments and international organisations as well as by non-governmental organisations – is at best a plaster and therefore an extension of welfare. Official aid, for very practical reason, tends to be a tool for implementing the priorities of the donor. As such neither form of aid cannot offer lasting economic development – just short-term relief.

CHAPTER SEVEN
The nitty-gritty of development

How did economic activity begin in our society? In 1776 Adam Smith, the Scottish philosopher and father of economics, remarked in *The Wealth of Nations* that in Scotland, where people made a living from making and selling meat, beer or bread, for example, such activities were carried out in pursuance of personal interest and not out of any concern for society at large. The result of each person's activity would indeed lead to the increasing prosperity of society, but that was the result of the individual activities, not the intention. Yet those observations and most of his work are inevitably coloured by the context in which the activities he was observing were taking place. We must remember that economics is very much part of society; different societies will generate different economic systems and relationships.

Britain has enjoyed some important geographical and social features that allowed a level of gradual prosperity. Economic activity has grown slowly but steadily from the end of Roman occupation in the 5th century. There was a period of persistent decline, including a decrease in population, until the end of the 8th century, but some elements of that earlier society remained; a few roads were even built as far back as the 1st century[1]. There are no mountain ranges that cut off sections of the population, there are plenty of rivers and lakes and no one lives very far from the sea – therefore there is relative ease of movement and fish to be harvested – and there is abundant fresh water. By the late 18th century, when communities had been settled for a long time, people had developed a tremendous sense of belonging. They spoke Gaelic in most small towns and villages in Scotland

and Wales and variations of English across the whole country. People were deeply religious with a strong sense of right and wrong, a characteristic shared by many poor societies around the world, in which both the rulers and the ruled knew their respective places. Local markets could flourish because there were both a level of skills, and a considerable degree of riches that had been accumulated over perhaps 10-12 centuries. They had over time acquired a sense of collective discipline that enabled an industrial revolution take hold[2].

Why has a similar pattern of development not occurred in the South? It is not the fact the people in poor countries do not possess the potential to develop necessary skills to make things or the willingness to produce a surplus they might be able to sell to others. It is the environment (in its broadest meaning) that is very different. The majority of poor societies are physically very isolated; poverty is so widespread that there is not much activity in remote villages on the verges of the Sahara or the Kalahari in Botswana because everyone is very poor and the land is infertile. However, there are skills even in the poorest villages of Africa. People fish on Lake Malawi and sell their catch inland. Women grow vegetables on very small patches of land in The Gambia and sell it in the hotels in Banjul, the capital city. Even the poorest have capacity and adaptability and can survive in highly competitive environments. I spent 35 years travelling around Africa and saw wonderful things everywhere that could have found a market in Europe or the US. There were wooden boxes and tables in Cameroun, wool hangings in Ethiopia, cotton weavings in Egypt, baskets in Rwanda and hardwood trays in Western Zambia. But transport is difficult, communities are isolated, the patterns of trade are very different from those of the North and there has been no organic economic development of local communities.

The force of inertia

In most of the North societies are very mobile; everyone is familiar with children moving away from home and with people moving to other locations, even other countries if their job requires it. These are very recent events in the history of mankind and they are themselves the result of a highly prosperous, educated and liberated society. Most of the world does not work that way; indeed the UK did not until perhaps 100 years ago – if you were born 'below stairs' in the Victorian era, that is where you remained for most of your life. This is still the rule in most of the poor world, where people do not question the rigidity of the system and the decisions of their elders. You can only stand up to local petty tyranny when you can see a way to escape it. You can only move away when you have an entrepreneurial spirit and a basic education and there is somewhere to escape to. For most Europeans there was the New World and, later on, there were colonies to which the most enterprising people could escape. In the present poor world you cannot do that. Health plays an important part. If you are poor and do not have regular access to food your body will not develop to its full potential. You are unlikely to benefit from education even if you have the good fortune to be offered it. This is why in both rich and poor countries those who have anything that resembles a balanced diet also are likely to be among the more intelligent.

A closed society cannot nurture change. A farmer who has always tilled the land with a primitive hoe that only scratches the surface of the earth will not be able to move to the simplest plough. She does not have the funds to buy it and even if she had, she would not know how to use it. For the same reasons neither will she use a new type of fertiliser. Without education or the inducement of a bigger market change will not occur. But one also needs to understand that the acceptance of change is a complex phenomenon even in the richest societies. In the last half century there have been profound changes in the North (for example in all fields relating to IT) and education has been an integral part of it. Yet a generation earlier for millions of people, for example in the UK, there was very little questioning of the 'natural' hierarchy of things. That approach was the product of a class structure that millions of people did not believe they had the right to question. Moving out of the mental framework of your society is a very courageous and unusual thing to do. Training blacksmiths in Tanzania would be considered undignified to most other people in the country because they have such low status. Malian musicians have found fame outside Mali but their status is so low that they would not be allowed into the homes of members of the higher castes in their country. Most Pakistani families in the UK would be ashamed if their daughters married outside their 'clans'. You certainly cannot do it in the caste system of India and in most tribal parts of Africa. That social immobility mirrors the economic immobility of most of the world; they are two aspects of the same phenomenon.

Lawrence Harrison[3] sets up a pecking order of groups whose internal dynamics provide the motivation for self-improvement; at the top would be the Jews, followed by the Protestants, and so on, with fatalistic societies – including Islam and Hinduism – towards the bottom. Gregory Clark argues that the stability of society eventually generated the changes in attitude, for example in work ethics and discipline, that enabled the development of the industrial revolution in England[4].

Skills and raw materials

In traditional societies people develop skills according to their environment; people who live near the sea become good fishermen within the limits of the capacity of their boats to travel or of the nets to haul the fish. But in many places there might not be any skills that would enable ratcheting up of the level of development. That might range from enabling the shepherd to skin an animal in a way that makes the skins a valuable commodity as a first step toward transforming it into leather, to training the forester to saw a tree trunk into useable planks. Too little has been done to develop skills at the right level of development. This is in great part due to the fact that the West has prevented the natural evolution of agricultural sophistication that would have enabled local people gradually to add value to their primary agricultural production. Then, in more recent times, donors and governments have basically ignored agriculture and related activities altogether[5]. If we encouraged, for example, roasting, mixing and packaging of coffee, or the juicing of fruit, or the tanning of skins close to the producers and not in the countries to which the goods are exported, there would be much greater incentive for farmers and their families to move gradually up the value chain into such agro-industrial activities. However, under the rules of imports into the richer countries of the North, namely the OECD countries, any processing that adds value to the primary product places those imports into different tariff brackets and they attract much higher rates of duty. Under pressure to gain foreign currency, governments in the South concentrate on those economic activities that have international markets. Policymakers are making it difficult to add value to such local produce or raw materials and therefore prevent any upgrading of local skills.

Exporting cash crops

The colonial powers repeated the sort of investment they had undertaken at home; if the land was good for planting tea, all that area was transformed into a tea plantation. In the early days of colonialism African lands offered to the colonial power the possibility of developing produce that was needed 'back home'; tea, coffee, cocoa, sugar, groundnuts for oil and fruit, for example. The entire production would have an assured market. To that purpose in most African countries the entire crop of cocoa, coffee, tea, cotton, and sugar was purchased by a relevant marketing board. These boards became the main purchasers, as well as sources of information and central players in the activities of all farmers. If you needed cocoa seedlings, you bought them from the cocoa marketing board. If you needed advice you asked help from the extension workers employed by the board. Small loans were disbursed against future deliveries. Such institutions became central to the entire operation. When one remembers that most of the farmers in Ghana depended on their cash income from the sale of their cocoa beans to the Cocoa Marketing Board, one can see how important it was. But that dependence carried with it the seeds of danger. Not surprisingly, after independence the boards became important sources of patronage. The new political elites were not going to allow 'outsiders' to take on the well-paid jobs as board directors, managers, regional directors, export managers and so on across the range. Corruption set in very quickly. Board after board collapsed because of lack of competence, inefficiency, huge debts and corruption. In most countries they were not replaced. Instead of trying to re-establish them with properly run institutions, they were dismantled by governments, often under prompting by the World Bank in the 1980s. The result was total anarchy and lack of assured markets for the small producer. Re-establishing them would break the rules of the WTO.

But there is a bigger problem. Eleven countries in Africa depend each on a major crop for their exports. This means that it becomes crucial to sell your crop at a price lower than your neighbour's. It leads to the sort of competition that might work well in the production of manufactured goods, where the manufacturer might improve production through more capital investment. We have seen earlier on that it does not work in the agricultural field, where there is no investment because the farmer is too poor. She receives no wage at all and depends entirely on what she manages to sell with an unchanging produce. There were periods of prosperity during the early 1970s in villages in Cameroun or Ghana (where the cocoa estates were once all owned by Cadbury). There were pretty local houses, decent village halls, there was even tarmac on some roads and all the children went to school. However, production then expanded across several countries in the region, prices went down and the farmers were not getting back what they had put in over many years of toil. This is where globalisation turns into local competition which turns into a fight for survival. There has to be some regulation of production, including the building up of stocks, not the encouragement of competition on price alone. Creating free world markets in produce where the end result does not depend on ability or hard work, but on capital investment, on the weather, or international competition is shorthand for ensuring that the poorest of the world will fight one against the other so that the better off in the North get a cheaper product. In these circumstances a cartel – a word that is unmentionable in the days of globalisation – would provide some degree of protection to the producers. OPEC, the Organisation of Petroleum Exporting Countries, can get away with it, the producers of soft commodities cannot.

In some other countries a different problem arises from the appeal of globalised markets. More and more land that otherwise might be devoted to farming to prevent starvation is being turned over to either vegetable oil or biofuels (for exports to the West) or soya production (for animal feed in China or India). These have become the new cash crops, whose viability is dependent on those in distant countries who have the purchasing power. It also raises another issue; more land is becoming the property of people who have no long-term commitment to a particular area. We are witnessing the emergence of the absentee latifundista in Africa; the locals are squeezed out.

Local markets

Without diversification and increasing orders, any local production will never develop into any substantial economic activity. For this to happen the very small sawmill in the village in eastern Zambia needs to receive regular orders of wooden planks from the furniture maker in the slightly bigger village down the road (if only they could reach it). For most people in the interior of Africa transport is a major problem. Small communities live in isolation; often they have survived precisely because they are isolated. Families have had to move as their land is exhausted. They have managed to avoid the attention of more powerful groups that could have raided or conquered their villages or homesteads. However, isolation has a downside. During the famine of 1984-85 it is thought that up to one million people might have perished in Ethiopia. Many died because the Marxist Government of the day did not allow the Northern parts of the country to receive food from international aid donors because they were trying to secede. Hundreds of thousands of people could not escape their villages. It was estimated at the time – and not much has changed since – that people lived on average about one-and-a-half days away from any main road. Not an asphalted road, just one that would be passable very slowly with a four-wheel vehicle. This meant that by the time the strongest men had collected food to take back to the villages many members of their families had died.

The same isolation makes marketing any product extremely difficult. The readers of The Guardian and Observer newspapers in December 2007 started to donate funds to help develop the Katine district of Uganda and the two papers regularly report what happens there. In some areas mangoes are so plentiful that the locals do not realise they have any monetary value. But just 20km away there are shortages and people would be prepared to buy the Katine mangoes – if only they were available. Unfortunately the poverty in Katine means that, even if they knew that there was a market for their mangoes they wouldn't be able to do anything about it as they do not possess transport with which to get the mangoes to market. The mobile telephone revolution that has encompassed the whole of Africa might to some extent reduce that profound isolation, but the capacity to respond to market demands is still hampered by distance, lack of storage capacity and lack of transport.

Policy-makers must become aware therefore of the need to develop markets that will relate to local demand and be under local control. This is not a question of advocating local monopolies, which in most cases would be to the advantage of the local bigwigs, but of advocating the priority of addressing local needs. What are needed are facilities for the local producer to reach a gradually widening local market. Some economists, such as Joseph Stiglitz[6], and campaigners, such as George Soros[7], would argue that there is no such thing as a perfect market. The mobile telephone might indeed help the local farmer to find where it might be more advantageous to sell her tomatoes, but she might well need more substantial capital investment, perhaps in the form of water or storage facilities before she is in a position to produce a consistent and marketable surplus. In The Gambia women farmers produce great tomatoes and heads of lettuce. For a long time they had no local market; the hotels in this small country were all owned by foreign operators who had contracts with European suppliers who received a subsidy from the EU to export to The Gambia. Eventually most hotels changed policy and some of the purchases could be made locally, but then another problem arose. Local intermediaries intervened to buy the produce from the women and take it to the hotels, offering them a pittance. The women tried to organise themselves into a cooperative, but were not able to as only men could be the heads of anything in this deeply Muslim society. Eventually the women formed an informal group and jointly hired a small lorry to collect the produce and take it directly to the hotels.

The stranglehold of the middleman

When the Dutch flower importers arrive at a farm on the shores of Lake Naivasha in Kenya, they create the opportunity for local farmers to grow and export beautiful flowers to the markets of Amsterdam and London. But local people seldom have the means to deal directly with the Dutch middleman. He does not want to become embroiled in local regulation, so he will deal with a well-connected local, who can look after the local production, sort out the details, and can assure regular deliveries. Some people involved in the process become very prosperous; the chiefs of villages on the shores of the lake will be palmed off with some money for allowing access to the water. Some headmen will receive money for the use of the larger patches of land to make flower growing economic, and so on, but money will not be spread evenly. The people working the local flower fields will receive a miserly rate per bunch of flowers and there is no control over the level of pesticides and fertilisers put into the land. Poisoning of drinking water as a result of pesticides is common. Nor is there any control over the balance of water being consumed. At every stage of the process of flower growing and exporting the most blatant abuses take place.

Another example involves the supermarket Tesco and its supplier of French beans (a farm in an unnamed African country, probably Zimbabwe), as reported in an ITV programme in March 1997[8]. The owners of the farm were white, the workers black. The workers had to collect beans and make them into 200 grams batches of exactly the same weight and the same length, for which they were paid a very small reward. If they had a complaint there was no vehicle to contact management. So many people in the area wanted to work that their reward was entirely at the discretion of the buyers. One of the workers was quoted as saying: 'Tesco must be a wonderful country. I hope to be given one day a visa to visit it.' On a farm in Northern Malawi cobs of corn are valued at 1p each, but the same cob is sold at £1 at any of the big supermarkets in the UK, a ratio of 100:1. There has been no value added between the farm and the consumer; only the packaging and transport cost, but six intermediaries have inflated the final price[9].

We have seen in a previous section [on page 85] the inequality between coffee buyers and coffee producers. This is true for most commodities that need a market in the North and it is very difficult to prevent the stranglehold that the middleman has on the market. This is the reason why wine producers in South Africa, almost 20 years after the end of minority rule in that country, are still overwhelmingly white. Likewise, all coffee exporters in Uganda, until Idi Amin came to power, were Asians. In Rwanda until the genocide they were Asian or European. In Malawi and Zimbabwe all the tobacco exporters were British. Members of the Lebanese community play a similar role in the diamond trade in Liberia and Sierra Leone. Many or all of these minorities have lived in those countries for years. They often came with the colonial masters, or are the descendants of the colonial masters themselves, and have faithfully served the new power elites.

Accumulating capital

It is very difficult to accumulate any capital when people around you are very poor. It is difficult to save when you are at the lowest level of survival – all your energy and time is spent on the fight to survive. In addition, in some societies the very tools of savings as the North understands them might not exist – there are no savings institutions and thus the better-off farmers invest in cattle that have to be herded around forever. The cattle are the money in the bank. Furthermore, if you have cash to save or invest, social pressures may prevent you from doing so. If you start a small shop in your village selling sugar your friends and family may feel that they are entitled to some free sugar, as will the village headman or your neighbours. Few people are able to create assets which would then become an investment for the future. The only way your trade can prosper or your shop succeed is if you move away from your society. This is one of the reasons why in every society in West Africa small-scale commerce is in the hands of 'foreigners'. In Senegal it is the Guineans. In Guinea it is the Senegalese. In Nigeria it is the Ghanaians. In most of East Africa most of the more complex forms of commerce is in the hands of Asians. In other parts of West Africa it is in the hands of the Lebanese or the Greeks. In most of South East Asia the Chinese control the bulk of commerce and banking. Within many cultures it is extremely difficult to borrow and feel an obligation to repay, in the sense that the richer nations of the world understand such ideas. And there is no sense of planning because people do not have the security or the resources to think long term.

The situation might be changing though; in many parts of Africa there are now professional people with decent jobs (often with foreign NGOs and international agencies) and there are more regular sources of money to governments. Local bureaucracies, voluntary organisations and the international agencies have created middle classes. There are people with a regular income. However, here another problem arises; the lack of local savings and investment vehicles that can be trusted to help channel those savings and invest for the benefit of all. The globalisation of financial markets makes it more profitable to use those savings to purchase bonds of foreign governments or invest in the financial markets of the North. Most remittances from those working in other parts of the world have not gone back into creating productive investment. In most societies the main tool for raising finance has been the ability to pledge some asset, usually one's house or land, as collateral against which one can borrow. That cannot be achieved where there is no legal system that ensures security of ownership.

The microcredit movement, which was instigated in the early 1970s by Muhammad Yunus, then a young professor of economics at the University of Dacca, has spread all over the world[10]. It is a genuine bottom-up process, refined over the years into a sophisticated instrument for borrowing and lending by some of the poorest people on earth. It works on a different principle of collateral; social credit – the sense of mutual and collective responsibility of members of a community. Before you can join a microcredit group you must fulfil certain conditions. Everyone must go through some basic training in business methods; that means some numeracy, grasping the concept of a business plan, the basic understanding of input/output ratios (what comes out must be at least equal to what you put in). For it to work there has to be a strong element of social cohesion among the members of the group. The group must also organise itself; someone has to be the chair, another person the secretary and yet another the treasurer. Discussions are held with all the participants present and everyone who borrows must repay before they can enter into a new loan. Most important of all, overwhelmingly the participants are women – the least mobile, most central, and most reliable members of both the family and the community.

However, the arrival of microcredit does not mean that millions of people in the poor world will suddenly become great entrepreneurs or multimillionaires. Not everyone is able to follow even the simple business discipline that is required. Not everyone has the entrepreneurial spirit that the system relies on. It is thus important to realise that there are severe limitations to what microfinance in all its forms can achieve. Its phenomenal success has shown that it can help the poorest. But it is almost designed to remain a system that can help petty trading and cannot scale up. It works well enough in the small-scale commercial sector because the turnaround is rapid but it is not able to provide the financial need of productive enterprises – in agriculture or manufacturing or house building. Some interesting new initiatives in these different fields are being introduced in countries such as Cameroun and Tanzania but there are as yet few clear lessons to be gained from such experiences[11]. It is a difficult nut to crack but new vehicles for gathering local savings and providing for local investments need to be instituted. It is a challenge for both external and internal policy-makers.

Education

The one basic tool for a society to develop must be education. The North has formed very specific views about education and has not been flexible about it. It tends to apply those views universally. International and bilateral aid donors have not given it the priority it deserves. Nor have governments in most of the East, except in South Asia. Education has been the cornerstone of development in China, Singapore, South Korea, Malaysia and some Indian States, such as Kerala and Tamil Naidu. By contrast, formal education in most of Africa depends on where you live and often on what pull you might have over those who can grant you the right to be educated. In Uganda, for example, you might have to bribe the teacher to let you attend the class. You might also have to bribe her to get your child to sit at the front of the class (if you sit at the back of a class with 80 to 100 children, you will not benefit very much from that education). You might then have to bribe the teacher to correct your papers so that you can get good marks in order to proceed to the next level of education. In addition, your family must be able to do without your contribution to the family income. All this is in a country where education is free and provided by the state. The rules are very different (and sometimes more coherent) where education is private, but then it is much more restricted[12]. The international donor community should make a much greater effort in this area.

Paradox of development[13]

A survey was conducted by the UN worldwide.

The question asked was: 'Would you please give your most honest opinion about solutions to the food shortage in the rest of the world?'

The survey was a huge failure, because:

1 In Africa, they did not know what 'food' meant.
2 In Western Europe they did not know what 'shortage' meant.
3 In Eastern Europe they did not know what 'opinion' meant.
4 In the Middle East they did not know what 'solution' meant.
5 In South America they did not know what 'please' meant.
6 In Asia they did not know what 'honest' meant.
7 And in the USA they did not know what 'the rest of the world' meant.

CHAPTER EIGHT

The process of economic development

The availability and usage of natural resources, labour, and capital are the key factors of economic development. Most countries that have succeeded in reducing the level of poverty of their people have managed to use to their advantage one or other of these factors. There are countries that have resources generating huge amounts of money that has been squandered. Angola, Equatorial Guinea and the Democratic Republic of Congo all have natural resources that have been appropriated by the elites. Nigeria has managed to squander most of the profit from the enormous amount of oil that has been extracted. In Zambia the government owns less than 3 per cent of the copper mines; in 2006 it received just 0.6 percent of royalties on total sales of copper – about £12 million. The President who negotiated the deals in 2000 was Frederick Chiluba, who was convicted in early 2007 in a London Court of having siphoned off millions of pounds of his country's money[14]. In other countries the bulk of the revenues from mining do not go back to the country where the mines are located; instead they go to offshore locations or in other ways escape local taxes and therefore local re-investment. The additional income to the country might push up the GDP data on world statistical tables; this is why so many African nations are showing impressive records of improvements over the last 10 years or so. Unfortunately this sort of flow of money does not enrich the nation as a whole; the picture is incomplete. We have to face the fact that in many societies there will never be enough capital accumulation to make investment possible from within. In other words, these countries will have to look elsewhere for the investment needed in basic infrastructure and for the many inputs of human capital and technology that are required to make their economies develop. Each of these inputs is highly complex.

The North is exporting multiple views on how to facilitate and achieve economic and social development based on the lessons and customs that represent the differing experiences of Northern societies. The approach to private enterprise, for example, will be different if you are French or German or American. Each country exports its particular approach to the different issues dressed up as theories with universal applications. This avoids the problem of having to accept the fact that there cannot be a single general theory. The lesson to be learnt is that different societies need different approaches and the theory or approach of one country or even one donor in one country might contradict the approach of another player. The only certainty is that economic development should be given priority and that will be achieved only through a myriad of private enterprises and initiatives. How to encourage and enable them to grow is a much more difficult issue.

What kick-starts economic development?

Let us look at some of the challenges that economic development poses. There have to be some factors that enable a society to take off into development. The first element is appropriate and relevant economic activity. You cannot develop agriculture if the land is not productive. You cannot improve agriculture if the people tilling it are not encouraged or even able to better themselves. It is a matter of availability of both raw materials and skills to make the necessary changes. Secondly, if there is no education at different levels it will be very difficult to implement change. If a society is unreceptive to outside influences, the process of economic development cannot occur. There will be stagnation – exactly what we see all over the poor world. Thirdly, the basic societal structures that exist in most places are simply inimical to development. There are many examples of this; local hierarchies that prevent change, religious structures that militate against any movement, tribal relations (for example, slavery or the caste structure) and political systems such as a dictatorship that make change impossible or very difficult. In those societies there cannot be any social or economic mobility and that puts a substantial brake on personal initiative.

Functioning formal structures that enable economic and social advance are essential to economic development. The North considers the key developmental agents to be the institutions such as police, army, judiciary, ministries, local government, banks, post offices and so on. If they do not function economic progress cannot occur beyond very rudimentary levels. Therefore similar institutions have been established (or at least the North is supporting the setting up of parallel institutions) in the South. Because this is the way that the North developed, the same recipe is being recommended to all societies across the world. The North works on the principle that one size fits all. It tends to forget that the institutions it now possesses are the result of centuries of evolution. But perhaps institutions as the North understands them are not the best way to foster economic advance. Certainly for any social historian the idea that institutions will help the advancement of the poorest in society is a matter of putting the cart before the horse. One could easily argue that social mobility is impeded by institutions, not facilitated by them. The North has forgotten that institutions have developed in response to demands from the people who wanted more justice or better services or more democratic institutions. Formal institutions in society arose from such demands from the base, not by imposition from the top.

Capital is needed for most economic activities. You can do very small things with very little capital – so long as you have labour and raw materials you can produce many things. But more substantial and lasting changes will require an input of capital (which is the way to introduce some form of technology). The key problem is that most of the institutions from the North, including banks, as we have seen, are simply not able to cope with the very different challenges posed by the needs of the South. This is why microcredit schemes, which began within communities of the South, have been so successful across most parts of the poor world. Applying the appropriate level of technology is another challenge that has to be faced. It is pointless to introduce a level of sophistication in an economy that is not ready for it – technology needs to be at the appropriate level. Water pumps are not maintained properly in most parts of the world because they are too often designed to a level of complexity that is beyond the capacity of most people to maintain.

There is an additional question that arises from those points; to what extent can development be externally induced? To achieve any development there needs to be either a powerful 'pull' or a powerful 'push.' We have seen in chapter 6 how the pull seldom seems to work. Where is the push to come from? Some of the most successful developments have been internally induced. The government of South Korea in the 1950s and 1960s prevented imports from killing off their weak infant industries, thus enabling them to grow. Then it gradually lowered the barriers. However, throughout this period it had almost unrestricted access to the market of the US. Even before South Korea, we have the historical example of Japan itself. In the late 1940s General MacArthur offered weak Japanese industries a protected market into the US. From a country that produced cheap replicas of cigarette lighters and poor quality sewing machines, within 25 years Japan grew to become the second-largest industrial power in the world. Both countries benefitted from the external pull. The internal push, however, was effective primarily because both countries had governments that worked and could enforce policies of protectionism and internal development before lowering external barriers. These examples will not be easily replicated in present-day conditions. For most countries an external stimulus can only be a small part of the whole development picture and probably cannot be the engine for growth, although a useful adjunct. If an internal engine is missing, one needs to look elsewhere for the stimulus to development.

We have already seen some of the elements that prevent economic development from taking hold. People do not have the opportunities, capital or knowledge to develop their natural skills. They might see opportunities: even in the poorest communities in the world people make and sell or exchange things. But when everyone is as poor as you it is almost impossible to start and maintain an economic activity that will generate a regular income for you and your family. There needs to be someone who can buy your services or products and this is the crux of the matter. There might be latent demand but there is no purchasing power. A continuing cycle of local purchasing power is essential for self-sustaining local economic development.

We need to go back to first principles. Poor countries and poor people have to set their own priorities to get out of poverty and meet their own needs, rather than follow what the outside world suggests they should do. The development of poor countries and the development of poor people demand different tools from current development in the North. Poor countries are encouraged to trade internationally and enter world markets while their people follow strategies of survival. Since the highest priority for any society should be to prevent its people from dying of starvation, poor countries that face food deficits should create a framework to achieve food self-sufficiency. It might run contrary to economic orthodoxy; most economists would argue that it is better to concentrate on producing those items that you are able to export at a premium and import what you are able to produce less well than your potential trading partners. But this implementation of the doctrine of comparative advantages works well only if the overall framework within which exports are being encouraged is able to guarantee basic food security to its poorest citizens. The very strong equity argument is that the needs of the poorest must be satisfied and must be given the highest priority. Agriculture must be given priority and its development facilitated. This means creating physical facilities such as irrigation systems, water storage facilities, feeder roads and warehouses. This is the area where aid donors should concentrate in helping Southern governments meet the survival needs of the poorest. A gradual widening of markets would then allow local people to start specialising in different skills, including services such as carpentry, plumbing, house and road building for example. For most of Africa, which is overwhelmingly rural – with some 60-80 percent of the population on the land – the basic priority should be obvious.

The development of agriculture

There are three major challenges that have to be faced in trying to develop local agriculture in most of the South. The first is to make small plots more efficient. The second is to develop commercial agriculture to ensure food security. The third is to establish a land tenure system. The increase in population means that every person tills an ever-diminishing patch of land, which is too dry without regular irrigation, too infertile without fertilisers and too small to be productive. It will be extremely difficult to radically change traditional farming methods, but efforts must be made to support the small farmer. Here the most effective vehicle for the transmission of change must be social organisations, above all cooperative societies in some form or other. If politicians, donors, international agencies and activists want to attack the shortage of food, however, they must encourage new, modern large scale commercial farming. Africa has the space for this. In such new and larger units of production it would be possible to make major investments in infrastructure, better seeds, improved farm machinery and introduce specialisation in the labour force. However, in order to increase production a clear land tenure system needs to be put in place.

Land reform has always been one step too many for international lenders. Joseph Stiglitz, a former Chief Economist of the World Bank, stated that this was because the introduction of land reforms would have been a challenge that the elites would not have tolerated[15]. The North finds it very difficult to understand the complexity of the principle of owning land.

When the Dutch settlers first arrived in the New World in the early 1600s, they asked the Native American Indians if they could buy the land; their request was laughed off. How could one buy land? One might as well buy water or air or the forest. But that is exactly what the colonists wanted and they offered a few bottles of spirit or beads or whatever and acquired the land and from then on defended it by force of arms. Land ownership in the New World was then inherited by the British colonists. A similar pattern was followed across most of the Anglo-Saxon world.

We cannot avoid tackling this enormously complex issue: it could be solved through various gradual stages[16]. Ultimately the aim must be

for land ownership to be placed in the hands of the farmers themselves, not remain at the mercy of the head of the village or the council of elders or the traditional chief. It would require the establishment
of land registries and courts that are able to rule on land issues in a
transparent way. The way to achieve this would be through intermediate steps of transferring land ownership firstly to collective organisations that would own the land on behalf of their members. It would
also be a way to transmit change and provide mutual protection.
Individual ownerships, if people wanted it, could then be introduced.
There are plenty of examples of purchases of land currently being
negotiated by Gulf or Chinese investors in Africa. Most of them are ad
hoc deals negotiated with local traditional chiefs or people in power
in government: they do not ensure fairness and continuity.

In the North some of the most important changes in the organisation of society as a whole were initiated by a wide range of collective
organisations, such as the cooperative movement, mutual societies,
trade unions, building societies and savings organisations. That is the
sort of system that should be encouraged in the South. As a social
force the cooperative movement has died in the North, but in the
South it might be the most important tool that could overcome the
more powerful forces of traditional social hierarchies. Because it is no
longer an important force in the North, most people who work in the
international systems are ignorant of their past role in Northern societies. Most people in the South have never been exposed to the ideas
of cooperative organisation. In the short time that I worked at the
World Bank it was evident that most of my colleagues – all products
of good international business schools and universities – had never
come across any cooperative or mutual institution. But such social
structures could be the best way to promote the substantial new projects that are required to ensure food security.

To encourage the development of such social organisations farmers need to be assured of a gradually expanding local market. Change
can occur only when there is a gradual increase in prosperity. One way
would be to set up funds that will buy from farmers a guaranteed
amount of produce over a number of future harvests. It would be
almost the re-establishment of the old marketing boards but for staple

crops, not just for commodities for export. Such funds would provide the local incentive and kick-start profound changes across the board. But only large-scale modern commercial agriculture on lands for which there is a clear ownership structure will reduce the vulnerability of the poorest[17]. Once ownership is clearly defined, both local and foreign investors will feel that it is worth investing in the infrastructure of water reservoirs and conduits, irrigation systems, warehousing, and so on. It might be unpalatable for the concerned and idealistic activist who wants to reduce poverty to think that 'commercial principles' should be introduced, but that is the reality if the intention is to prevent the most desperately poor people on earth remaining exposed to the vagaries of their physical and social environment or the generosity of foreign donors.

Meeting local needs at the local level

I have mentioned above that the equity argument – namely social justice and fairness – demands that the first political priority must be meeting the needs of the poorest. But the main economic argument I want to put forward here is that meeting such basic needs would also create millions of jobs and that would enable the economic cycle to start. After food security, the most important requirements in all poor countries are water and sanitation. Demand for water is as old as life itself; there are local traditions of water conservation all over the world. Approaches and policies must be changed so that local needs are satisfied through traditional ways where possible and that means working as closely as possible with local communities[18]. In some countries, including Colombia and South Africa, European water companies have introduced water supplies to households in the main cities, but the result has been that end users have to pay as much as 20 times what they had previously paid. That quite clearly cannot be the way forward. We need better local solutions. In rural areas the need is for simple pumps that can be made with local materials, such as discarded tyres and bits of broken-down cars, not pumps made in Europe or the US that no one can maintain. We need low tech not high tech.

Energy requirements would be the third priority that needs to be met. In the South for many generations to come, energy for heating the pot and the home will be through wood and charcoal. Forests can be developed, but that again demands security of land tenure so that local communities have an interest in protecting the plant seedlings, irrigating them, felling only reasonable amounts and ensuring the long-term survival and sustainability of the forest. Conservation organisations all over the world have found that the only way to ensure the survival of local animal species is through ensuring the involvement of local communities. The same applies to forestry.

The fourth major need is for housing, which is again linked to land. Not only would millions of jobs be created by the construction of new housing but value would be added to the land, because most building materials required for housing (wood or bamboo poles) can be harvested from the land. It is not sufficient to rely on the simple operations of the market to kick-start this range of activities. The market is not an efficient tool for the satisfaction of the needs of those who do not have purchasing power. It has to be done through the careful management of demand in the economy as a whole, exactly as the US did under the New Deal in the 1930s and Europe has done for the best part of 40 years, until the mid 1980s.

The role of foreign investment

The bulk of Foreign Direct Investment (FDI) that goes to the poorest countries in the world, from Angola to Zambia, goes there because they possess essential raw materials. Extracting raw materials is relatively simple for the companies involved; they can strike the best deal with the local elites, do the minimum amount of work on site, remove the raw materials and export them as quickly as possible to be processed elsewhere. This rapid exploitation of non-renewable natural resources is what will inevitably happen where national governments do not make economic development their priority. Economic development requires a government that has a sense of responsibility towards all its citizens, bureaucrats who feel an obligation to help everyone in society, citizens that feel responsibility towards one other, corporations that feel a responsibility towards local people and the ability of governments and their international backers (mainly international financial institutions) to choose the right path of adding value locally. It also needs – and this requirement is essential – the involvement of local communities. Unfortunately in reality they rarely have any voice.

Foreign companies should not only bring capital that is immediately translated into buildings and other investments, which in turn generates the local multiplier, but also new goods, new production methods and new technologies. They are all vital steps for change and progress. The multiplier is a well known economic concept in the North; every job that has been generated will in turn generate other jobs, because we all employ one another. One person's expenditure is another person's income. What is required is not a free competitive market for the cheapest product destined for the international market, but a series of links between companies in the North and potentially capable partners in the South to develop jointly a range of products over a period of years. There are a few examples of such practices, but they are the exception, such as IKEA (described below). Japanese companies have also often developed excellent relations with small-scale suppliers across East Asia. The majority of companies follow the pattern of international chains such as Gap and Walt Disney. They put out to tender contracts for items they require, from T-shirts to soft toys, and producers in the South fight one other to bid for them. In order to win the contract they squeeze one of the few elements over which they have control – the wages and the conditions of the workers. It is a race to the bottom. The people who make the trainers or the T-shirts in the Far East are not those who market them. They rely on the owners of the big chains to award them orders. Most policy-makers in international organisations seem not to understand this. In the South it is not the producer who matters, it is the marketing intermediary who plays off one manufacturer or one country against another. Look at the case of China, which has been a crucial player in world trade for the last 20 years; not a single Chinese brand has become known internationally. The only brands that exist are those that existed before manufacture transferred to China.

But there are exceptions. IKEA, the Swedish house furnishing company, one of the largest companies in its field in the world, set up various partnerships with local workshops in Bangladesh. The head office sends designs to their partners, as well as seconding some of their engineers, advancing funds for the machinery and entering into a long-term contract that guarantees the training side as well as long-term purchasing agreements. Similarly in Lesotho, a small country completely surrounded by South Africa, American and international garment manufacturing companies have established long-term links with local workshops and are committed to train, invest, maintain orders over long periods with local producers. These are genuine partnerships and they should be encouraged as a way out of poverty. Small countries cannot achieve economies of scale and do not have the resources to enter world markets. If you are a small coffee producer you cannot develop the roasting facilities required to start exporting. If you have a small area of land that grows beautiful flowers, it does not mean that you will be able to export them. In both cases there has to be a minimum economic capacity to develop and to work together. Let us look at one example. There are several countries in Africa that could produce and export wine. South Africa and Ethiopia are two that already do; the first on a large scale and the second on a minuscule scale. But to expand their markets both would have to set up distribution facilities and acquire the means to transport those wines. In July 2007 the European Commissioner for Agriculture and Rural Development announced that approximately €120 million (over $150 million at the time) would be spent to promote European wines outside Europe. This figure is way above what non-European wine producers (except the US and Australia) could ever contemplate spending.

A coherent approach

The basic assumption made in the North is that development is a process of general economic responses that it can understand from its own experience and its own past. Northern countries have the bulk of the voting rights in the major international organisations (World Bank, IMF, UN Security Council, OECD, EU, WTO) and therefore their policies, approaches and philosophies exert a disproportionate influence in the thinking about DEVELOPMENT issues. Their views and their priorities pervade international policy-making, of which aid is a small component and trade and international investment are very large components. Their assumptions about growth and development thus affects key decisions regarding aid and the future development of the poor world. What most of those who care deeply about the fate of the poor of the world should be concerned about is that the poorest are seldom consulted, and if they are at all, they are not listened to. The mechanism required to make things work to suit the poor does not exist.

Economic development is possible. Several countries in East Asia have shown that it can be achieved. But to achieve it in most other countries requires a quite different approach from what has happened in the North over the last couple of hundred years. The North developed organically. The South requires joined-up action in the body politic and in the body economic, but international rules of trade and sectional domestic political priorities militate against such cohesion, especially in Africa. Some countries in South East Asia, as we have seen, were able to benefit from economic protectionism. This would no longer be possible under current international treaties and agreements. The result is a series of contradictory priorities that hamper development. International donors may have good intentions, but are constrained by their own rules, and if they are governmental bodies they have to negotiate with governments. International financial institutions such as the IMF, the World Bank and the regional development banks follow the diktacts of the international financial rules – namely financial stability, protecting currencies from inflation and maintaining external financial stability. The main problem is that they work on the principle of one size fits all. Bilateral donors sometimes listen to their partner governments, regardless of how badly chosen or appointed those might be, because there is no alternative, but most of the time they follow their own set of priorities. Private corporations look at the cheapest and most effective ways to get their investment in and out. If that means that they have to bribe their way in and out, so be it. They are not there to adopt moral stances; that is not what their shareholders pay them for.

No one can be sure that governments and the institutions of the state (ministries, police, courts, postal system and the providers of basic services) can over time deliver the range of services that people want and nations need in order to function unless such institutions reflect the local capacity to cope with them. Currently one has the impression that, regardless of the capacity of local structures to cope with them, the North is being highly prescriptive. In dealing with the countries of the South, the North should start not from where it would like them to be or what it would like them to achieve, but from where they are now and address challenges at their level of need. That assessment requires a different, practical and realistic approach, rather than a theoretical one. Consider one set of choices that shows clearly the dilemmas that many poor countries have to contend with. Most countries need foreign currency; it is necessary to buy oil, pharmaceuticals, chemicals and machinery, among others items, from abroad. The foreign lender will be keen to lend the foreign currency that will go into a project that will generate income in foreign currency. How will they be repaid otherwise in foreign currency? The government thus wants to go for tourism. Local people would choose water.

The priorities of the South should be obvious; poor countries must concentrate on developing the primary sectors (agriculture, mining and quarrying) and the secondary sectors (processing primary products) of the economy; this is where the bulk of the jobs are to be created and where the majority of local needs must be met. The ordinary person in the North has become so dependent on the services provided by the state in basic areas such as health, education, social services, pensions and so on, that most people are not even aware that economic and social progress in their economies started by riding on the back of the economically productive sectors of society. Countries that are rich now tend to forget that they did not start with nurses and doctors and teachers, but ended up with them once societies had become prosperous enough to pay for the education and the remuneration of doctors and nurses and teachers. The South needs to go back to basics.

International trade
Northern policy makers have come to think that international trade is the key to development. That might indeed be true for rich societies

now, but it is not the universal remedy. You can start to trade only when you either have some natural assets (preferably high value minerals or oil) to trade with or you have produced something that you can trade for something else. Governments around the world have been concentrating on trading, because that is what the economic power of the North has forced the global economy to do. Indeed, the success of China has hidden the fact that in China there has been, for at least three decades, a massive investment in education and huge improvements of infrastructure. It has all been done at breakneck speed and in the process it has often destroyed local societies and habitats. For example, the Three Gorges Dam, the largest civil engineering project in the world, resulted in the displacement of a million people, but it has provided huge amounts of electricity for central China. Many of the items the North imports from China embed scarce water and expensive power that has gone into manufacturing those items. In other words, China invested in the Three Gorges Dam as much to satisfy the North's needs as its own.

Production requires different factors that together enable someone, some entity, some corporation to produce something to trade with. Then, to move out of the cycle of just producing what you might need for yourself, you need to become a better, more efficient producer than your neighbour or the person down the road. This is another example of comparative advantages – one entity for some reason or other is better able to produce an item than another entity. Through the process of continuing adjustment they each will eventually specialise at what they are relatively better at producing. The one that has access to more water might start producing a surplus of rice (which requires a lot of water) and the one that has drier land will produce potatoes. They then start to exchange what they are producing. The Northern world has enlarged that simple doctrine of comparative advantages to one of global exchanges, forgetting to ask the basic question of how some of the advantages came about and whether the basic factors are immutable. For example, will the producer of rice always have enough water? Will the producer of computer chips always have a ready supply of cheap educated workers? Should transport costs always assumed to be nil?

CHAPTER NINE

The role of government in economic development

Economic development should mean improvements across a broad front of economic and social activities – that is, more clean water and new schools and health clinics and improved nutrition at the same time as new income-generating activities. The latter will enable the former to improve and multiply. But to achieve all of these, one must look to some powerful and consistent direction to the economy. There has to be a concerted effort to get an economy going; you cannot leave it to each of the myriad of individual enterprises (many of which will have great difficulties in gearing up) or to the larger units (which will tend to control entry in the sectors in which they operate) to pursue their own aims in the hope that somehow miraculously it will all come together. Things are not the same as they were in the days of Adam Smith. Economic development that also brings some sort of social justice can only be achieved through such concerted action over a medium- to long-term period of time. One must believe in some form of dirigisme (a French word best translated as 'interventionism'), a system in which it is possible to make the different players move in some sort of unison where the state works to prevent bottlenecks that might arise in the development process. It is a process of joined-up thinking and action.

Dirigisme is the approach that Keynes introduced in economic thinking in Northern societies in the 1920s and 1930s. He saw the state as the body that would employ some people to dig holes in the streets and others to fill those holes. In the process of being paid for their work, those millions of people would of course get an income which they would spend to feed, clothe and house themselves and their families, thus generating other jobs in the process. This is the process that he called the 'employment multiplier'. In the current economic crisis this would again appear to be the process that politicians favour as a solution to the credit crunch.

The system that Northern societies enjoy of untrammelled freedom of action for individuals, for corporate entities, for the different institutions of society, each in perpetual competition and adjustment with the other, simply cannot help poorer societies to develop. It might work where a society has already achieved a substantial level of complexity and therefore different players have emerged that balance one another, but it will not work in a poor country where those who do not have any voice will simply fall between the cracks in the system. If you do not have strong unions, the weakest workers (not the professionals) have no rights. If you do not have pensions for older people, once you cease to have any employment (if you ever had any) you are condemned to starvation.

Since the end of the cold war and the dismemberment of the Soviet Union, in Northern economies the role and function of the state as the central pillar of society has greatly decreased[19]. In other societies it has increased. Government in the BRIC countries (Brazil, Russia, India and China) remains a powerful interventionist entity; it has become the centre of economic transformation of Russia and China. In key geographical areas of the world, fragile states are run by plutocracies that are self-absorbed, certainly undemocratic, ineffective and self-serving. They are unable to encourage growth, tackle poverty or offer any social justice to their own people. The numbers are not small – there are 40 to 60 such states, which are home to almost two billion people. In the current economic depression the likelihood is that the private sector will decrease in importance and that more people and more entities will look back to the state as the spine around which the body as a whole will move. But what will happen in those societies where the state is so weak that it hardly exists?

The trickle down approach

It might be unavoidable that elites run countries; elites are self-perpet-uating even in democratic societies. In most societies of the South there is an innate elite capture and there is no entry into that elite; there is no advance through meritocracy that most of the North now enjoys. And there is something else that needs to be taken into con-sideration. Government is, by definition, a complex set of activities that is managed by the people at the top, the people who govern. They include politicians, their immediate advisers and courtiers, the top civil servants and the top people in institutions such as universities and hospitals. When you think of better governance, it is these people who take the decisions and need to be better able to govern. To improve the police force in any country, the politicians and the police-men at the top think of instituting better offices for their own needs to fulfil their duties more efficiently. That means better computers, the best secretary/personal assistant, a decent all-weather four-wheel car. It means good filing cabinets, safes for important documents, good telephone communications and so on; it is a cascade of interests and needs that comes from the top down. It is natural in the systems that the Northern world has devised. Mr Manhoman Singh, Prime Minister of India and himself a distinguished economist, stated that the mechanism of delivery alone of any basic improvement of servic-es to the poor in India will consume 90–95 per cent of any money that has been allocated to that improvement. This cascading down of ben-efits is also one of the fundamental weaknesses that exist in the sys-tem of aid delivery. All this would happen even without adding the elements of mismanagement and of corruption, both of which are deeply entrenched. By helping any government the external donor is adding to the division between the people at the top for whom govern-ments work and the people at the bottom for whom governments are irrelevant. Money from central coffers, including aid money, will be mired in the quicksand. This is the key issue; there has to be a viable mechanism for delivery – and most of the time that is totally absent.

The remit of government

Governments can do and should do lots of things, but there are three basic functions that impinge directly on the economic development of a country, and those should be the priorities: establishing a planning framework within which the economy as a whole should develop; providing the basic services (public goods) that cannot be left to the private sector; developing the key elements of a physical infrastructure. Before we can look at these three requirements we need to address the far more basic issue of the priorities that should be set by those in power. Here again one needs to accept that the economies of the OECD countries and those of the poorest countries simply operate on different principles. The kind of political decisions that the North expects it politicians to take do not apply to the South. In the UK there are endless discussions regarding the building a third runway at Heathrow airport, extending a motorway or lowering the voting age to 17. Poor countries need to make choices that represent not the priorities of a political party to guide the state – both of which at best are very vague and indefinable concepts – but the needs of their people. For anyone who visits any poor country, the priorities are self-evident and overwhelming. That tallies with their own peoples' perceptions of what their priorities should be. We have seen earlier [page 20] the large-scale consultation undertaken by the World Bank in 2000 to ascertain the views of some 60,000 people in the South. If you wish to attack poverty, the priorities are clear; physical security, enable people to grow their own food, provide water, the possibility of shelter and the provision of wood for fuel. The choices become technocratic rather than political; you need to find the most efficient way to carry them out, not discuss endlessly the order of 'political' priorities.

Establishing a planning framework

Governments need to be able to plan and find ways to implement plans. To achieve those aims they need qualified and trained personnel and able administrators. A government cannot provide all the schools, hospitals or community centres that might be needed across a country, but they should be able to provide the basic framework within which these entities can be built by local communities or by outsiders. The planning function of the state is therefore vital. The need is for the state to be in control and able to enforce that control –

to impose its will. Yet in too many countries that function is very weak and the donors become far more important that host governments. After the UN General Assembly of the year 2000 when the Millennium Development Goals were set, each country was encouraged to produce a document setting out its own priorities for development. Yet there are so many of these Poverty Reduction Strategy Papers (PRSP) which are supposedly written through local consultations that use the same language that one suspects they have all been written at the World Bank in Washington.

The provision of public goods

Economists refer to services that the community as a whole needs as 'public goods'. These include the police force, the army, the judiciary, prisons, basic education and health systems, an inspectorate of public health, and so on – services and goods that should be provided by the state for the benefit of all. The problem of course is that the state in most poor societies provides such services for a very small number of people, namely its immediate clientele – the clan or ethnic group in power, the metropolitan entities and the employees of the state. This is often due to the lack of financial resources. But it is also too often a function of the fact that those at the top do not care for their wider population or are not fundamentally accountable to them.

One essential public good is a legal system – laws, courts, a police. If legal rights and property ownership are not properly understood, codified and applied, the rest of the edifice will crumble. The world has done nothing to confront the very fundamental issues of the law and of property rights. The Chilean economist Hernando de Soto identifies these as the key difference between the North and the South and the key reason for the development of rich societies[20]. De Soto has for many years argued that capitalism works in the West and in the North where countries understand the rule and concept of law – if you cannot enforce a contract, it is not worth entering into a contract. He applies his ideas mainly to commercial rights, but the principle relates to all forms of property ownership, particularly land. As we have seen, the issue of land rights is extremely complex and this is why international organisations, both governmental and non-governmental, and aid donors have avoided squaring up to it altogether.

Developing the physical infrastructure

There are some physical facilities that all governments should provide for everyone. The problem was clearly highlighted in the report of the Commission for Africa, which identified the lack of a physical infra-structure as one of the gravest impediments to the development of the continent[21]. It is also one of the key arguments in Paul Collier's book *The Bottom Billion*, in which he notes that most of the poorest countries of the world are landlocked and that being landlocked is part of the recipe for poverty[22]. Such countries are at the mercy of neighbouring nations in exporting their produce and importing their essential needs. This is where we need to look for international involvement. The governments of the North could afford to pay for the construction of the roads, by putting them out to international tender, so long as local firms are deeply involved and local training becomes an integral commitment. That remains one of the great challenges for the international community to confront: how to pay the private sector to undertake work for the public good[23].

The government's income

I have argued above that in a poor country the driver (not the engine) of development should be the State. But let us go back a step or two. To improve conditions in any of the fields in which development should take place one needs capacity and capital. For capacity you need a competent State. It is not that competent people don't exist; it is that the State, in most cases, does not have the resources to employ them nor the ability to direct them. A competent State in a poor country is a contradiction in terms. In some countries the State is so weak that there is just a 'phantom State'[24]. In many societies about the only mechanism that works is the army and sometimes the police. We have seen both working even in nations that are otherwise hopelessly without rudder, such as Nigeria or Zimbabwe. They are controlled through the mechanism of power and money. The planning mechanism of the State at different levels needs to be reinforced everywhere.

Capital is needed to create or improve facilities (roads, hospitals and school buildings), resources (school desks, books, blackboards, operating theatres and x-ray machines), people (doctors, nurses, managers and teachers) and so on. Quite a few of these require significant sums; a modern hospital must be built to a good standard, although perhaps the same does not apply to a school. Where is the money to come from? In a rich and sophisticated society like the UK it comes from the State itself; the government raises taxes from individuals, corporations and imports, and then redistributes it to the society as a whole. In most poor countries the number of people who earn enough to pay tax is very small and the system of tax collection very weak. Those few who should pay do not pay, or if they do pay they pay only a small percentage of what they should. Most poor countries raise the funds they require to undertake the most basic work through import and sales taxes. Naturally enough, the goods that are imported through smuggling do not get taxed and that can account for a large percentage of goods in circulation. But the gravest injustice of any sales tax, when applied, is that the poorest pay as much as the rich; it is indiscriminate. It is unjust because for many people it means that the goods they require are more expensive than they should be.

The injustice aside, raising funds through sales tax is a very weak base on which to raise substantial finance if the bulk of your economy is not monetised. The inability of most poor countries to raise any income from internal sources is one of the most intractable issues that the poor world has to tackle. It forces such countries to borrow from international bodies such as the World Bank or the African Development Bank. We have seen the horrible consequences of the huge amount of borrowing from the World Bank in the 1970s; the level of indebtedness of the poorest countries rose dramatically over the years, firstly because they had to borrow to keep basic services going and secondly because to repay those debts they were forced by the same institutions to sell off their few public assets. Furthermore, under the Structural Adjustment Programmes (SAPs) imposed on debtor nations by the World Bank in the 1980s, countries were told to lay off thousands of state employees. That reduced even more the limited purchasing power within poor economies and also weakened the capacity of many bureaucracies to deliver basic services. Poor countries remain poor in the provision of basic services because they do not have the resources to invest in public goods, the sectors which could make a society function and give the State any sort of legitimacy.

The inability to raise income from taxation has had two other unintended consequences for most poor nations. One is that governments have had no basic sense of engagement with their own people. If you tax people, they have some sort of hold on you[25]. You create the right to challenge those who levy taxes on you. Those who levy the taxes are often the primary beneficiaries of them; the taxes pay their salaries. These bureaucrats sometimes develop an interest in maintaining some integrity and indeed some distance from the political powers. They might judge any set of politicians to be a transient phenomenon and consider that their future might depend on integrity and acceptability by the next government, the next set of politicians. This happened in countries such as India, South Africa and even Zimbabwe for some years after independence. But the other unintended (or perhaps intended) consequence is the reverse of the very issue of accountability and democracy; you owe political debts to those who have lent you or donated money. The donor becomes more important than your people.

The debt of several of the poorest countries to the rich world has been cancelled in part. That has been a partial success. But the poor world will still have to go begging to the international community for new funds for development. In her book *Dead Aid*[26] Dambisa Moyo argues for poor countries to go to international money markets to raise funds for their development. In theory that might be an appealing approach; it would make governments behave in sound commercial ways, as an alternative to the lack of sound democratic principles. One suspects, however, that this is the approach of the World Bank and international banking, in whose world, if you behave, the reward is that the international investor will fund your requests for investment. If not, you fall flat on your face. But the reality is that in most countries governments actually neither understand commercial responsibilities nor are able to govern – in the sense of being capable of enforcing their rules. Therefore the poorest countries under such a formula would remain poor forever because they would be assumed to be too great a risk to attract commercial funds. Additionally, there is no guarantee that the cycle of borrowing-going-bust-debt cancellation will not re-emerge. It is for this reason that offers from the Chinese Government become so attractive; they will buy the minerals of the poor countries and they offer to help them spend the money they have pumped into their economies. There are few political conditions. Most of the OECD world in 2008-2009 is going through what will be a traumatic period of recession. There will be less money for aid and less willingness and ability of the international banking fraternity to lend to what they would consider to be 'dodgy' projects or nations. Governments of the South will be far less able to borrow the money they need for their development. This could provide the non-governmental community and the private enterprise sector with a unique chance to play a leading role.

Making governments work for development

The key economic function of governments in the South should be the manipulation of demand to generate jobs in the economy. They should join forces with every agent who is willing to achieve that aim. In a war you have to subjugate all activities to one particular aim. Achieving economic development requires a similar concentration of minds and resources. Building roads and water reservoirs, as well as housing estates, schools, government buildings, prisons and so on, should be the main vehicle through which local jobs are generated and local expertise built up. The Singapore Agreement of the World Trade Organization forces countries to open up competition for state contracts to everyone. The rich world is preventing the poorest countries from using the creation of demand as the key tool for the development of the local economy. To achieve development at a level that responds to the needs of their people, the North should encourage the nations of the South to make things work at a more basic level. That means targeting governance at the district or city level, rather than at the top which is at best unresponsive. At that lower level you can have accountability and effective auditing of the authorities; this is where there should be more power. This can be achieved within a concept of nation-building, which remains a valid principle so long as it means building up society as a whole, for which establishing a sense of national identity is vital. There should be more conscious and active democratic participation in the life of the community. If we want the State to function as a viable unit of local or international governance cohesion is vital. This is as true in the South as in societies of the North.

In the 1980s in the UK a Conservative Government under Mrs Thatcher moved many of the powers of local councils to central government, indeed abolishing some of the layers of local democracies, such as the Greater London Council. Power has been centralised. This is not an example that nations in the South should follow; it is exactly the opposite. Making local structures work is both a more democratic approach and a more effective development process.

> The Member of Parliament Vince Cable (the Liberal Party Spokesman on Finance in the House of Commons) tells this joke about his period as adviser to President Kenyatta in the early 1960s. He warned the President that his opponent was promising free land and beer to all the voters and was likely to win the election. The President, realising the danger, had him arrested and jailed just in case![27]

CHAPTER TEN

The mirage that is the state

The concern in the North for the people of the South and the initiatives undertaken to address their problems manifest themselves at two different levels. People want to do their 'own thing' to help and want their governments to do the right things to help. Governments in the North work through governments in the South, because that is the way things happen in the North. Governments of the North want governments in the South that can do what the governments in the North do – plan, legislate, hold elections, improve administration, resist aggression, control imports, raise taxes, appoint police, inspect the production of medicines, ensure that criminals are locked up, and so on. Many governments in the South do have similar aims and welcome that sort of help, but let us be realistic: the first concern of those in power in most countries is the fulfilment of their personal priorities. Even in those countries in which the governing classes do care, their priorities are, unsurprisingly, often different from those of Northern countries. Economic progress of the poor is seldom a government priority for the simple reason that the poor have no power.

What is the state?

In a new nation with an embryonic state apparatus the mutual relationship between those who are in government and those who are governed that is necessary to make any system function properly does not exist. There is no trust and there is no feeling of mutual obligation. It is more complex than 'them and us' – it is a matter of parallel existences. The concept that the State is composed of different constituencies, including what the North considers the three fundamental estates of society – government and the executive, the legislature and the judiciary – that are in existence precisely to balance one another is a totally abstract construct in most of the South. The State is a mirage as far as most of the world is concerned. In most of the poor societies in the South – certainly across almost all of Africa – the pool of educated people who form the elite is so small that these people would all know one another and would probably not be willing or able to challenge, criticise or oppose one another. Ethnic considerations, as well as loyalties at other levels, would not permit it. For example, there is deep respect for older people, as well as for traditional authorities: this respect transcends most other structures, particularly those that could lead to modernity. In some of the larger societies, where there is a larger pool of educated and capable people, the power of those at the top is such that they can quash any attempt at criticism; they would view it as a challenge to their power. This reality is a notion that most of our politicians and decision makers do not appreciate at all. In many Southern countries, what the State is and stands for is what an Eritrean friend of mine summarised as follows: 'What do I want to do with the government? The government is made up of a bunch of people who want to take my money away and my money ends up in their pockets. If anyone from the government comes to my home, it is because they want my money or they want to take me to prison. Keep them as far away as possible.'

In developed societies the government and the people are very often the same body. People own the government and the government is connected with the people. In poor countries what happens at the political summit has no impact on what happens at the economic base. The lives of the poorest in South Africa – the overwhelming majority of people in that nation – are no better now than it was under apartheid. In China people do not expect anything from government in terms of health or pension provisions; they save for themselves. The reliance in the North on its limited understanding of the concept of the State can also lead to a dangerous misperception of what amounts in fact to fragile entities. In Africa there are five countries that really matter in terms of population, size and military might: Egypt, Nigeria,

Ethiopia, the Democratic Republic of Congo and South Africa. Only two of these – the first and the last – are likely to survive intact for the next 10 years. There must be serious doubts that the other three will survive as we know them now. There is too little internal cohesion and there are too many interests that could pull those countries apart. There has been no nation-building as such; any movement in the future will be on the political, not the economic front, because these governments will have, above all, to keep the elites on their side. Yet the world acts as though they can be long-lasting entities and partners.

The role of democracy

In few poor countries does the genuine view of an informed population affect the election of government. Democracy needs to have firm roots in literacy, institutions and traditions. Democracy is far more than voting every few years for one candidate or the other; it is a deep-rooted acceptance of differences and submission of minority views to the will of the majority. In turn the majority must accept that there are differences and must be willing to compromise and accommodate such differences. But democracy is also a large network of institutions that continuously challenge one another.

International policy-makers seem to measure democracy in terms of the existence of different political parties. This simply cannot be the reality in most parts of the South. In most countries of Africa governments are so weak that they cannot provide what must be the first priority of any government – namely ensuring the physical safety of their citizens. Thus what the North understands as government is absent from the start. In those countries in Africa where multiparty democracy has been introduced there has been an increasing level of corruption for the very good reason that political parties need a lot of money – to print posters and leaflets, to organise rallies, hire airplanes and cars and so on. It is unfortunately a problem with which people in Britain are familiar as well; both the Labour and Conservative parties over the last 10 years have been plagued by the difficulties of raising funds for their own coffers. It has raised issues of corruption at the heart of government and has substantially damaged the trust that the public has had in politicians in general. In most of the South the problem has been compounded by the fact that political parties have become the conduit for the expression of different ethnic groups. It has had little to do with ideology – it has to do with grabbing the levers of power and having control over the spoils.

I do not wish to give the impression that there has been no genuine change at some level in several African countries. There is fighting, but most conflicts are internal and not between nations. Ghana, Tanzania, Malawi, Mozambique have held elections in recent years that were reasonably free and fair, but how deep is democracy when ethnic groups in Kenya feel so disenfranchised and excluded that they go on the rampage as they did in early 2008, leaving 1,500 people dead and perhaps a quarter of a million displaced? Elections become a distraction for the elites. Richard Dowden in his book *Altered States, Ordinary Miracles* is surely right when he questions the 'winner-takes-all approach' of Northern societies as a tool to be used in the South[28]. It is not a way to encourage unity within the limited pool of people who could all contribute to the political and economic development of society. Southern societies need more transparency.

What is governance?

For many poor countries of the South the capital or main city is the beginning and the end of the state. This is where central government is based, where the ruling elites reside, where the key decisions about the entire nation are taken. The university and best hospitals will be here, foreign embassies and perhaps international bodies and their representatives operate from here, the airport will be here. There is no identification with people in other parts of the same country; there is no connection between the rural areas and those in the metropolitan areas because of the dominance played by the capital in the life of government. Yet it is at the level of the provincial city and the district that one should be encouraging governance; local bodies are needed to ensure viable and democratic local economic governance. Otherwise DEVELOPMENT might be something that affects state structures and not societies.

The concept of governance has become one of the primary considerations of the Northern world, not economic progress or development, which should be the real goal in order to attack poverty. And of course it is assumed that good governance is something that can be delivered only by governments. Governments are given tasks and attributes that in most societies simply have no meaning. It is part of the Northern obsession with its own priorities. From that comes the Northern obsession with the concept of how you deliver good governance, how you create governments, the limits of governments and the whole paraphernalia of democracy. The UN and other intergovernmental agencies – built of and formed by governments – not surprisingly reinforce the perception that governments are and should remain the only unit of decision making and responsibility.

Homogeneity

The most fundamental of all forces that have enabled governments to perform their tasks has been the development of formal or informal networks of mutual obligations, linking people one to another within the confines of a state or region. It has created in the North the reality of a governing class, which, regardless of political priorities, views the state and its institutions in similar ways. Even if their range of political priorities might be different, they will not want to destroy the institutions – they might wish to change them, perhaps amend their functions, even abolish them and then create new ones. That feeling of obligations and the concomitant feeling of reciprocal rights is the result of an homogeneity that long-term stability of institutions, customs, language and common external wars have brought to Northern societies. It might not be an homogeneity of backgrounds, but certainly an homogeneity of behaviour which has led to trust, a fundamental cohesive force in society. Institutions and structures in Britain are representative of that homogeneity. There have been forces at work that permitted the people from various parts of the country to feel they belonged to the same nation. In most of Europe, for example, the development over the centuries of a strong monarchy, a system of vassals and hierarchy gave way slowly to a strong central government. The cohesion of the state enabled the transmission of commands and it enabled the state gradually to enlarge its activities and provide more services for individual citizens. It also created an order in society in which the higher classes have a strong sense of noblesse oblige – obligations due to their privileges.

That enormous complexity of networks, unity of language, adherence to common institutions and the other forces that create a backdrop for a successful system of democratic government are totally absent in most new countries. Indeed, such obligations are becoming weaker in our own ever more mobile societies. There is no society in Africa (with the possible exceptions of Ghana and South Africa) where one could genuinely say that one political party is representative of a majority of the different ethnic groups of that state. Loyalty is still primarily to one's tribe or ethnic group. Consider the mass killings in Rwanda in 1994 and the continuing killings in Burundi. The main reason why people kill their neighbours, their friends and their schoolmates is that they have disregarded loyalty to their communities, their neighbours, their friends, even their faiths, choosing instead to obey the orders of their elders[29]. It would take enormous spiritual and physical courage to break the injunction of the most important people in your traditional society and resist their orders. There are a few exceptions of course, but the massacres continue and an enormous number of people are killed because they belong to the 'wrong' tribe.

Developing the institutions

There are many ways of defining economic development but it is indisputable that it is a series of interconnected processes and activities, under which different parts of a society all move forward to deliver increased prosperity to both the individuals and to the institutions of that society. The reason why the individual and the institution must develop in tandem is very simple: you cannot have rich people and poor institutions. Institutions, in the form of government departments and ministries, hospitals, schools, prisons, a police force and so on, must be capable of providing for everyone the services for which they were set up. If you have a ministry that cannot deliver higher education for as many people as can be encouraged to go to school, then that institution is not up to the task it was set up for. It is not fit for purpose.

In the North the complexity of multiple demands on the state has led to emergence of new bodies. This has meant that there are more and more institutions that control every step of our lives, but also control one another. Corporate power – be it at the private corporative level, at the state institutional level or at the level of the interest group – has become the principal and often the sole vehicle of delivery of services. The North has thus come to view any aspects of governance as requiring institutions and has tried to create them in the South in its own image. In the UK there are functioning ministries and departments, such as Customs and Revenue or the Medicines Agency or the Railways Inspectorate; policy-makers assume that this machinery of government will work in other societies. Inspectorates for the control of medicines and the quality of food produced, controls to prevent exploitation of workers in factories, of miners in their underground tunnels and so on are all the tools through which governments are expected to function. If you take the view that only the top man can change things, you appeal directly to him; he does not want to delegate power. That is the way to dictatorship. The North takes the view that the more institutions, the more solid the democracy. In Britain for example, government works through almost 800 quangos (quasi-autonomous non-governmental organisations), which together received around £34.5 billion of public funds in 2007-2008. They range from the Olympic Games Delivery Authority to the BBC, from the Medicines Agency to the Independent Police Authority. Collectively they employ well over 100,000 people[30]. It is as in any construction: the stronger the foundation the stronger the edifice.

But the conditions in the South are so different that this approach in unlikely to work. The North has an enormous reservoir of educated and talented people; the South does not. The North has a long tradition of service to society and of societal homogeneity, including common languages and education; the South does not. The North was able to develop in the absence of international economic institutions that impose restrictions and rules on the functioning of different fields of human activity. The UK, US, France and Germany would never have developed in the way they did if there had been a World Trade Organization that told them what to do. In most countries of the South institutions that mirror those of the North might thus come into existence, in response to the demands of the international community, but often exist on paper only and not in reality. Most of them represent a widening of 'elite capture' of the state. These institutions are not able to perform what they are set up to do. Just look at one example. As the world becomes more and more interdependent and it becomes easier to buy medicines on the internet, preventing the production of imitation drugs becomes more and more urgent[31]. Nigeria is a major exporter of fake drugs to the entire West Africa region. Within the police in Nigeria there is a body that is supposed to prevent the production of fake medicines. But the police force in Nigeria has shown itself totally incapable of action on this front. In fact the police in Nigeria are a force of such power in their own right that most politicians fear them deeply[32].

Here again one forgets that institutions need to develop from the bottom up – they must reflect common needs and aspirations. The UK has not gone the way of most police forces across Europe and has 43 different police forces. They are very much a community force, with governing bodies that include locally elected personnel. The police force in the UK, deeply rooted in local communities, is one of the best in the world and is one of the most efficient tools for the delivery of their specific remit within British society. In most African countries the police forces are an expression of state power, not of people's needs. Yet the North carries on insisting on more democracy in the South, not at the level where it matters but at the national level, where it is the least effective. The international community does very little to encourage democratic voices to emerge through the village, the community and the city. This is primarily because Northern societies have lost the ability to encourage and develop democracy at local level. In the UK local democracy is moribund. Most people have no idea of who their councillors are. Local policies are being undertaken usually with little local involvement. This is the result of a structural clash of interests and responsibilities between central government and local institutions. Local people cannot establish and control their own priorities. The mechanism of local democracy does not work sufficiently well for the North to export it as a model to the South.

Government as kleptocracy

In most of the South people are in government or seek to be in government because they wish to appropriate the spoils that result from being in power. The result is corruption. In states that are not democratic – the situation for most of Africa – the power elites will simply appropriate the riches of the state, be they oil, minerals, control over trade, import permits or licences to build. There is little incentive for the elites to encourage democracy for the simple reason that it is not in their interest – they don't want to have to share the wealth[33]. Yet international policy-makers and donors maintain their approach despite this basic fact.

Corruption is rampant in China and India. Money from corruption in the South comes back to the North; the North does very little to prevent illegal money from entering its economies, being laundered by its high street banks or their owners being protected by crooked lawyers and accountants. Massive corruption occurs at the international level in all civil engineering contracts and arms deals. Very little has been done to protect people who are trying to expose the corruption from within their own countries. It took a non-governmental organisation, Transparency International, to place the issue of international corruption squarely on the map. But it is not limited to the South: by not actively blocking corrupt funds that come into its economies, the rich world is complicit with frauds committed against the poorest. In January 2008 the Norwegian government established an international committee to look at international corruption. It excluded Britain from the Commission because it claimed that it had become an offshore financial centre[34].

Corruption in most parts of the poor world is omnipresent. Country after country has seen officials in ministries of education setting up phantom teachers and heads and even schools so that those salaries can then be diverted. 'Grand corruption' (to use the terminology of Transparency International) is being perpetrated in arms deals, civil engineering projects, mining and of course aid. But there is continuing petty corruption that is commonplace at airports and throughout every bureaucratic transaction in offices in the South. My friend and neighbour who originates from Sierra Leone is trying to collect computers in London to give to schools in her home country. She is forced to pay bribes to customs officials and their 'agents' to get those donated computers into the country. They are being donated for free and the law in Sierra Leone is clear that such items are not subject to sales or income taxes, but who do you appeal to when there is a powerful barrier of vested interests that prevents you from giving a tool that could help hundreds of children?

Local power not national power

At one end of the political spectrum we see that nations cannot be insulated from changes taking place across the world, and at the other we see forces within nations pulling the nation in different directions. In Europe the nation state is weakening. The old-fashioned City State is re-emerging. Less and less is under the control of central government and more and more is subject either to the forces of the market (such as where activities have been privatised) or to the forces of local democracy. Paris is doing more for its citizens now than it has done for the last 100 years and so are London, Berlin and Barcelona. Marseilles is home to a far larger proportion of Muslim people than Paris and yet did not suffer from the racial riots of Paris in 2006[35] – it has been able to adapt its policies to suit its particular needs. We should take this on board and encourage poor countries to move towards more localisation of services and decision making. The city of Nairobi and the municipalities of Calcutta and Dhaka need more autonomy to improve the lives of their citizens. They should be able to develop their schools and hospitals, or at least to provide a framework for the development of such facilities perhaps by the private sector, perhaps by foreign aid agencies, perhaps by their own expatriate citizens. There is likely to be far more loyalty towards a city than towards a state, and loyalty at this level will galvanise and empower people.

In poor countries, and this phenomenon is the more obvious the poorer the country is, the issue is not the prioritising of different grand political issues, but the effective provision of basic needs. It is about generating income and ensuring survival. For the latter you need efficient administrators and technocrats, not politicians. In fact, the more practical the operator is the more he/she will be able to implement solutions. We need more emphasis on issues such as delivery of education to all, provision of water facilities, improving agriculture, delivery of fertilisers at local level. At this level we can talk about efficiency and transparency. For example, in Uganda it was found that providing a decent lunch at school had an incredible range of positive consequences. More children were coming to school, more parents were keen to send their children to school, children paid more attention in class as they remained awake, their health improved, their education prospered. That sort of basic improvement was not the result of some grand policy, but the decision of some local funder or perhaps an enterprising school head. Another decision radically improved the role of schools: each school was given public information about the amount of money that it should receive from state coffers. Schools published the amount due to them on a blackboard placed outside the school building. This meant that far fewer of the people delivering the miserable pay to the teachers could help themselves to some of it – a regular occurrence in most poor countries. It made local people ask questions about school buildings and school facilities. This is real democracy. The same successes cannot be achieved if the Ministry of Education in the capital is strengthened to deliver education across a country.

Cheapest is not necessarily best

The best way to kick-start economic development is the creation of physical infrastructure. This underpins the rest of the economy[36]. In most countries since local capital is not available that means attracting foreign investment. Properly executed it will bring not just the foreign capital and expertise, both technical and managerial, but could also ensure training of local people and thus ensure technology transfer. Under present rules established by the World Bank and other international financial institutions tenders are encouraged from companies on the most basic principle of competition on price. The lowest tender would normally be awarded the project. But that surely is not enough; tenders for public works of any size need to be awarded on the basis of technology transfer, a very difficult aim to achieve. The cardinal point is that we must move away from awarding contracts on the basis of the cheapest tender. Tenders need to include a serious and detailed component of training of local people. It is not an easy set of priorities and here one might have to resort to complex formulae and approaches that at present do not exist. For example, a project involving 500km of roads needs to be broken into 50 contracts of 10km. Each of these contracts needs to have different local partners. There needs to be education in road building associated with the work. Local engineers and surveyors need to be involved. Each of these steps will require close control to ensure that the money is not wasted. Many such projects will be less 'profitable' – as a lot of the costs will be incurred through providing non-profit-making services. There is deep resistance to this approach because it does not make 'economic sense'.

This author was involved in tendering for an enormous project in North West Angola involving the building of a massive new oil exploration and refining complex in 2003. When initially launched the project was budgeted to require as much investment as had been estimated originally for the 2012 London Olympics, about $10 billion. The project entailed employing several hundred local people initially to undertake unskilled jobs, such as road building and jungle clearing. There would eventually have been more complex building jobs, including housing for the staff, work canteens, security walls, storage, and docking facilities. One could have trained local people to become proficient in all such tasks and there could have been upstream contracts under which local people would have been encouraged to produce food for the canteen of the workers who were eventually to be stationed on site. Had local farmers been guaranteed a market for their produce for some years ahead, with perhaps a little help in planning they would have been able to produce all the items. There would have been both forward and backward integration that would have benefited many thousands of families. I have no doubt that there would have been some exploitation along the line – but at least some change would have been initiated. Unfortunately the Government was not interested in the long-term planning and vision required. The project was put out to tender on the basis of the lowest price; none of the social and educational ramifications were included in the project. It is more than likely that somewhere along the line considerable sums of money changed hands. The foreign contractors brought skilled people from around the world into the project, with an enormous amount of machinery and plant, and the locals were left to do the least skilled jobs only.

Governments are not good for development

Governments are the basic unit of running a country, but, as discussed above, in too many instances are obstacles to development because they have to pursue the interests of those within government. One should look at alternative approaches to the role and functions of government. One could think in terms, for example, of Switzerland: a nation of four languages and 34 cantons, each with great power, but with power based on its citizens. Or one could look to the US, comprising 50 States with an average of six million people per state (and 20 states with fewer than three million). The individual states are consequently run much more democratically than the Federal Government could ever be. These are the models one should encourage in the South, where the competition of different ethnic groups over vast territories for the limited resources available only leads to wasteful use of resources, including scarce human skills. Governments are not very good at development or running businesses. In Britain one needs to look no further than the example of the Millennium Dome, built in London to celebrate the new millennium. It was built at a cost of around £800 million, far more than originally budgeted, and completed very late. It failed to engage the imagination of the British public and then lay unused for six years until bought outright by a private operator. Within three years it had become one of the most successful venues in the world in terms of attendance. The private sector has adaptability and the capacity to take risks that those employed in the state sector simply do not have. The lesson to learn from this is that policy-makers need to find a balance between the development of a general framework for planning and that for detailed planning (which should be delegated to local bodies) and then for execution, which should be left to the private sector.

CHAPTER ELEVEN

The role of the private sector

In the last three decades there have been some undoubted successes in economic development in formerly very poor parts of the world. Development has taken hold in some countries, including a few that used to be called the Newly Industrialised Countries (NIC), such as Singapore, Malaysia, South Korea, Indonesia, the Philippines, Uruguay and Mexico. In both China and India there has been a dramatic increase in the numbers of people who have been able to find employment in the manufacturing sector and in some service industries. Yet the North seems to have been mesmerised by the successes and to some extent blinded to what it means. We have already seen in an earlier chapter [page 53] that the work of Dr Ha-Joon Chang using World Bank figures would indicate that, if we exclude China in the manufacturing sector and India in the service industries, the benefits of globalisation have been considerably overstated. However, the main engines of advancement in each case have been private enterprises, most of them local entities cajoled, encouraged and protected by the policies of their governments. A few of them, particularly those from Japan and South Korea, have managed to grow to a global level[37]. In the other cases, the initiative has been taken by international companies based in the North who have brought Foreign Direct Investment (FDI) and formed partnerships with local entities to take advantage of cheap labour.

Governments in the OECD countries in particular have been happy to work alongside corporate bodies from the North, the true agents of globalisation, who are extending their production facilities across the globe in order to reduce their production costs. It is a process that is not seriously threatening the future of Northern entities (at least not just now) and probably adding to the general well-being of the people of the North, as it lowers everyone's cost of living. The very same phenomenon is spreading the interests and reach of the North, through international service providers such as banks, insurance companies, accounting, auditing and legal services, all of which originate in the North. While one would be blind not to notice that there are substantial benefits to some of the poorest on earth in this process, there is no guarantee that this is the one solution for poverty. There is also the real concern that the recession in the rich world will threaten globalisation. It will reduce purchasing in the North and create a call for some measure of protectionism. Those issues were frequently raised during the 2008 US presidential campaign. Protectionism will reduce the amount of certain types of goods that will be purchased from the South. This in turn will exacerbate the poverty in the South. One of the main mental blocks for most people who work in the field of development is a proper understanding of this challenge of creating jobs and viable economic entities. Because job creation has not been made a priority, the world is sitting on a time bomb. China alone has to provide an estimated 35 million new jobs every year to prevent an increase in the number of unemployed youngsters. The millions who will be losing jobs in the current recession and will therefore add to the pool of unemployed will make the situation much worse for the Government of China. The rich world will buy fewer items from China. China will need less raw materials from Africa. More Africans will lose incomes and join the ranks of the poor.

But there is another fundamental lesson that we tend to ignore in the field of development. Only the private sector, the millions of individual initiatives that this sector represents, can provide the billions of jobs all over the world that are required to lift people out of poverty. There is no other sector and no other tool that can fill that space. It is the private sector that has to be helped to develop and take off.

Self-sustaining economic activities

The key challenge in economic development is how to generate, nurture and sustain local economic initiatives that will gradually generate a circular flow of income and will sustain that cycle within the poorest societies. Through sustained economic activities commercial entities can generate surpluses, as well as employ and train staff and gradually improve their skills. This then raises the level of production to a higher and more sophisticated plane. Sadly though, those working in the development field seem to fail to understand the nature of this challenge. Most governments in Africa certainly do not give priority to economic activities at the base, activities that could become permanent and employ the poorest members of their communities. Governments have been encouraged by international institutions, by foreign advisers, by international and bilateral lenders (the people to whom they owe huge amounts of money) and by big businesses to concentrate on what they can export. The purpose of exporting will be for the poorest to get some income and for the country as a whole to obtain foreign currency to repay the loans that have been raised to buy imported items. But if you want to export successfully, your prices and the quality of the product you wish to export need to be as good as or better than those of countries you are competing against. This is again something that has not been properly understood in the South (possibly not in the North either); enterprises from the South will not be given a share of the market in the global economy; they will have to claw it, they will have to compete against others who wish to achieve the same successes[38]. It will be incredibly difficult and for Africa probably impossible because its cost structure is so high.

It is very easy to produce biscuits and indeed many countries do produce them. In Ethiopia, however, biscuits are expensive to produce. The special flour, chocolate, and the wrapping paper, have all to be imported, as well as the energy to power the mills. The cost base of Ethiopia, because the country is virtually landlocked and transport costs are very high, means that the minimum amount required to live the most miserable life is deemed to be $1.25 per day. In Bangladesh the equivalent minimum is deemed to be $0.50. Ethiopia will never be able to compete with imported biscuits. Or indeed with a thousand other items of production.

The reason why most attempts at the economic development of Africa have failed is this basic major error of approach. It is not macroeconomic export policies that will make or break the poverty cycle, it is support of a myriad of micro-initiatives started by individuals in response to local demand in very challenging circumstances. These must then be supported by state structures that will gradually ensure a permanent developmental activity. Economic development would result from the scaling up of such activities. Even the recent successes in the flotation of government bonds for Nigeria or Gabon for example are to meet general government needs, not to create jobs at the base[39].

Development of industries

Industrial manufacturing must be the long-term aim for substantial poverty reduction as there are already more people than can be accommodated on, or fed from, the available land. However, for the time being, satisfaction of basic needs for food and so on through agricultural improvements has to be the priority. The key is to add value to local produce by canning and preserving tomatoes and green vegetables, roasting and mixing coffee blends, producing fruit juices or packaging tea, refining sugar cane. This is the field of agro-industries. Currently such activities at the global level are the preserve of large multinationals in the North. Only in Malaysia and Chile have local producers succeeded in any serious way in exporting value-added produce to the North. In both cases their governments have provided the platform on which the private sector has flourished.

The North will never significantly reduce its tariff rates on semi-processed exports from the South. There are very good strategic reasons for this; there needs to be a food cushion to protect the North and at times of recession there is a call for food to be purchased locally to encourage the small domestic producer. Economic development in the South must not rely on a policy of export-led demand, but be built from the base upwards, in other words it must be made to fulfil the needs of the South first, in spite of international bodies advising the South to take the export option. Even now, in the area of niche agricultural products, which African countries are advised to pursue, there are several examples of outright exploitation by middlemen, as we have seen in the section on commodities. There is scope for improvement here between concerned retailers in the North and their 'partners' in the South. But a longer-term shift is also starting to develop. In the long term it makes more sense for Malawi to export food (it has the land on which to grow it) to China than for Europe to do so, as the latter does not have the space on which to grow the millions of tons of vegetable and animal protein that China requires. There is a much stronger argument for trade and exchanges between countries that are within the same bracket of economic development.

How can government encourage private enterprises?

Microscopic, small- and medium-size individual enterprises are the essential base of development. It is not the large-scale corporations that the North knows and perhaps even understands (although most Northern governments do not always seem able to control them) that will generate development. Large-scale investment from any source will not be made where the terrain for such investment is not fertile or where there has not been any experience on which the foreign investor can build. To achieve real growth in the economy the first step must be to translate the needs of communities, with the tools required to meet these needs, into demands for local products. This means strong planning at local level, so that in the early stages the needs – food security, the provision of water, rural roads, better housing – can be met locally. If governments do not have the resources they should look to foreign aid while maintaining control over the planning and overall execution. Governments in Northern societies ensure that people with special needs are provided with jobs in sheltered workshops. These workshops are given exclusive contracts to produce items such as hospital beds or uniforms for the armed forces. It is a series of simple steps that should be encouraged in the South as well. The parallel is not that people in the South are disabled – they need to be able to protect their own limited markets from competition from outside.

To put this right we need institutions that are able to respond to the needs of local people in an appropriate way. In one project in

Ethiopia that I was involved with a group of blacksmiths produced good quality hand tools that the farmers needed but neither the agency I was working for nor the farmers had the funds to purchase the tools. The enormous distances that the farmers had to travel in order to purchase the tools added considerably to the cost. The lack of any local system of gathering and investing local savings or the lack of appropriate institutions made it impossible for poor farmers to scale-up their productivity. Intervention from a donor at the right point in the cycle (providing, for example, a small fund for that sort of loan) could have remedied a key issue. But the donors found it easier to give food – usually only after a few thousand people had already perished.

Businesses need to be encouraged to develop systematically – an extremely difficult process. [On page 34] we have seen some of the very real barriers that societal forces create for the person who might wish to start his or her own business. Governments might want to develop a business class but do not know how to do it; in most cases they have only introduced a level of unnecessary bureaucracy that has killed initiatives. In several African countries development agencies to promote small-scale enterprises have been established but these have usually been little more than ways of extracting money from tiny little businesses. In one East African country the relevant agency, when approached for financial help by the small businesses that paid an annual subscription to belong to it, just wrote a letter to the bank to support an application for funds. It could do nothing more; it had no funds and no trained personnel to evaluate the requests and thus speed up the process. In many other countries the process of collecting the subscription fee is the beginning and end of the operations of the agency. That fee more often than not goes into the pockets of the bureaucrat who collects it. In most countries in the South the key elements in enabling individual businesses to develop are missing: there are not enough training centres, no power generating facilities, no marketing back-up, and no purchasing power to direct towards the producers. The economic system is simply not fit for purpose and governments do not have the proper tools. In order to survive, micro- and small-scale businesses must break all the rules – they have to work against the State. They must ignore safety rules, employment legislation concerning minimum wage, employ members of the family who should be at school, hide their profits.

Why has business failed in Africa? There simply was no business class at independence that could take advantage of opportunities[40]. The only way in which an ambitious and capable person could therefore think of advancing was to gain political power; there was no other avenue to advance. We ignore this when we talk about the development of individual commercial or business initiatives in poor countries. If you want to get into government contracts you need to bribe someone. If you want to have a future in that country's DEVELOPMENT, you need to become involved with one political party or the other or several. Private enterprise does not have to be another word for greed (although sometimes it undoubtedly is), but private individuals and, much more importantly, corporate bodies must work in very different ways to become really useful tools in the development of the economies of the South. They must work within structures that should restrain their natural proclivity to make as large a profit as possible. The farmer should be able to make a decent living but not to take advantage of food scarcity. The importer of fertilisers similarly should be able to import and sell at a level that makes the risk worthwhile but does not restrict fertilisers to a few people through price competition alone. Or, to use economic jargon, the externalities of working in weak economies need to be taken into account. These would include reducing damage to soil, water, and to the environment in general, training local people in management and development, helping to grow the infrastructure and be willing to pay taxes. But, even more fundamentally, it must be accepted that the law of the markets will not provide the best balance of interest. To achieve this, one needs a strong legal framework that makes the fight an even one.

What the business community must do in the poorest countries is to be able to extricate itself from the political classes, govern and improve itself and be visible at the forefront of economic development. It is not an agenda that the political classes would adopt without a fight as it collides with the interests of the ruling elites. A 2007 World Bank study showed how difficult it is doing business in Africa. Out of the 35 least business-friendly countries in the world, 27 were in sub-Saharan Africa. The Bank showed how complicated it was to establish businesses across the continent. In the Democratic Republic of Congo registering a business takes 155 days, while enforcing a contract in Angola involves 47 procedures and takes over 1,000 days[41]. All such processes are hindered by the need to pay bribes to people in various ministries, all of whom have the capability to slow down the process if no bribe is forthcoming. It is not surprising that small businesses remain small; they have no incentive to enlarge and come to the attention of the authorities.

This is the sort of agenda that foreign companies should take on when investing in poor economies. It is a daunting list of responsibilities and it is not surprising that foreign investors are scared to sign up to it. To do all this and also add value of the primary produce in the country of origin is generally not possible through the tool of the private company. FDI is very badly needed as it brings to the receiving country a combination of capital, machinery, knowledge and skilled labour, but it must also lead to technology transfer and to the enrichment of the local receiving communities through adding and transforming the primary product, be it oil, coffee or wood. Private enterprise has no natural proclivity to do any of these things and under the present climate of rules and regulations it will never do it. There is also a different but related and also unresolved challenge: how can private enterprises carry out work in the public interest and be rewarded at an appropriate level when it succeeds and yet be punished when it fails? It is a challenge that the North cannot meet in its own societies either – it is not just a problem of the South. There appears here to exist an opportunity to create a new sort of partnership; this could be three ways; the host community, the foreign investor with the capacity to add value, and a third party (perhaps a non-profit body) that can meet the costs of what a pure commercial partnership cannot provide (e.g. education and training).

I appreciate that many readers would see this as advocacy for a neo-liberal approach to development – one of unfettered capitalism. It does not have to be and I do not believe that family responsibilities and loyalties will be totally destroyed by this approach. Those who work in the field of development always talk about the need for people in the South to 'own' their development. Why not advocate a form of ownership along the lines of private ownership in the freer societies of the North? After all only the private sector can provide the billions of jobs that will lead to people living a bit better. Here again there seem to exist an opportunity for bold new initiatives by NGOs from the North; why not offer to intervene in some projects in the South and offer to underwrite some of the non-economic elements of FDI by companies in the North investing in the South? They could pay for the education and training components; they could support local subcon-tracting to enable local businesses gradually to scale-up their activi-ties; for some of the needs of the families of the workers, such as nurs-eries for mothers at work. There should be more partnerships between small businesses in the North and small businesses in the South. Yes, all this could amount in the eyes of the WTO to unfair subsidies. But these are the sorts of initiatives that are needed if we want to prevent continuing marginalisation of the poorest.

CHAPTER TWELVE
The role of civil society

In the North there is a constant balancing act between those in power, running and closely benefiting from institutions, and those who are set apart from the state, the opposition between the various organs that serve the state and those whose task is to question it. The media would be one such group of outsiders, as are the various faith groups, trade unions, many of the professions and components of what one now usually refers to as 'Civil Society'. They have powers that derive from their members, their followers, their believers, and sometimes their economic muscle. This plurality of forces that the North considers necessary to balance the power of individuals and institutions in our societies by and large does not exist in the South.

There are examples of vibrant civil society in the South, but it can be very different from the society the rich world knows. The Christian churches have many followers in the South and they have played an important part in the development of schools, hospital and clinics. But the situation is changing. Southern Christianity is increasingly different from the Northern version. The North is tolerant of homosexuality in its midst and does not tolerate polygamy. The South tolerates polygamy but not homosexuality. The North seeks to ordain priests who have a theological training. The South requires priests who are able to understand the daily lives of their parishioners. Muslim missionaries from the Middle East are paying individuals to convert. In Kenya or Ethiopia a Christian would be paid around $200; it is an enormous sum and highly persuasive to a poor person. Islam does not ask for much; it is extremely easy to convert and it is also, despite what many in the North might think, a serious social progression for many people in that it rejects, for example, the caste system. It also gives women rights – even if the rights might seem limited to people in the North. These are some of the reasons why Islam is the fastest-growing religion in the developing world.

A different force has been the increasing independence of bodies such as trades unions and professional associations. This has come about as the direct result of the increasing growth of specific groups within society, a reflection of the increasing growth of the middle classes or of growing employment in certain fields. In India teachers form the most important single group in the political system, just as lawyers are in the North. It is natural that they should start to organise and wield political muscle. But all such groups are inward looking; no one could accuse lawyers of caring very much for the rights of the common man who cannot pay them. They might like the law, but not necessarily those who need it.

Professional bodies

In recent years Northern societies have, to a large extent, developed through the growth of specific interests emanating from professional bodies. It is the increased professionalism of the different fields of medicine and surgery that has led Northern medical services to improve so much and help save ever more lives. The pressure of the different branches of science, in which the physicist is pitted against the chemist, the haematologist against the oncologist, and so on are the very essence of professional life in advanced societies. It has led to the situation where the very expression 'professionalism', which should simply describe the work of the professions, has acquired the meaning of striving for excellence. This is one of those forces that is necessary in rich society and yet adds to the splintering of societies in the South. Just look at medicine; the South does not need more specialists in oncology or HIV/AIDS or rheumatology – it needs more people who can treat general diseases and people who can work in the field of prevention, which is both cheaper and far more effective at saving lives. They need fewer pills and more clean water.

The strength of the professions has also led to excessive power given to groups in society that take advantage of those positions. It has led to what economists call 'producer capture'. In the Northern world in 2007 and 2008 the banking profession allowed the breakdown of the financial markets that they controlled. It led to excesses in lending and risk-taking which no one could foresee because it was not in the interest of the bankers themselves to let anyone from the outside look into the arcane mysteries of their trade[42]. In the US the different groups involved in the medical fields – doctors, dentists, surgeons, pharmaceutical companies – are preventing any reforms of medical insurance. As a result, the US is the only industrialised country that does not have a comprehensive health service and some 46 million Americans do not have medical insurance cover. The legal profession, the medical profession and police forces across the world are just some of the professions that are often guilty of taking advantage of their power and position to reap benefits for themselves, at the expense of the general population. To prevent their exploitation of the poor in the South, professional bodies need to be moulded to serve society at large and not their professional interests alone.

The media of communication
In the North the role of the media is to expose the worst excesses of those in power; the corruption of politicians, their bias and their favouritism. But to be able to withstand the power of politicians the media need to be independent and well resourced – a luxury that in most parts of the world does not exist. Even in the UK and US the press is not as independent as it might appear. For example, Rupert Murdoch, who owns several newspapers and has an interest in television stations in the UK, can in effect stifle criticism of any government or any policy he chooses. The BBC World Service was transmitted to China through a satellite that carried Sky TV, also owned by Rupert Murdoch. When the Chinese Government started to object to some of the contents of the news coverage of China, the BBC World Service was dropped from that satellite because that activity clashed with the longer-term interests of the proprietor[43]. In Kenya the press has reported very little of the enormous corruption within government; the papers are owned by businessmen who rely on government for

most of their advertising income or their long-term contracts for other work. If there was any adverse criticism the Government would cut off advertising and the paper would probably be unable to survive. In those circumstances it becomes impossible for the general public to learn about corruption or unfair electoral practices.

The let-down by Northern academia

The academic community in the North has always been one of the most important components of civil society. It has enjoyed traditionally freedom that other groups have always envied. It has also been one of the greatest beneficiaries of the expansion of aid to the South. The amount of money that has been spent on research of all types within the North 'to help the South' has increased more than proportionally to the total aid increase. Not only has there been an increase in the number of people who can take up development studies at universities in the UK and in the US, but the number of consultancies that have been commissioned by international agencies and national governments under bilateral aid has increased to the extent that many respectable academic bodies in the North see such contracts as a continuing form of oxygen to keep them going. Think-tanks, university departments, research institutions and specialist consultancies have mushroomed. This is not to argue that research is not necessary – it is – but a lot of it is research for its own sake. It is built into the DNA of any academic to demand more time and more support for more research. What is needed is less research and more implementation. If academics in the North had done more to help academics in the South, there would have been fewer reasons for the latter to leave their societies, and everyone in the South would have benefited. Instead we have a seemingly unstoppable brain drain from South to North. There is a very strong argument – as the Commission for Africa made – for more tertiary and advanced education in Africa. That argument, however, to my mind is nullified by the fact that Africa can retain so few of its best scientists or graduates in general; they go abroad because the research facilities in most African countries are so poor. Let us train many more Africans at primary school level and build up that way and let us encourage many more research institutions from the

North to relocate in the South and qualified Africans to return home.

The invisible resources that the North has accumulated in institutions of higher education and research in various fields, through sophisticated equipment and patent rights, together with the capacity to invest ever higher amounts of capital required for new research, has meant that the North is becoming more and more dominant in intellectual research and capacity to innovate. The patents for future generations of GM seeds, medicines, electronics, arms, nuclear research, alternative energy sources, and so on are in the hands of Northern companies and Northern governments. This will mean that the North will receive the benefit for generations to come from licences and patents for products that the whole world needs. The Northern domination of some of these fields is already insurmountable. Governments of the North but also academics from the North should help governments of the South undertake research locally and register the benefits locally. If that means seconding good people from the North to work in the South, their posts and pensions in the North should be maintained and kept open so that working in the South is not seen as second best. If we go on as things stand now, it is impossible to slow down this brain drain and, as in other instances we have seen, the poorest lose out most.

One of the most important documents to have been produced in recent years in the whole field of development was the 2008 World Bank Human Development Report, which was all about agriculture. It is an excellent piece of work and should be obligatory reading for anyone who cares about the issues at the core of underdevelopment. It has the most incredible range of references to the most obscure studies undertaken in various parts of the world. It is so sad that clever minds have devoted so much time and energy to study in great depth some of the issues that are so blindingly obvious. It is even sadder that money from the aid budgets has gone to support such studies.

Voluntary aid organisations

In the delivery of aid voluntary organisations from the North are still a junior partner to official bodies, but they play an increasingly important role, accounting for about one-third of total aid[44]. The role of voluntary organisations in the North has been fundamental in determining the relationship between the North and the South. Most people have no way of understanding what poverty in Africa is or the extent of the damage due to flooding in Bangladesh or the abuse of human and political rights in Latin America except through the work of voluntary organisations. Unfortunately, in some countries and circumstances agencies from the North have become important if unwitting agents for 'their' governments. They deliver an exclusive Northern vision to the whole world.

NGOs are not the solution to the underlying challenges of underdevelopment, but they have an important capacity to think and act in independent and innovative ways that no other player has. They can adapt to local needs, and in the field of development that is an important virtue. They perform a number of functions that at present no one else is performing or could perform. Their role in involving local groups and democratising the process of development has been crucial. But to be truly constructive they should be able to show that common agreement on identifying and attacking the key problems is possible. Incoherence in policy-making and aid delivery is one of the main problems facing the North's approach towards the South; the fact that NGOs cannot show greater coherence in their policy-making reflects poorly on their criticism of governments and international organisations. There are several issues and approaches on which agreement must be found within the NGO community and which in turn they might foist on the governments of the countries from which they emerge and of those in which they work. In my view one of the problems of voluntary organisations is that they have been too timid and not demonstrated their willingness to lead.

From about the mid 1970s certain organisations in the North, such as Amnesty International, started to create sister organisations in the South. A decade later it was the turn of international environmental bodies, such as Greenpeace. In the 1990s a number of international gatherings, such as in Cairo in 1994 the International Conference on Population and Development and in Beijing in 1995 the International Conference on the Status of Women, started to generate independent groups in several Southern countries to tackle specific issues. Then, throughout the late 1990s, there was a fundamental change within those Northern NGOs that were working in the field of development as a response to changes on the ground. Bodies such as OXFAM in the UK, the Save the Children Fund, CARE in the US, Concern in Ireland, and others changed from being Northern-based and Northern-dominated organisations to genuine federations of national organisations, enabling local bodies to participate in the discussions concerning the development of their own societies. It was a genuine development from the grassroots upwards. A parallel development occurred in the Catholic Church; in the last 20 years it has become a truly global organisation, reflecting much less its predominantly European origins[45]. The setting up of the Millennium Development Goals, which encouraged the establishment of Poverty Reduction Strategies, has been another important encouragement to local civil society to become more engaged. For the first time ever in many countries non-state actors became officially involved in defining the ways in which their societies should develop. But there is a great deal of controversy over how effective many of the local representatives of international federations have actually been. Many of them do not have very deep roots and organisations from the North are forever involved in propping up the capacity of their sister organisations in the South. In some societies local NGOs are the only alternative to government and as such they can easily become the focus for political dissent, which then brings them into conflict with their government. In some cases the local workers of the NGOs talk more to their partners in the North than with their own constituents.

As a general point, one could say that the more people become involved with the problems confronting the South the better. The more people in the rich world realise that those in live in deep poverty are fellow human beings, the better. Yet there are some very obvious limits. The work of civil society from the North in the South is not always a fair representation of the priorities of the South; it is inevitably biased by that organisation's priorities. Fewer and fewer senior staff of voluntary agencies in either the North or the South have any experience of commercial activity and therefore do not understand the key problems that confront the poorest people in the South.

Their experience is based on white-collar employment that promotes fund-raising in the North but not economic activities that will ensure a bit more wealth and a bit less poverty in the South. This is in spite of the most dedicated and selfless work by thousands of men and women in the North and in the South. It is all part of the over-arching problem of using the wrong tools.

In their continual search for funds the voluntary organisations in the North have become trapped in their alliances with celebrities and this might eventually lead to some of the worst possible consequences for their work in the South. The logic is simply that, if celebrities have the ability to attract the attention of the media and of the politicians, one should harness their power. But the downside is that so few celebrities have any understanding of the real issues of the South. The profound and substantial needs of the South have become sound bites for the media. Celebrities can attract the attention of US presidents and European Prime Ministers. No respectable celebrity can be seen without attachment to some good cause or other. I would not wish blankly to condemn all celebrities; having had the pleasure of working briefly with Bob Geldof in Ethiopia in 1985 I know that he does not pretend to know a great deal (although he does know far more than he shows), but accepts that he can attract the media and this is what he does. He acts as an intermediary. But this is not the impression that most star performers give. Poverty cannot be overcome with a little bit of money to those that have fallen through the cracks. It needs patient and long term investment in capital, resources and education. A lot of the work that is being undertaken to raise money in the North is deeply demeaning to the peoples of the South. It is an enormous challenge but the NGOs in the North must tackle it. The Northern world cannot leave the challenge of poverty to be met by people who rely on comic activities to convey the enormity of the problems. The issues of world poverty encompass environmental, physical and social security for the world as a whole – not just the peoples of the South, well-intentioned as such initiatives might be. These issues deserve more than the superficial and very vacuous support the world of pop stars and celebrities can offer them. Far more in-depth education is needed.

The development of an endogenous civil society in the South has been one of the most exciting aspects of 'development' in the last decade. The links the members of civil society have had with their sister bodies in the North has been of fundamental importance. But the context is so different that the relationship has not always worked. In the North fundamentally the role of civil society has been either to pursue its own thing – as faith-based organisations or the professions have done – or to enable the weaker members of society to stand up against actual or perceived exploitation by the more powerful, as trade unions have done. In the North they are incredibly important as persistent examiners and critics of the more powerful, as has been done by human rights groups and the media of communications. In the South, in the absence of any other tools by which protest and dissatisfaction can be expressed, civil society organisations very often become the only lung of society – but to what extent they are representative of a wide group is questionable. Most of the time they are a challenge to the government of the day; they then become alternative political parties. They are too often the expression of very small groups of people within the middle classes. They can be very brave and even successful, but do not perform the same role they perform in rich societies and the alliances Northern organisations seek to form are often based on incomplete understanding. No society can happily breathe with just one lung.

There is a more fundamental issue that needs to be explored concerning voluntary agencies emanating from the North; they have been too willing to follow the path dictated to them by the governments of the countries from which they emerge. They need to carve a different path if they wish to attack world poverty. That means extricating themselves from the blandishments of the Establishment, because that very Establishment is part of a continuum of activities and policies that encompasses the World Bank and the WTO, bodies that at their very heart do not help the poorest, but fundamentally damage them because they are powerful tool to tackle the wrong illnesses. If the international community can change direction – and to my mind it is essential that it should – it is the voluntary organisations that have to show the way.

CHAPTER THIRTEEN
The role of aid

A great deal has been said about aid in development, that it is useless, has a corrupting effect, and so on. Certainly the figures are staggering: according to Paul Wolfowitz, when President of the World Bank, the enormous sum of $2.3 trillion had gone into aid to Africa from the 1950s to 2006 and Africa of course is the one part of the world that has become poorer over the years[46]. However, in his excellent book, *Does Foreign Aid Really Work?* Roger Riddell reveals that less money goes to Africa now than in the past because a great deal of the aid allocated to Africa never leaves the shores of those who give it. It goes on studying issues of world poverty at universities and research institutions, on conferences and on disparate initiatives aimed at looking at possible interesting ideas on growth, on fair trade, on social justice and on other new areas of DEVELOPMENT. A lot of aid goes to international institutions that inevitably also undertake research and have to pay for expensive administrative overheads. Some of it goes on scholarships to promising youngsters from the South – and that can pay back in goodwill and long-term links. Thabo Mbeki, the former President of South Africa, was on such a scholarship at Sussex University in the UK. There is little doubt that research into, for example, improving agricultural seeds or migration or solar energy development will be eventually of assistance to African countries, but not in the short term. The problem is that too many people are involved in the process of aid and that the focus of aid is becoming less and less clear. The agents involved, particularly the economists and the researchers in the DEVELOPMENT community, all distort what should be the ultimate purpose – development as the tool for poverty alleviation.

The key study undertaken on the role of aid in changing the macro-economic environment of poor countries has made the point that aid has not resulted in any fundamental change[47]. Aid has played a positive role only in countries that are reasonably well governed and adopt sensible economic policies. The most important criticism of aid in its present form is that it is mainly a way in which rich countries reassert their priorities. Aid is spent mostly on what the rich countries think is good for poor countries. It seems not to occur to the people who are planning for emergencies that perhaps if there had been a bit more spent on prevention, there would be fewer emergencies and thus more funds available for development. And those who are aware of the challenge can do very little about it. This should be self-evident in all cases of famines that seem to reoccur with ever greater frequency in the South; the emergencies occur because of the fragility of the economies of the South.

Aid as welfare and not as development

In most societies there has been a mismatch between the needs of the poorest and the intentions of the donors. Everyone is, by and large, moved by the most horrendous examples of need; emergency appeals with appalling pictures will always generate a much more positive response from the public than the more complete picture. The reality is that in most normal situations there is indeed a great deal of obscene poverty but in most situations there are also ways of getting out of poverty. Here people of good will face a serious dilemma. The individual who might like to help cannot do so directly; how do you help someone who is obviously desperate for some food or clothing or housing in some remote part of the world? You rely on the intermediary, either governments, which, as we have seen, most of the time are not a tool for the development for ordinary people but for the advancement of those who are in government, or the voluntary organisations. The latter are in turn caught in a dilemma. They raise more funds by presenting extremes of poverty through images that will prick the conscience of the people of the North than by encouraging the long-term approach required to develop those societies. This leads to a serious lack of balance in the perception of the South by the North. NGOs are encouraging charitable giving because that is an easy way to appeal to the better nature of people in the rich countries, but they are not encouraging the investment that is the long-term answer to permanent improvement in the lives of the poor. Nor do they have the capacity to encourage the development of a commercial or industrial culture that will lead to self-sufficiency.

The unintended consequences have also been extremely damaging to poor countries. The commercial success of China has radically changed the world's perception of the Chinese. The world now thinks of them as being less wealthy than the North, but with huge potential. Not so about Africans. Most people do not realise that Africa is a huge continent with an enormous variety of peoples, issues, problems, and potential solutions just like most other parts of the world. Zimbabwe is in turmoil but Ghana is giving genuine vent to democratic forces. Rwanda is not a democracy by Northern standards but is trying to achieve some sort of reconstruction. This negative image means that people in many countries in Africa have to overcome the deeply held images of poverty and incapacity that the culture of aid has created. Given the presentation by the aid lobby most people are not able to differentiate between different countries and different situations.

We have seen in a previous chapter [page 108] how the development of Northern societies has been the result of the cumulative and parallel development of government, business community, and civil society. These have subdivided further and further to the extent that each tentacle has assumed a life of its own. They still control, check, and balance one another through the combined institutions of society. The number of footings supporting rich societies has added to their stability. That is not the case in many poorer societies that have not developed this network of institutions. In most of Africa the aid and development communities (which at the end of the day, well-intentioned as they might be, have become powerful interest groups in their own right) have been more powerful than the business community and often more powerful than governments themselves. Stephen Browne estimated in 2006 that there were around 100,000 people working full-time in the field of development[48]. For these key people aid is obviously seen as more important than any other aspect of development and in so doing they have retarded development by their very presence and importance.

Lack of focus

The problem with international aid efforts is that inevitably everyone pursues their own priorities, not those of the recipient. The case of the official (i.e. governmental) aid community is instructive. Intergovernmental bodies were initially established to serve the needs of the rich countries and all of them were headed by representatives of the rich countries – in the 1940s the poor world did not exist. Help to the poor world was a low priority. What has happened in too many cases is that those organisations have become avenues through which the richer or at least the more privileged members of the poorer countries have managed to join the world of the more privileged international community. This is not to say that no good whatsoever is being done, but the end result is less important than the internal dynamics of the organisations themselves. The very nature of the set-up is one that engenders competition which at the end of the day consumes scarce resources. If you deem that education (UNESCO) is more important than agriculture (FAO), or health (WHO), or more than the environment (UNEP), you then have a race between those different agencies to influence governments of the donor countries to fund their particular operations and of the receiving countries in adapting their programmes accordingly. Any attempt at coordination by the United Nations Development Programme (UNDP), which is supposed to bring them all together, is frustrated by the system. At the highest level of policy-making the World Bank seems to have been locked in for almost 30 years into a fight to control the macro-economic heights of world economy with the IMF. This has led the Bank, the most important single agency in international development, to neglect the needs of the poorest.

Aid can be a huge burden for receiving countries to deal with. One of the most extreme cases is the well-known number of official donors to Tanzania; there are reputed to be over 2,000, several sometimes from the same country (e.g. the US Department of Agriculture or the US Department of Commerce or the US Agency for International Development)[49]. Each of these will have their own requirements in terms of auditing and reporting, with the result that there are over 2,000 accounts in the Central Bank of Tanzania, one for each donor. Reports have to be provided to each donor monthly or quarterly or yearly or whatever. For a country that has limited skilled manpower it is very time-consuming and for the entire development process it is plainly absurd.

There is another set of dangers to which the endless subdivisions of responsibility leads. The head of FAO at a meeting at the House of Commons in October 2008 gave a talk in which he described his organisation as near perfect as one could ever want it to be (it would have been surprising if he had said otherwise!). When challenged as to why there was a world food crisis, he explained that he could only give advice to member countries. That is plainly an abrogation of leadership and responsibility. The World Food Programme (which deals with emergency food relief), the International Fund for Agricultural Development (which is supposed to foster long-term agricultural development) and the FAO, all based in Rome, continually blame one another for the failure to prevent people from starving. The truth is that they are set up to be in permanent rivalry one with the other[50].

The same is true for the private voluntary agencies. If you are raising money among animal lovers to help a dog sanctuary in Sri Lanka that is what you will get money for. The community of donors will thus expect the money to be spent to satisfy that particular objective. Or it could be for people who are blind, or polio victims or disabled people. While there are clear cases of need where charities play an important role, such as helping polio victims in the poorest societies, what we must aim to achieve in the long term is to enable communities to become self-reliant, so that they can eventually look after their own. This is not something that individual organisations, except the largest, can deal with. The central core of the problem – trying to overcome economic poverty itself – is not being addressed at all, because that responsibility rests with 'someone else'. Organisations, once set up, very seldom go out of existence and collectively they do not address the key problems. Each addresses a very small segment of the whole panorama of needs.

Most of us would assume that where there is not enough food, the priority should be to grow food. That is what the poor really want and they need the opportunity to do it themselves. It is strange that the international community has not managed to make the growing of more food the highest priority in the countries that are always short of food. Global assistance to agriculture decreased from $6.2 billion to $2.3 billion between 1980 and 2002, even though official aid overall increased by 65 per cent during the same period. Multilateral aid to African agriculture fell from 32 per cent of total aid in 1981 to a mere 7 per cent in 2001[51]. We know that there are periods during which food is scarce and that the international community will often react positively (if not always very rapidly) to the lack of food and that food will be bought on the international markets to meet the emergency needs of some of the poorest countries on earth. That lesson should be enough for all concerned to make agriculture the first priority. But it is not.

Aid of course has to be seen within a wider context of political and economic ties. A factionalised and divided approach leads to serious conflicts and sometimes to the most absurd results. An extremely good example of this is the genocide in Rwanda. The Northern powers did not intervene in 1994 when probably between 800,000 and one million Tutsis were murdered in 100 days[52]. But in 2008 a French judge issued a warrant for the arrest of the President of Rwanda, Paul Kagame, accusing him of war crimes. For years there have been suspicions that the French armed the Hutus who were responsible for the massacre of the Tutsis in Rwanda, but the French Government granted immunity from arrest to several people who had been accused of taking part in the genocide. Kagame and other members of the African Union would simply see this as the forked tongues of the North. The North fails to help prevent hundreds of thousands of murders but is prepared to intervene when it decides that some principles of its own making have been breached. This smacks of a highly partisan approach to justice[53]. This behaviour is also characteristic of the North's general approach to DEVELOPMENT.

Aid in emergencies

In cases of emergencies both voluntary and official aid can be extremely effective. The very vigour of, and lack of restraints on, voluntary organisations can be a blessing. They were, for example, far more effective than official US Government agencies in intervening after Hurricane Katrina hit New Orleans in 2005. Governmental bodies did virtually nothing for four days[54]– the very period when most people were at their most vulnerable. The tsunami that hit South East Asia in late 2004 was one of the best examples of the speed and efficiency that voluntary agencies are capable of. Foreign governments were slow and joined the relief effort several days later. We must remember however that the efforts of national governments have always been greater than the efforts of outsiders. Emergencies show that when the need is clear and obvious, the international community can react positively and can help solve problems. People need water and clothing, shelter, emergency latrines, and usually these are rapidly provided both by official aid bodies and NGOs. It is like fighting a war: you put all your energies and resources towards tackling that aim. One accepts the command structure commensurate with the challenge; a war cannot be fought by committee. But such well coordinated action is absent in the field of development as a whole. The aid given in emergencies has saved millions of lives and here aid is clearly an effective tool, but in most other cases aid is unfocused and inevitably wasted.

Let us come back to the example of the World Food Programme (WFP), which is mandated to provide food to populations that are faced with food emergencies. It does so by distributing food donated by rich countries (traditionally including the US, Canada, the EU, Argentina, Australia). These countries buy the surplus food from their farmers and give it to the WFP to distribute. The result, of course, is that starvation might be alleviated but that the long-term damage to the receiving country's agriculture is incalculable. WFP does receive some money and buys a growing proportion of its annual requirements from some African countries, but it is a small part of the total. Its policy destroys the livelihood of the small farmer across many parts of Africa. The Gates Foundation has recently given enormous amounts of money to enable the WFP to buy more food from African farmers, but one wonders why it took an admittedly very rich private body to subsidise the work of an intergovernmental body that for at least a decade has ruined the lives of millions of poor people in Africa through its policies[55]. The WFP is American dominated and it is unlikely that its policies are going to change radically any day soon. For example, the US dictates that all official US aid should be spent on US provided goods and services – from the purchase of grain to the bags, from trucks to ships, as well as intermediaries and brokers. This all adds enormously to the costs of US aid. In 2007 it was calculated that aid from the US cost $800 million more than if it had gone to international tender or purchased within Africa[56]. Such policy was introduced by Bill Clinton when President and George Bush tried unsuccessfully to alter the terms[57]. The Chicago Council on Global Affairs calculated that in the 1980s the US was spending $400 million per year on boosting African agriculture. By 2006 this had gone down to $60 million per year. It calculated that the US Administration spent 20 times more on food aid than on long-term schemes to develop indigenous food production[58]. Small farmers whose food could have been purchased by the WFP and by other food donors would have been encouraged to grow more. They have instead been ruined and have joined the ranks of the extreme poor. Had the Gates money gone to a local structure or helped to develop local structures, if would have been still more effective in the long run.

Aid from NGOs

It is difficult for someone who comes from a background of work with international voluntary agencies blankly to criticise the work of the Northern agencies in poor countries. For example, one might question the motivation of missionaries from a range of Christian churches, yet they have brought literacy and basic health services to countless villages. Their people have died in large numbers in areas affected by malaria and the tsetse fly. By and large, hundreds of NGOs have been doing good work; they have engaged countless people in the North in the challenges faced by people in the South. Many people in the North genuinely want to help alleviate poverty in the South. They join voluntary organisations at salaries lower than they would get in the commercial or financial worlds. They have prevented millions of deaths – of this I have no doubt and I am sure no sane observer from either the North or the South would question their efforts – even if occasionally one might disagree with their motives. But one could also argue that NGOs from the North, and some from the South, have unintentionally vitiated the attack on world poverty. People with social service and humanities backgrounds constitute the majority of staff of NGOs and they are often extremely ignorant of all things to do with money and uneasy with the concept of private enterprise and income generation. Many such people believe that the State should take on most economic functions, functions that governments have nowhere been able to discharge successfully. NGOs generally do not understand the need for creating economic activities that will enable peoples and communities in the South to become self-reliant and self-sustaining.

At a wider level the work they perform is still a small part of the total picture and this is the key criticism against aid in general; it is a small dyke set up against a very powerful flood. There is a long list of sins that Northern governments and Northern interests (in the widest possible sense of the word) commit daily against the interests of the poor. The North receives qualified people who should be working in their countries, allows money laundering, supports subsidies to Northern agriculture, encourages trade liberalisation, and so on. It is a long agenda of issues that rich nations do not adequately address and which combine to underdevelop the South. Aid is very small compensation against such complex and powerful forces. Voluntary organisations therefore in many countries can be accused of being there to assuage some of the damage that the economic neoliberal approach pursued in the North – by its governments, official aid and international bodies – has caused to the South. These policies have weakened trades unions in the North and pressed down wages in the South. When NGOs from the North arrive in the South to relieve the extremes of the damage the North has caused to many people, it smacks of hypocrisy. In other words, Northern NGOs have become agents involved in repairing some of the damage caused by the policies and institutions the North controls.

At the other extreme there is the criticism of the destructive independence of voluntary organisations. A devastating criticism of foreign NGOs in Afghanistan is given in Ashraf Ghani and Clare Lockhart's book *Fixing Failed States*[59]. The authors give a picture of a large community of foreigners, much freer to operate than even their home governments and certainly more so than the different government ministries in Afghanistan. For example, some NGOs are able to offer salaries that would obviously attract good local people, but such salaries bear no relation to the salaries that either the host or the donor governments could offer. Good people who should work for their country's future end up working for foreign employers instead. The book contains the criticism of two people who care about the failure of Northern voluntary agencies to help countries that desperately need help.

It is too easy to set up a voluntary organisation, and certainly in the UK there is no mechanism to check whether someone is fit or qualified to run an organisation and appeal for funds. Hundreds of organisations replicate each others' work and there is no legal or even moral pressure to make them work together. The bureaucracy involved in running NGOs is sometimes problematic; running costs of many organisations are very high and the process of making applications to grant-making bodies is time-consuming and expensive. In the UK, charities typically have to employ specialists to fill in applications to major trusts such as the National Lottery or the Department for International Development. Some organisations no longer apply for funds from bodies such as the European Commission, probably the most bureaucratic institution on earth, because of the costs and time involved in applying. World poverty is too important an issue to be sidelined by such procedures, yet they have become the hallmark of dealing with the poverty of the South. At the other end of the scale, too many organisations are too small to make any lasting difference.

The right level of operation

In too many cases aid is being given at the wrong level. To develop at the grassroots you need the right tools. Donors seem to have forgotten that, if they want to develop agriculture, people need to be able to start with better hand tools, not sophisticated machinery that they will not be able to maintain. In the highlands of Ethiopia, where the land has the potential to grow more food, the depth of the blade of most ploughs is only a few centimeters because that is the depth that a man pulling the plough can manage. Only a traction animal could pull a plough with a deep blade that does more than just scratch the surface of the soil. It quickly becomes a vicious circle; to be able to ensure better production, the farmer needs the capital to buy that animal, which would also need to be fed and maintained. She cannot do that before she has generated enough surplus to purchase and maintain the animal for which she first needs the deeper blade. The North has paid very little attention to what for the rich are low-level obstacles, but for the farmers of the poor world are insuperable barriers. Most of the best examples of problem-solving have already been developed somewhere in the South; in some Indonesian projects, vouchers were advanced instead of money by way of credit to enable the farmer to acquire a limited quantity of good hand tools. The first lot of vouchers had to be redeemed and subsequently repaid before any new set of tools, seeds or equipment could be obtained. If the farmer did not either return or pay for the first set of tools in this way, he or she would not be allowed to borrow again.

Lack of coordination

The key element that militates against effectiveness in aid delivery is the lack of coordination in aid giving. A friend who was head of the UN Development Programme in one small African country invited all foreign and local agencies involved in the supply of water – both official aid donors and NGOs – to a meeting. He suggested that for the good of everybody they should try to supply one type of water pump across the entire country. This would mean that it would be simpler in future for the government to obtain spare parts since all pumps would be standard. It would also mean standardisation of maintenance and simplifying the training of the operatives and the communities in which they were working. The proposals were totally unsupported. Since the country had been a French colony, the representative of

France pushed for his country's model to be adopted. Theirs was a good pump, but expensive and thus replacements and maintenance would be costly. Local communities would not have access to the funds required to purchase the spare parts. For diplomatic reasons the EU representative could not back the choice of a non-EU model, so the French pump was selected for official aid purposes by the EU and European donor governments. However, none of the other donors accepted the recommendations, which they accused my friend of having supported for 'diplomatic' rather than practical reasons. Both the government and the voluntary organisations continue to install whichever pump they individually prefer.

All too often what one organisation or institution proposes militates against the intentions of another donor. The result is a great deal of chaos and even more often undue weight on the shoulders of weak administrations or economies. Coherence in international aid giving and policy advice has been totally lacking over the last 50 years. Only in education does there seem to have been a reasonable joint effort by the OECD countries in a few countries of the South. The example of Bangladesh is always trotted out: members of the Development Assistance Committee (DAC) of the OECD donors were able to join forces to deliver a substantial plan of education to the country for a 10-year period, during which time it is claimed that around $1 billion worth of aid will be given to foster the development of education. This particular case is interesting because it involves the largest voluntary organisation in the country, the Bangladesh Rural Advancement Committee (BRAC). It is well established and well respected, certainly far more so than the government itself which is near the top of the Transparency International corruption index, and has wide coverage across the country.

Donors are obsessed with the need for logical frameworks in their work and yet miss out the most basic issues of policy and delivery coherence. In most development work the right hand does not know what the left hand is doing. The very number of private aid agencies (over 500 after the tsunami in South East Asia in 2004[60] or around 250 in Kabul when the Taliban collapsed in 2003[61]) clearly shows that the voluntary aid community is no more capable of coordination and coherence than the official aid agencies. Voluntary agencies were the first to champion the rights of women and children, fought for the rights of minorities, for the conservation of the environment, for more participation of the poorest in development. They championed such causes among governments that by and large would not have cared very much for any of these issues because they would have been seen as destabilising to their own powers.

There are hundreds of Northern agencies that work in the South, but there is very little evidence that they cooperate or work together at the grassroots. If you are promoting water-saving methods, best practice in agriculture, small animal farming, maintenance of equipment or tools or clinics for mothers and children, the priority should be to achieve results across the board. Yet the NGOs do the very opposite in order to protect their territories. In order to 'sell' their particular message and fundraise effectively they stress that what they do is more important than what anyone else does[62]. It is understandable then that the Government of Ethiopia (a country that has never been colonised by foreign nations but only by voluntary organisations), is taking steps to restrict the freedom of voluntary agencies. This is an action that is highly repressive, yet there are many ordinary Ethiopians who deeply resent the approach and the arrogance of the aid agencies.

Making aid the powerful tool that it could be will be complicated, but it need not be impossible. However, there has to be leadership, but at present it is not clear where it will come from. At the G8 meeting in L'Aquila in 2009 it was obvious that the rich countries of the world were not honouring their pledges, made only four years before at Gleneagles, to double the amount of aid. The World Bank has become so self-absorbed and so complacent that it has lost any leadership role and the EU has shown no intention of taking control either. In the current climate of recession that leadership will not come from multilateral or bilateral aid donors, only from private donors and voluntary agencies.

Social protection

For the last 10 years in some poor countries there has been a serious new approach to reduce extreme poverty through the provision of social protection. Several national governments, backed financially by donor Governments and organisations from the North, including ActionAid and OXFAM in the UK, have designed programmes under which a minimum amount of cash is provided to some of the most marginalised and therefore most vulnerable members of the poorest countries. They identify people who are in danger of landing in emergency need and then give them food and money – 'smart aid' – throughout the year. NGOs have been pioneers in this, but more donors in general have now become attracted to this approach. It enables them to tackle hunger and vulnerability with predictable cash transfers to the chronically poorest social groups, instead of just having to deal with the extremes of hunger and need that arise repeatedly in emergencies[63]. This social protection is vital and is to be welcomed; it is also cheap. It costs about one-third less to offer social protection throughout the year to a family in Ethiopia than to supply food aid in an emergency[64]. This fits in perfectly with the analysis offered by Amartya Sen that in case of famine what happens is not necessarily that food becomes scarcer; it is that access to food by the poorest becomes prohibitively expensive. The idea of social protection has been further developed by some Southern governments in the form of regular pensions, or food stamps, or food for work and often they are able to do so much more comprehensively than Northern donors. Lesotho for example, through the provision of modest pensions, is able to help thousands of poor families achieve a basic minimum safety net. Yet social protection can only be seen as a short-term remedy. It will always remain a means of support that can be given only to a small proportion of the total number of people in need. In the ongoing recession of 2009 the problems will be exacerbated. Governments of the South will have less income. The NGOs that started this process and official aid donors who have backed it will have less aid to give. More fundamentally, this extremely important initiative has not been transformed into effective sustainable demand. It has not led to investment in productive resources that should eventually assist self-sufficiency.

Aid from non-OECD countries

Do other countries help? Every time the oil price went up by $0.10 in 2007 and the first half of 2008 the members of OPEC received approximately another $500 million per week. Islamic countries have grown incredibly rich. According to Moody's, the international credit rating agency, by the end of 2007 the combined wealth of Islamic banks was $97.3 billion. The amount of official aid Islamic countries have given to the poor world is miniscule by comparison[65]. There are occasionally grand donations; in early 2008 Saudi Arabia gave some $500 million to the WFP. But such unplanned one-off gifts are not the solution, which has to be long term change and investment. There is no tradition of individual giving in China or India – in fact, apart from deep family obligations, giving is very rare. In the past the Chinese Government was probably one of the largest donors (as a proportion of GDP) to liberation movements and fragile governments – see the chapter on China [page 198]. Now, both India and China are more likely to invest rather than give aid. In June 2008 the official Chinese Exim Bank and the privately owned China International Fund pledged upwards of $7.4 billion in soft loans for infrastructure projects in Angola alone. This compares with the World Bank's offer of $500 million[66]. Obviously the Angolan Government has had to accept certain economic conditions, including the allocation of the building contracts to Chinese companies, and the employment of Chinese labourers and skilled people. This is no different from the normal behaviour of the North and the World Bank which have always imposed conditions as well.

Aid v investment

Aid in emergencies is clearly something that should be given and should be increased. In fact everyone needs to be better prepared due to the increasing number of calamities that will occur. But more fundamentally the aid givers need to rethink their role if they wish to achieve development; the way they are operating is to provide bandage after bandage without addressing the fundamental underlying problems. There has to be a more focused and, I would argue, a more 'commercial' approach to aid giving, with very clearly defined goals and the capacity to measure results. It would make the donors more aware that they have to generate results and that the receivers would be encouraged to view aid as investment. That might generate the discipline that a finite flow of income would induce; at the moment it is all viewed as a ceaseless stream. But neither can be achieved from a distance; it has to be done locally. In my view there is still a reticence to say and do the right things; support for development is too vague and too remote. Let us look at one important initiative.

In 2002, under the leadership of Kofi Annan, who was at the time Secretary General of the UN, a new initiative was launched to encourage the development of agriculture in Africa with the name of AGRA (Alliance for a Green Revolution in Africa). It received a substantial donation for the Gates Foundation. Its head office is in Nairobi. It has brought together good people from various disciplines – scientists, economists, statisticians, researchers in different fields – to look at the various problems. Yet, at the end of the day, all these people, who collectively represent a vital chunk of the most skilled manpower of Africa, have only a limited role – they can only advise because they have no funds to invest. In spite of being almost entirely an African initiative, AGRA cannot make African governments take sensible measures to prevent famine within their own borders. It is doing valuable work, for example in training distributors of fertilisers so that they can provide the valuable services needed by farmers. They target small-scale farmers, which they see correctly as the main tool of transformation of African agriculture. It is prevented from implementing sensible policies because it comes up against the barrier of 'national sovereignty', which is all too often used as an excuse for governmental inaction. AGRA has thus become another intermediary. It would be difficult to identify something new that AGRA carries out that could not also be done by the FAO or IFAD or the WFP. But, as this example demonstrates, in the field of international development it is easier to set up a new organisation than improve an existing one. The real issue, to repeat this point, is actually to do something practical and thus ignore the traditional boundaries of the institutions. They each do good work but the collective effort amounts to very little change.

In her book *Dead Aid*, Dembisa Moyo condemns all aid as having corrupted Africa. There is inevitably corruption in most fields of government intervention and public investment, but it has not been caused by aid alone. In the field of aid, corruption has been caused because, by necessity, in the way it is disbursed, it has led to the enlargement of the bureaucracies and the clienteles of the State and of the donors. It has enlarged the middle classes and not relieved poverty at the village level. To avert this problem, a combination of the roles of straight commercial investment (focused and demanding returns within specified time frames) and aid (driven by generous responses) is required. The Gates Foundation, with its approach to business school evaluation of input/output in aid projects and intermediaries, is probably providing a useful example for all development agencies. But in more general terms the required discipline is more likely to come from China than from the North. It is an area in which the voluntary sector in the North could and should become far more interventionist. We will return to this subject at the end of the book.

I worked for the Commonwealth Secretariat in 1981-83. In 1982 I went with the director of my Unit to a middle-income Commonwealth country to draw up a list of projects in the field of industry that needed to be evaluated. The director was so desperate to obtain such a list of projects to take back with him to London that he made what I considered an improper offer to the senior official of the country whom we met at the end of the visit. As a result we returned with a long list of requests for projects to be evaluated. I reported the incident to the director's superior. The complaint eventually went through the whole chain of command. I was dismissed. But the Unit had fully justified its existence because there was a long list of requests for assistance. Its budget was increased. None of the projects that we had been asked to study were ever realised, because they did not justify any assistance. Three years later, having realised that nothing had been achieved, the whole Unit was disbanded by the Heads of Governments[67].

PART THREE

Living in a
Changing World

Governments of the North and their bilateral aid bodies, the international institutions controlled by the North and even many of its voluntary organisations have not realised that not only there are profound changes taking place in the world arena, but that the role of the North is rapidly diminishing and that other forces are starting to dominate the global agenda. Or perhaps they have realised it and cannot get their act together to cope with the changes demanded by the new situation. These forces might ultimately play in the same direction as those of an earlier period – the search for energy sources and minerals, cheap sources of food, markets for manufactured products – but the geopolitical framework is changing very rapidly. In a few years' time, particularly as the recession in the North forces retrenchment, decreases the employment of nationals from the South that cuts the flow of remittances, increases protectionism and reduces aid and lending to the South, the role of the North will become much less important than that of the new players. Even many of the poor countries are starting to question much more fundamentally their relationship with the North, sometimes for good reasons and sometimes for bad ones. But the speed of change is very rapid and the North is in danger of losing the positive results, limited as they might be, that it has achieved.

CHAPTER FOURTEEEN
The paradigm is changing

The entire basis of the dialogue, of the paradigm for development, is changing as we speak. The North has entered a terrible financial recession which will lead to long-term structural reforms. For example, there will be far less bank credit available in the future, be it for private enterprises or for governments, including those of the poor countries. China and India are now making the running, and Africa possesses minerals and land that everyone needs and wants – and they will get it at the expense of the ordinary African farmer. The emergence of new players and new forces is changing our world before our eyes. The Northern world and its values no longer rule the roost or set the standards. The power of the World Bank, of the IMF and of the many organisations which the North has created and through which it has dominated the global agenda is diminishing. Economic power is slipping from the hands of the North and with it the capacity to dictate the agenda for the world. The priorities of the new players are supplanting the older order. Furthermore, the increased muscle of the new powers provides the opponents of the North with the security to voice their dislike of the peoples and governments of the North.

Some 40 years ago everybody thought that Africa would develop and that the real challenge was poverty in Asia. At independence Kenya and Ghana both had a higher per capita GDP than South Korea, the Philippines or Brazil. One of my professors at Uppsala University in Sweden, Gunnar Myrdal, wrote the first comprehensive book on world poverty under the title '*Asian Drama*' published in

1968[1]. But China and India now are doing all the things that international financial institutions are telling less powerful countries not to do, such as protecting their crops, shielding their markets, copying products, ignoring patent restrictions, subsidising bank loans, ignoring bankruptcies, and so on.

A world of four economic speeds

The world is no longer driven by one economic engine; there are instead four different engines moving at different speeds and with different characteristics. We thus could say that we have four parallel economic worlds. Of course there are overlaps, and a lot of advantages have accrued from links between one world and another – from the rich world buying white goods from China and China buying copper from Zambia. But at the same time part of the mess in which the world's economic system finds itself is due to the mismatch between the very same economic worlds.

The OECD world

The rich world could be characterised as one in which there is a relatively low level of unemployment – at best around 3 per cent and at worst in the forthcoming recession it might go to up to 15, event to 20 per cent. Populations are ageing and they have substantial needs for medical and social services. Their economies need a lot of capital, they are highly industrialised, and they export a great part of their services. They produce only a proportion of their total food requirements. They posses a large private service sector in areas such as finance, banking and health. There is a high level of personal security with a developed system of individual rights and freedom. Great powers reside in groups of professionals, above all lawyers, but also bankers, doctors, teachers, policemen and accountants. Their economies are flexible and sometimes volatile, and exposed to external currents and unforeseen events[2]. They are the home of powerful corporations that their governments back and which act as surrogates for the new economic imperialism. They are reliant on imported energy; energy security will be the main driver of their external policies in the forthcoming decades. They currently control the international institutions. The middle classes dominate and set the priorities, which means that there is an emphasis on health and education and on expecting equality, and there is the luxury of principles (including ethical approaches to trade) and vibrant civil societies. Bureaucracies – particularly state bureaucracies – generally work effectively.

The BRIC countries

Brazil, Russia, India and China have substantial populations – they are large countries with a high proportion of young people (except Russia, where the population is ageing as in Western Europe). They therefore have huge potential internal markets and their economies are growing rapidly through the process of satisfying them at a rate two to three times as fast as the economies of the OECD countries. They are much poorer than the OECD countries and their economies are not as solid as those of the OECD. They have weak physical and social infrastructures. They need technology and, with the exception of China, capital. They are driven by their governments, which have enormous powers of intervention which they use without restriction. The media of communication are not free and the independence of interest groups is often thwarted. There is very little independent accountability of banks, companies and state institutions; these are centres of patronage. They are developmental states, in the sense that they can use their State-run corporations to drive their economic agendas. They are also therefore very corrupt, hospitable to international mafias, and witness enormous and growing differences between the very rich and the very poor. Civil society is very weak. In the present economic recession they will do their utmost to remain as independent of the OECD world as possible. They do not want to be sucked into that world.

Resource-rich countries

These are countries that are rich because of the oil and minerals they possess. They cannot spend their wealth because their populations are very limited. They import huge numbers of labourers. They are all dictatorships or autocracies and inevitably corrupt. Many of them are dominated by the interplay of powerful theocracies and traditional elites, with a weak concept of the division between the State and religious authorities. They are generally allied to the West because their elites have been educated in the West and therefore their outlook is westernised. There is no civil society and no government independence. They have weak physical infrastructures and their economies are unlikely to develop because their populations are so thin. They are so rich that they can waste their money – Saudi Arabia is buying weapons for non-existent armed forces; Dubai before the financial crisis was enlarging its landmass by building islands in the Gulf and developing indoor ski slopes and underwater hotels. They are buying up the companies that the West is unable to support or that have become cheap because of the financial crisis. Their state-sponsored Sovereign Wealth Funds were estimated to be worth between $1.9 trillion to $3.5 trillion before the financial crisis of 2008-09 and should at least double within 10 years[3]. With that wealth they will be able to buy up the rich world. They do not grow enough food and are buying up land in various parts of the world, particularly in Africa, on which they will grow food to be exported back to them. They are tied to and indeed depend on the world trade system because they need to sell their raw materials in exchange for the import of basic foods and other essentials. Although the Democratic Republic of Congo, Nigeria and Zambia could be part of this group, the DRC has a government with very limited control over its territory, Nigeria has a very weak central government and most of the resources of Zambia are not in Zambian hands. Angola and Equatorial Guinea are however already part of this group.

Poor countries

These are small in terms of population and economic size and have very little to sell. The whole of the GDP of sub-Saharan Africa is about the same size as that of Belgium and several of the London Boroughs have larger budgets than individual countries on the continent. Their populations are very young and growing younger by the day. They have no tools to fight endemic poverty and thus diseases linked to poverty – including HIV/AIDS and tuberculosis. They are run by kleptocracies, even if some have acquired a vestige of multiparty democracy; indeed the birth of their multiparty democracies has often been at the expense of financial rectitude in their society. They have a highly skewed social structure, with a few people in what is generally referred to as the middle class (who benefit from external aid and from the state) and a large proportion of very poor people. Most are highly heterogeneous and thus the state is at best the representation of a small part of the total population. They are highly dependent on aid and on international structures because they cannot control their own economic environment. They thus have tended to gravitate towards the existing economic blocks. They are quite happy to ally themselves with the countries that put the fewest conditions on their political priorities. They have little to trade with. Agriculture, where they might have a natural advantage given the available labour force and the amount of land, is underdeveloped. The only part of the service sector that is developed is that which centres around state expenditure in health and education.

Economic tools of the rich world

The continuing economic growth of the North has always relied on a *minimum critical mass of activities* in order to develop. You need a certain number of houses being built to generate an economic body of activities and specialisations. Rich countries develop *magnet economies*, in which those who were the economic instigators or have acquired primacy became the magnets. Globalisation has made it virtually impossible for new companies to grow organically in the way in which existing Northern companies grew and eventually begat the multinationals. The best that new entrants can hope to achieve is either to become suppliers to the main producers (this is the line that India has taken in many aspects of the automobile industry for example) or to encourage companies that are already in that field of activity to relocate. The latter is the option that China has been taking for the last couple of decades. Chinese companies are also very good at *adapting to changing circumstances*; one day a company that produces bicycles will start producing scooters or vacuum cleaners, not because it has built experience in that field, but because it has the resources[4]. But adaptability can occur only where you have access to markets where you can offload such new products; if the market disappears, so does your production. The North, however, still possesses knowledge and trained people; it will survive even a serious downturn.

Another force in rich societies that does not exist in poor societies is *specialisation* that in turn leads to *efficiency*. Efficiency means that you create the same volume of products with ever fewer people. This generates a surplus of people who can then go on to produce other things. Economic specialisation started perhaps 10,000 years ago with the farmer producing what the hunter needed and vice versa. One could say that economic progress is, above all, about increasing output and benefiting from economies of efficiency and of scale. Increasing output always requires some change, perhaps in management or additional capital or improvements in technology – indeed usually all these things at the same time. In the early 1800s the UK witnessed an enormous increase in productivity: within the course of one lifetime the level of economic productivity increased by a factor of up to 10. The developed world has witnessed another period of revolutionary growth in productivity over the last 20 years with the advent of computerisation – a process that is not yet complete. Such levels and speed of change are caused by changes in technology but they also require an institutional base that enables change to take hold. It needs to be supported by financial facilities such as fixed or variable rates of interest in money lending. And that in turn demands a working financial system, not necessarily the banking system as the North knows it. In fact that banking system has shown that it has developed far beyond the framework designed to regulate it. Bankers have run away with the loot.

The rich world has been obsessed by the pull of *gigantism*, a combination of economic and managerial forces, which has tended to make 'big is beautiful' and has led to capital accumulation and growth the yardstick by which most developed nations judge all sorts of institutions, both commercial entities and statutory bodies. Managers in both the for-profit and not-for-profit fields have felt driven by the need to be big. Sometimes this tendency has been inevitable by the process of manufacturing (you cannot build a small chemical plant), but in most cases it has been driven by the egos of managements. This has generated its own standards of measurement; it has brought rationalisation, computerisation, streamlining in areas of work that would have probably benefitted from different approaches[5]. Very few of these concepts can be applied to small- and medium-scale enterprises, particularly in the Southern context, where the market is too small.

Living in a changing world

If the analysis in the preceding pages is correct, the Northern way of doing things in the South is doomed. The work of the North will become marginalised in the poorest countries because above all its roots have not been sufficiently deep and it has achieved too little. In the inevitable last page of the colonial saga the North left governments of some of the weakest economies unable to cope with the range of problems they faced, and that often the colonial power shaped. Since then the North has created even more problems for them. Some of the reasons for the mess in which they might find themselves are of their own making. The North might be almost totally over the colonial phase, notwithstanding the intervention of France on the side of the Hutus in Rwanda or that of Britain in Sierra Leone, but China, on the other hand, is becoming far more active. Its intervention and investments penetrate much more deeply than the North ever did at all levels of economic life and has a much greater effect on ordinary people. China might not be liked by all the people in the countries where it is present, but there will be benefits to them that will be far more obvious than those the North has offered over the years. China will provide major public buildings, roads, railways, water reservoirs, factories and farms. The Chinese back home are not concerned with some of the niceties of life that so dominate the agenda of the North. Rich countries have tried only very late in the day to export the ideals of free speech, human rights, democracy and the rule of law in their dealings, which have been primarily with the more privileged members of the poor societies. Much less power will be devolved to the non-governmental community and to civil society in general. The outcome of deals negotiated with central governments will be less respect for the rights and desires of local communities and, in consequence, less individual freedom. However, the poorest will have more jobs, and one could hardly argue with Ghandi that for a poor man freedom is a loaf of bread.

This is leading us back to the nature of the state and of democracy in nascent societies. Clearly none of the colonial powers expected the colonies to become independent so rapidly and the countries of Africa were simply not prepared for their independence. I am conscious that to some extent this is a rehashing of the arguments that raged in the early 1970s when Elie Kedourie, a noted writer of the day, criticised the influence of Arnold Toynbee on the policies of the British Government that precipitated the rapid departure of Britain from its former colonies. Toynbee had been director of studies between 1925 and 1955 at Chatham House, the most influential think tank on international affairs in the UK. The argument centres on whether it was right for Britain, in the name of radical democracy and retrenchment from the colonial past, to leave the colonies at the mercy of rampant nationalism. The result was a rapid departure from countries unprepared for self-government whose new leaders had enormous political and often ethnic debts to repay and did so at the expense of the wider good of their nations[6]. This lack of democratic roots implies also that the power of the rulers will be reinforced by the Chinese approach. They will be the people whom the Chinese will buy off. They will acquire powers that, to some extent, Northern policies in recent years moderated. The world will witness a reversion to a less sophisticated phase of the state.

Migrants' remittances

We have seen in Part One how there is a continuing migration from poor countries; in 2005 it was put at 200 million people and it was estimated that some 60 per cent of these moved to richer countries[7]. They send a lot of money back to their families; the global volume of remittances in each of the last 10 years has been about three times as much as the net value of global aid. It was estimated at $167 billion in 2005[8]. The figures, when they become available, will show an increase for a couple of years and an inevitable slowdown after mid 2008. Remittances have been a grassroots phenomenon. They have gone to some of the poorest people on earth. They have often gone to projects that lead to no permanent economic improvement; weddings, christenings, medical expenses, house improvements and so on. These remittances have provided foreign currency to many poor countries of the South. Given the right vehicles they could be a powerful tool in changing development at the grassroots, but governments of the South have not been able to provide those vehicles. Unfortunately it is likely that in the next few years things are going to get worse, with a decrease in remittances from the North to the South as the North will make it more difficult for people from the South to find jobs in Northern economies and Northern labour unions will resist immigration. It will make things far worse for several countries, including the Philippines, Malaysia, Pakistan, Bangladesh and Nigeria.

Budgets of Malawi and London Borough of Southwark 2009-10

Southwark (Population; 260,000)

Total expenditure:	£995.9 million
Health and community services	127m
Children's services (including Schools)	347.9m
Planning and economic development	27.6m

(Source; Council literature)

Malawi (population 13.89 million)

Total expenditure:	£959 million
Agriculture	135m
Water and irrigation	32m
Rural development	36m
Pro-poor expenditure	33.8m
Health	131m
Education	109m

(Source; Ministerial Presentation to Parliament, 23 May 2009)

CHAPTER FIFTEEN
The age of retribution

We have seen over the preceding pages how the North has imposed its rules and regulations over the economic and political world and in many ways shaped that world, simply because it has been so powerful. But changes are occurring. The BRIC countries are flexing their muscles. The OECD countries are increasingly dependent on imported energy. Those countries that can supply it from the Middle East, Africa, Central Asia and Latin America are acquiring power and influence well beyond their size and economic sophistication. In Latin America the local people are dictating changes and electing as leaders people from their own backgrounds with often strident anti-Northern policies.

There is, however, another very important factor that we never see as it operates below the radar. It is hidden, very powerful, and might surprise many in the West; most of the people of Africa, Asia and Latin America do not like most of the people of the rich world. The point is this: why should the South trust the North? It is not a hypothetical question. If you listen carefully to African voices in their environment and read African newspapers, this issue comes through quite clearly and forcefully over and over again – even if often in coded form. The North is always promising so much and delivering so little in trade matters, in security and in aid. It is becoming increasingly a matter of challenging the North and the rich and the whites (terms that in many languages are interchangeable, just as the initials UK, US, EU, UN are all interchangeable to most people's ears). To be seen to agree with the North or to be on its side is not acceptable to the vast majority of the people of the South.

The animosity towards the North

It is very easy to dismiss resentment against the people of the North as being something that should be left behind. The world has moved on. But of course it has not necessarily moved on everywhere and there is a heavy baggage that the North has to carry. Racism in Northern societies is still very much in evidence, even if most people have become much less aware of it or pretend to. Barack Obama may have been elected President of the US, but this was because he is clearly a remarkable man and the Democratic Party political machine ensured that, once he was selected as a candidate, it would bring in the votes. The majority of middle-age and middle-class white people voted against him; it was a coalition of minorities and young white people that ensured his victory[9].

There has always been animosity towards the arrogance of the white man and resentment for the tools at his disposal. Now things are changing radically because in some countries the real power no longer lies with groups that the North chose, but in groups with deeper local roots. They have new champions that have no links or obligations to the North. People from many parts of the world seem to want to distance themselves from the former colonial powers. In Africa the countries from which the North drew slaves, are looking for partners with which to establish new and different relationships. In Latin America the descendants of European colonisers are losing their privileged positions in the political order. In Asia the vibrancy of local markets makes them link forces one with the other, not look exclusively to Northern markets. There is a seismic change of power; the people of the poorest countries on earth are finding that they no longer have to follow Northern diktats. In Bolivia, Colombia and Venezuela powerful local movements are emerging to fight the powers of the international companies that by and large have been Northern dominated. They are voting into office people such as Evo Morales in Bolivia, who have their roots in the native population, not in the Europeans who took over the reins of power. China's need to obtain Africa's raw materials is forcing it to adopt a different stance in the continent, which is enabling Africans to approach China for funds and disregard Northern entreaties. The 2007 Annual Meeting of the African Development Bank was held in China; that is perhaps the most blatant evidence of the shift of power.

One of the elements in the latent resentment among many black people across the world is slavery. Slavery began at the dawn of mankind; one tribe waged war on another and made slaves of those that they captured. Even the word 'slave' is a corruption for 'Slav' which denotes that most slaves came from Eastern European tribes. Slavery still goes on in certain parts of the world; in India, for example, millions of people are enslaved by the system of bonded labour. But by far the largest numbers of victims of the Europeans were Africans enslaved by other Africans to be sold to Europeans. It was slavery on an industrial scale. Some 12 million Africans were forcibly removed from their villages and towns to work against their wishes in other parts of the world[10]. This was not a million years ago; the appalling trade officially did not end until it was outlawed in the last third of the 19th century. The bicentenary celebrations that took place in 2007 in Britain were of the end of the slave trade, not of slavery itself. Slavery continued in the Portuguese colonies until later that century, well into the Victorian era. The US Civil War was about slavery; that was fought as recently as the 1860s.

All the associated acts of enslavement – rape, branding, cutting off of feet of those who had tried to run away – are acts of brutality that might be subsumed in the enormity of the entire trade, but it would be strange if all had been forgotten by people who descend from those who suffered. Many Africans who are in the diaspora in the West are calling for reparation, which is nonsense of course; how can you make reparation to people who you cannot identify? Do you give money to current dictators or corrupt politicians so that they have more money to stash away? But some moral responsibility must remain with the former colonial powers and their allies not to continue the exploitation.

Many people might think that racism does not exist in any persistent way in the UK, but that is wrong. There is example after example of how it exists at all levels. Just one thought; social workers in the UK discourage allow white couples from adopting black children. Why? Most people would consider that it would be good for race relations if more such cross-colour and cross-racial adoptions took place. But social workers know that black people will experience far more prejudices throughout life because of their colour. It is therefore important that the adopted child be brought up in a family where the parents understand the hurdles they may well have to overcome and prepare them for it. A survey in mid 2005 in the UK showed that fewer than one in four white Britons had ever been in contact, other than in the most casual manner, with someone from an ethnic minority. The British National Party, which is fundamentally racist, is constantly improving its position at local elections and achieved two Members of the European Parliament in June 2009.

Racism continues across most of Europe. In France at every presidential election candidates of the right do extremely well and in 2000 they were the runners-up in the presidential election, ahead of the Socialist Party. They still got close to 20 per cent of the vote in the French Presidential elections in 2007. Black people are constant victims of assaults by the resurgent nazism of Russian nationalists. One of the key figures in Austrian politics for most of the last 10 years was the late Joerg Haider, whose party is avowedly racist. He regularly made remarks that were clearly sympathetic to the Nazis and their racial ideologies.

Putting across Northern values

For many people in Africa the basic injustice of Northern exploitation is not over yet. This point is crucial. The images that peoples in the South form of how the North considers them is not dictated by lofty ideas, by grand pronouncements made by the President of the United States when he visits two or three countries in Africa over a period of five days or the Prime Minister of the UK when he visits a country for a conference lasting a couple of days every couple of years. That is the level of grand theatre. Opinions are formed by the continuing reporting from one person who lives at the bottom of the pile in societies of the North to another person who is in a similar position back in Africa or Latin America. Most of the people in most African countries hold views that are formed from messages and communications they receive, most of the time through word of mouth, or perhaps brief conversations on a mobile telephone, with their relatives or friends who have managed to enter a country within the European Union. That is the level of the village – where change should take place but does not.

In its dealings with the South and in its DEVELOPMENT work the message that the North is trying to convey: 'We are here to help you develop,' comes up against a huge credibility gap that it has to surmount, something that will probably take generations. What people in the poor world hear of Northern people is not that they are generous and kind. On the contrary, they hear that black and brown people in the UK, Germany and the US – those who were born in those countries as well as asylum seekers – remain marginalised. These people frequent strange religious sects because they give them the moral courage and the sense of belonging that most other 'European' traditional religions do not offer. They borrow from loan sharks masquerading as kind moneylenders. They are more frequently stopped in the streets by the police than white people. When they appear before courts, they are more severely punished than home-grown white criminals. Disproportionately more black people are in jail in the UK than white people for the same crimes. Northern societies are institutionally racist.

Africa v the North

Over the last few years we all have seen the tragedy of Zimbabwe unfolding on our screens. Robert Mugabe, the man whom many liberals in the UK and throughout Europe supported in his bid to become President of his own country against Ian Smith, the colonialist who had declared independence from the UK in the 1970s, has descended increasingly into the extremism of dictatorship. The North has raged against him and asked its African friends to intervene, but they have not. South Africa, the giant neighbour to the South, ignored for a long time requests from the North to intervene. It placed solidarity with an African leader above criticism of Mugabe's actions. Britain at first tried to intervene, but the action was cleverly exploited by

Mugabe to claim that Britain was supporting the white farmers against a liberation movement. All Britain's actions since 1990 have been presented in that light by a very wily operator. African nations have seen any attack on Zimbabwe as an attack on the dignity of Africa as a whole. One of the spokesmen for the African Union in 2006 stated that the protests from Britain were another manifestation of the innate racism of the West.

But there is a more fundamental difference of outlook between Britain and the peoples of Southern Africa. The problems of South Africa go back to the days of apartheid, when the British Government opposed sanctions and Margaret Thatcher chastised the Commonwealth for imposing them. Mrs Thatcher opposed the freeing of Nelson Mandela in 1990. For 20 years Angola was pulled asunder by a civil war waged by Jonas Savimbi who was backed by the North. Millions of people were killed. Many more were displaced from their lands. Many thousands will continue to be maimed because the country is littered with unspent landmines. The tragedy of Angola occurred because NATO, to which Britain has always belonged, supported Savimbi because he was anti-communist. In both South Africa and Angola the policies of Britain and other OECD countries (except for the Scandinavian group) were running contrary to the interests of the majority black population. The British Government's actions have understandably not endeared Britain to the peoples of Africa. Europe might have changed considerably, in the same way that the US is clearly heading for a different path under President Obama than under the previous administration, but have the poorest in those countries really seen any benefit from this change?

Looking to the future

What is happening in the world is no longer dictated by the North. The notion of democracy that has led to greater individual freedom, some of it illusory, in the North (illusory because it has not always been accompanied by economic freedom), is also realising more and more divergent views in other parts of the world, views which are often very different to those held by the North. Resentment has been building up against what domination the North still has; it is in part a sense of resistance against the North and in part a new-found solidarity within the peoples in the South. In South America one country after the other is nationalising energy sources and other key assets. To some extent it is an anti-American rhetoric, but it might be a more profound antagonism to being bossed about by the international community. The growing economic power of China and India, the energy sources at the disposal of Russia, the economic leadership provided by South Africa within Africa – all these realities are bringing to the fore forces that the North will not be able to contain. The North is not used to having political power defined outside the Northern sphere of influence. It no longer has the monopoly of purchase over scarce minerals and resources, the media, professions or sources of wealth that it once enjoyed. Even the suggestions and lobbying of the international NGO community, fighting for human rights, for more trade justice, and for control and restrictions on the arms trade, are increasingly seen as the products of a vision that basically supports the European and wider Northern points of view or at best a way to assuage the damage that it has caused in the past. Many non-Europeans see this as a continuation of the colonial attitude of having the God-given right to run the world. But that was a Northern God; a vision of a society in which religious and secular principles are not so clearly defined will lead to other approaches. Non-Christian religions become a way to assert political independence.

The North is continuing with policies that ignore the feelings of the masses of the South and too often concentrate on the demands of a few of their unrepresentative leaders. This is not an option that will make much sense in the future. Northern governments continue to support governments in the South who are its allies and whose support they need because these Southern governments are key players in the war on terrorism – a war that is defined as being anti-North/West. Dictators do not want terrorists in their countries and the North wants them to control their home-grown terrorists, yet those terrorists will at this rate be increasingly seen as freedom fighters by their own compatriots. At the same time the North is trying to export visions of democracy that it understands but which may not suit highly factionalised and heterogeneous nations, which are currently feeling their way hesitantly towards their own multipolar national formats.

The first rumblings about the changing role of the North can already be heard in the world of information; that world is now multipolar and new voices are being heard. Al-Jezeera is increasingly the station to which the Asians in the UK would turn to in order to obtain information on what is going on in the Middle East. They assume, rightly or wrongly, that the BBC will not give the same weight to Palestinian as to Israeli views. The North is not trusted as it once was. (At the same time it is interesting to note that a survey by al-Jezeera among its listeners in the Middle East – mainly young educated Muslim people – showed that their long-term aspirations were basically to reach the levels of material comforts and freedoms that the people in the US enjoy at present[11].)

The North ignores other forces at play, such as the multiplicity of short wave radio stations in countries such as Uganda, where they have far more power and relevance in the democratic process than the written media – all controlled by the government. Democracy is indeed being developed, but it is being developed in forms that are strange to people in the North. Islam, in a more fundamental way, is challenging the North's approach to free speech. Recently in the UN, Nigeria challenged the right of the organisation to question Shari'a law. The North in general has given considerable weight to evidence-based decisions since the days of the Enlightenment. Now, however, more arguments are being put forward on a religious and ethnic basis.

The battleground for the meeting of these contrasting world views is already to be found in societies of the North. There is daily evidence of this in demands from Islamic communities in Britain and in other countries in the EU for their views to be taken into consideration.

CHAPTER SIXTEEN

China

China, through its economic development, is lifting more of its own people out of poverty than any nation has ever done throughout history, and at the same time it is proving that globalisation can work in its own interests. Its process of industrialising is also benefiting other poor countries; in the case of Africa through enormous purchases of raw materials and investment in infrastructure. As a result of its industrialisation China has become far more active in Africa than European powers ever were.

China is using pure economic forces to lift itself out of poverty. There are no idealistic approaches to development and no respect for human rights and democracy; the overarching aim of the hierarchy for the last half-century has been to forge international political alliances. The Chinese people above all, subject to centuries of local dictatorial rule, have become the ultimate pragmatists of the world. It is not a newly discovered love affair with Africa that has brought them to the continent; China has been consistently, in its own terms, the champion of the poor of the world. Together with Yugoslavia it led the non-aligned movement (which, from the North's point of view, was probably far more aligned to the communist world) from the early days of colonial emancipation. At the same time it desperately needs raw materials and Africa can provide them. It has a strict policy of non-interference in the internal affairs of others and does not comment publicly on the leadership of any country, although privately it is likely that things are quite different.

China's economy

With political stability within China and a positive approach to private enrichment, overseas Chinese families started to return home during the 1980s and 1990s. The influx of such families provided a major bridge to the outside world that facilitated the economic development of the country enormously. Allied to this has been the realisation by multinationals that political stability and continuity offered them the markets and the possibility of doing business that they need. The Chinese economy has been growing at an average of around 9.5 per cent each year for some 25 years. (Some commentators have claimed that it has been at about twice that rate[12].) The exact figures are impossible to ascertain; national figures from China indicate a growth rate up to 2007 of around 11 per cent per year and in 2008 of 8 per cent, but the results from individual provinces would indicate that the growth was probably a couple of points above that. GDP quadrupled between 1980 and 2000 and has possibly doubled again since then. It is too early to be able to judge what the current recession will do to China, but the country has enormous reserves of cash. It will not go through unscathed but is likely to be able to take more concerted action than the North, because of the way in which the political and economic priorities can be joined up. It will probably be one of the few countries in the world that will be continuing to grow economically.

There are immediate consequences for the world at large from such growth. Not only did the price of most basic hard commodities in the 1990s and the early years of the present decade go up – iron, manganese, coltan, zinc, titanium and copper – but also the price of foodstuff worldwide. As the Chinese people acquire more purchasing power, they want to eat better so they buy more food rich in animal protein. China started to import cereals in 2006 for the first time in 20 years. This is one of the key factors in the growth of basic food prices that we have seen in all economies throughout 2007 and 2008. Virtually all items of fresh food have gone up substantially in price across the world. Those who will suffer of course are the poorest of the world who have to compete in the global marketplace for the same staple foods. Good land is being used to grow food that will go to feed animals.

Increasing wealth within China will mean that its demand for new goods will grow at a faster rate than in Northern economies. Currently a large proportion of the goods produced in China are exported, but this will not continue. The range of goods that people want when they become slightly richer – cheap cars, televisions, radios, CD players, air conditioners, refrigerators, and so on – will come from inside China for Chinese-produced goods. This will mean a slowing down of the pace of globalisation, a force that the North has assumed will continue to grow because of its demand for goods and services, but the North will not be able to supply and compete with Chinese goods. One suspects that the development of India will lead to a parallel economic growth and generate huge demand within India. We can expect to see India, China, and Russia at a later stage, having parallel rates of economic growth and making policies that the North will not comprehend and at the moment cannot envisage. This is not to say that China will overtake the economy of the US any day soon; the US has an economy of some $13.5 trillion and China of around $3 trillion, but the rate of growth is important. China will need to generate production to meet both the increasing demands of its middle classes in terms of improved standards of living and of jobs from new graduates (as well as people losing their jobs due to the decrease in external demand).

China is changing the rules and the discussion concerning economic development

For those who are concerned about the poor world the problems take on a different dimension. The sort of industrial and commercial protectionist policies that were pursued in the 1930s in the countries that were colonies of the North can no longer be pursued, although it is clear that political forces as a result of the recession will encourage Northern countries to become more protectionist towards the South. The capacity of China to supply very cheap items and to invade the markets of poor countries makes protectionism in poor countries virtually impossible. From the Chinese point of view of course things look very different. China is doing something very close to what the North has been doing for many decades. If you have cotton, which many African countries have, you should be able to produce cheap material with which to make T-shirts or vests or uniforms for the police force or the Army. But these products are not being made in Africa; domestic markets in many African countries are being swamped by donated second-hand clothing from the North or by extremely cheap new items from China. This twin assault immediately kills off the majority of local initiatives.

China does not look up to any former colonial power. Most countries of the poor world have been colonies; from Kenya to India and Jamaica to Fiji the elites look to Britain for their models of education and behaviour. From the Ivory Coast to Vietnam and Algeria to Lebanon they look to France. From Brazil to Mozambique they look to Portugal. But not China; the Chinese upper classes might have at various times been exiles in various parts of the world, from the Philippines to the US and from the UK to France, but they look to China as their spiritual home in a way in which no other expatriate minorities seem to do towards their home countries. China has been united in some form or other for 2,200 years, in spite of the many warlords who dominated its political panorama at various times. It has had one dominant language, one unit of currency, one unit of measurement for all of that period.

Some of the more liberal thinkers in the North might resent the total lack of respect for individual liberties but the truth is that such elements for most people are not as important as having enough to eat. Northern liberals might resent the intervention of China, which in many countries in Africa, particularly in Sudan, Zimbabwe and Angola has resisted the creation of more humane and transparent societies, but they tend to forget that the North has not fared very well either[13]. On the one hand, under pressure from NGOs, in the very recent past Northern governments have tried to rein in the excesses of the corrupt governments of these countries, but on the other hand they have done nothing to prevent its own commercial interests from exploiting and making deals with all of them. China takes the much more unified approach; commercial companies do not voice opinions or take action on issues that the Chinese government does not agree with.

China would argue that basic rights to food and necessities are more important than political priorities[14]. China has always been suspicious of the North's intervention in Africa and it has always emphasised how it has shared the fate of many African nations in being marginalised or ostracised and then in breaking free from the subjugation by the North. It turns a blind eye to corruption among African leaders, but then so has the North. In the North's case private corporations rather than governments are continuing to fuel that corruption, even in democratic countries. In Nigeria, for example, Western oil companies have been quite prepared to 'buy' their safety in many parts of the oil states by paying off local politicians and local mafias.

Setting new world priorities

The North has long framed the world's problems in the way that suits it and China is showing the world that it does not really care about other countries' points of view. This is something that India could also do, but for the foreseeable future India is likely to have a point of view that agrees to some extent with that of the North. The main language of communication in India is still English, many of its structures (law, parliament and political parties) are based on the British system and many members of the upper classes are British-educated.

What the North has not yet realised is that with the changing economic priorities in China, new alliances are formed, alliances of interests that are outside the traditional sphere of control of the North. For example, the need for energy might well create closer links between India, China and Russia. The first two need energy and the third has plenty. Brazil and South Africa (the last one is often referred to as the next member of the BRIC group), are more likely to be interested in joining those three than in turning to the North. There are two main reasons for this; firstly, because there is a more equal relationship if a country enters into pacts with other countries at its own level of economic development than with more powerful economies that will overshadow it. Secondly, a state can retain greater flexibility if it has the power to intervene than if it has to rely on multinationals with allegiances outside its control. China and Russia have governments that will not hesitate to intervene to make a deal work rather than leaving it to a multinational with outside investors from foreign lands.

Here the NGO community of the North is being outflanked. The BRIC countries have powerful governments that are not susceptible to political influence in the way they are in Europe or North America. At the time of the Tiananmen Square massacres in June 1989 humanitarian agencies in the North protested loudly and vehemently against the Chinese government to no effect. NGO influence will count for far less not only in the BRIC countries themselves, but also in the countries in which the BRIC have reach as well. Not a single African leader raised a word of condemnation regarding Tiananmen Square. China's leadership, which does not change very frequently, has long memories. Another example of the power of the BRIC countries is the way in which Yahoo! and Google have had to change their policies. Nowhere in the world do they censor the internet and cooperate with governments to restrict freedom of expression apart from in China where, rather than losing the lucrative Chinese market, they cooperate with the authorities.

China in Africa

China has staked its claim to be one of the leaders of the South since the days of the first Afro-Asian Peoples' Solidarity Conference in Bandung in 1955. At the time China declared its support for the peoples of the South, for their independence from their colonial masters and pledged non-interference in their internal affairs. It is also undoubtedly true that China, then one of the poorest nations on earth, for very good reasons of its own, always gave more aid to liberation movements and poor governments than many far richer countries in the North[15]. In other words, the interest of China in Africa is not something new; it has been present for a long time. For example, not long after the independence of Tanzania, back in the early 1960s, the Chinese built the Tazara (Tanzania-Zambia Railway Authority) railway, enabling copper from Zambia to reach the sea at Dar-es-Salaam on the Indian Ocean coast of Tanzania. But now the policy of China is to invest rather than give aid.

At the end of 2007 China became the most important importer of oil from Africa in the world. It is also an enormous importer of copper, aluminium ore and manganese, and again Africa is the main supplier. In 1999 trade between Africa and China was valued at $6.5 billion, but by 2008 it had risen to $107 billion[16]. But the Chinese do more than just importing raw materials; they offer to get involved in infrastructure building in order to recover some of the foreign currency used to purchase the raw materials in the first place. It makes perfectly good sense for China to do so and they are more effective and cheaper than any other country would be. In Tanzania, for example, they have recently constructed a huge national stadium, the place where large public ceremonies, as well as sporting activities, will be staged. The downside was that the engineers were mainly Chinese, as were the surveyors and supervisors during the construction period. Of the labour force of around 1,000 people, some 700 were Chinese doing the more skilled jobs, from laying electric cables to driving forklift trucks. The Tanzanians were doing the least skilled jobs; cooking assistants, night guards, cleaners. One might criticise this allocation of duties, since the very essence of investing in a developing country should be to generate and upgrade local skills. But one of the most important functions of any economic activity is to generate income and even the 300 people employed on this site and their families would have had a bit more money to spend.

The main criticism that commentators in the North have against Chinese investment in Africa is that the lending is done more or less without political questioning, the very essence of the relationship between the North and African nations. The Chinese Government is not asking the Sudanese to stop killing its people in Darfur and is in fact providing weapons, including fighter planes, to make the killing more efficient. It has also opposed any UN resolution condemning Sudan for the genocide. In Angola corruption is rampant and again China does not seem to care; China is building new roads, three railway lines and a massive new airport that will be able to take 30 large planes per day. It is not difficult to envisage who might get the contracts for building the control towers, the airport navigation systems, supplying the engineers and the air controllers, as well as the train drivers and other skilled jobs that the railways will need. There is a dilemma; should one protest that the Chinese are not doing what economists and NGO personnel from the North think should be done to encourage the development of skills and so on, or does one accept that the development of infrastructure is better than no development at all? The poorest are still excluded because they are not given sufficient opportunities to benefit from the investment. These developments are not happening without some hitches; in 2006 a visit by the Chinese President to a copper mine in Zambia had to be cancelled because of a demonstration against the Chinese by local workers. The police fired on unarmed demonstrators, causing a number of fatalities.

The importance of non-economic calculations

The Chinese Government has been able to make very good use of its control over companies that work within the Chinese economy. Very often these work both within and outside China, with the rules as to who owns what not always clearly defined. In many parts of Africa the Chinese have been willing to bid for oil, road building, hotel management contracts and other projects not because they make much economic sense on their own, but because once you are in a country, you are there for a long time – you have a toehold. A company might not make a profit from a single deal, but if it does not have to repay the loan it has incurred because the Government back home has 'fixed' the cancellation or partial reduction of a debt, the project in Africa can still go ahead. China needs oil and is willing therefore to exchange a contract to obtain oil for the building of a few hotels, a national stadium, a railway or a regional airport. More than pure economic considerations come into the picture; profit margins may be as low as 1 to 1.5 per cent. China is able to ride roughshod over the increasingly tough standards demanded by the international organisations. The IMF is asking for greater transparency in government accounting. On the huge $7.4 billion loan referred to on page 175, the interest rate demanded by the Chinese was just 1.5 per cent over 17 years. But it also asked for approximately 70 per cent of the building contracts so that there would be a considerable amount of work allocated back to Chinese companies.

The North has no cohesive plan for how to deal with the growing economic power of China and the associated consequences. China and India are both trying to develop the first really cheap car, likely to be below $2,500. If it comes into production, planned for the late first half of 2009, the level of pollution in the world will greatly outweigh anything that the world might manage to do to reduce pollution to adhere to the Kyoto Agreement or any successor. What we do know is that China, simply to keep up with the growth of population, let alone reduce the remaining widespread poverty in the west of the country, will have to carry on creating jobs, at home or abroad[17]. If it does not, it encourages growing dissent at home.

The BRIC countries account for 22 per cent of the $60 trillion world GDP. They have been bailing out the rich countries by investing in their governments' bonds that has kept low the rates of interest in the rich world and fuelled the rich word's consumer boom[18]. They are now demanding more power within the IMF. They formally met for the first time in Yekaterinburg in mid June 2009.

PART FOUR

The Agenda for Change

The context of the fight against world poverty is changing rapidly. Population is rising extremely rapidly in the countries least able to support the increase. There are increasing numbers of poor people worldwide. Food is becoming scarcer and more expensive and will remain so because of the different forces described in Part One. The rich world is ever more preoccupied with its own priorities. The rate of degradation of the physical environment in which we all live is accelerating and might already have reached the point at which it is irreversible. The planet is really facing cataclysmic physical challenges that we are unable to resolve because we do not have the necessary tools, but above all because of the short-term political horizons within which decisions and considerations are made. Global security at the physical, social and environmental levels that affect everyone have now come together in an unprecedented way. Yet we have not realised the enormity and urgency of the collective challenges that are upon us. Doing nothing should not be an option for the North, but political systems that rely on politicians who have to consider being re-elected or rejected next year or the year after or in four years' time, cannot take a long-term view[1]. Therefore there is a terrible risk that the world shall do precisely nothing.

Realistically no law or authority will succeed in decreasing the rate of consumption of everyday goods in Northern societies because there is such in-built resistance from all interested parties. In the North the poorer members of the community need improved material circumstances and the richer will not accept brakes on even their most conspicuous consumption. The perpetual competition between corporations and other interest groups engenders continuing demand on other groups and entities in society. The weakest societies in the world are real losers in this entire scenario. They are the 'third party', 'the outsiders'. They will be left to sink or swim and the poorest among them may very well sink.

In this concluding Part, I would like to make the case for a new set of priorities that the North must adopt if it wishes to protect some of the weakest people on earth and at the same time build on the little it has achieved so far in regard to development. Those in the North who care must apply to development activities in the South the North's unique flexibility in supporting, partnering, linking and developing groups across the face of the poorest economies. But we need to identify the tools that have to be used for the purpose.

Political avenues may no longer be the route to change. But there is another instrument to achieve change; that is private action – the private company and the private voluntary organisation. Because they are responsible to smaller constituencies they can adopt a much more targeted aim and stand a better chance of achieving results. They can be the exponents of the flexibility needed to rise to the challenges, but this would entail playing a different role in society – to include the transformation of long-term objectives into short-term acceptable targets that politicians can sell to their electorates. In the South they need to change from being agents of welfare to agents of development. I will concentrate on the latter point because this book is concerned with the development of the South. But the transformation of these intermediaries will have to be profound; from facilitating the process through which the poorest can express their priorities and encouraging education in all its forms, particularly on the subject of family planning; to building community support structures that are democratically accountable because that is the only way to enable equitable development to take hold. This is not the concept of democracy as the North expresses it, primarily through the ballot box, but a series of more flexible and down-to-earth consultations.

More fundamentally at this stage, in a world that is going through very profound economic changes, there are powerful forces within Northern societies that fight against the interests of the poorest of the planet or at best resist changes that will reduce their role and benefit. The voluntary organisations that are part of the development community need to take courageous initiatives that stand against those. Some of these are explored in this final part.

One overall message is very clear: urgent practical action is required.

CHAPTER SEVENTEEN

A matter of principles

We need to be clear about what we should aim to achieve. The priority must be to work for global social justice: what we want from our society for our own benefit we should wish to be available for the benefit of others in their societies. The principles are simple; even the poorest have the right to a decent life; every human being is born of equal worth; the power that some have over others must be derived from legitimate democratic means and must not be at the expense of the weakest; and our institutions must be made to work towards achieving such aims. If some people interpret such priorities as being challenges to their beliefs – that women are inferior to men; that power is inherited and not merited; that some people can push the weaker aside without redress – we need to be prepared to confront those who advocate such views in order to achieve development. In the words of the American Constitution, 'we believe these truths to be self-evident.' Such principles also demand that one should help others where help is needed and where one is able to help; that one should respect other people's priorities if freely determined and not impose one's own. Any aid must enable others to stand on their own; unthinking aid is wasted charity – it can cause dependence and not relief. This is as valid in London, where a few coins to a homeless man might well end up in the hands of the drug dealer, as it might be on the streets of Lagos.

Yet the implementation of such principles demands a deep commitment to making change work and that can have grave consequences. It calls for a separation of long-term aims from short-term targets. For example, ensuring that women have the right to owner-ship of land (or anything else) will upset long-held traditions and reli-gious beliefs and will simply not be achieved by sitting back and wait-ing for things to change of their own accord. NGOs have to find ways to offer intermediate solutions on the route to the longer-term goals.

Tackling the big picture

There is a long list of international issues that affect both the North and the South detrimentally. Because of the differences in their respective stages of economic development, these issues affect differ-ent parts of the world – the four different groupings that we looked at in an earlier section of the book – to differing extents. It is only when they affect the North that they seem to be treated with any degree of urgency. They include: the continuing existence of tax havens, many of them (18 out of 50) within the jurisdiction of Great Britain[2]; failure of most European nations to subscribe to the OECD agreements on the prevention of bribery and corruption; banking and legal affairs that facilitate the laundering of funds siphoned off in the South; liber-alisation of exchange rates which lead to capital volatility; restrictions on imports from poor countries; subsidies to exports that vitiate the economic viability of some economies; the brain drain; the worsening global climate; arms and narcotics smuggling; tacit cooperation of bankers and lawyers in the UK with international drug traffickers and money launderers by invoking 'client confidentiality'; subsidies that encourage the growing of tobacco; and so on. The list is very long.

These are issues that destabilise security at the core of everybody's life, namely financially, physically and environmentally. The power to achieve change by redirecting the international agenda lies with peo-ple such as President Obama and President Hu Jintao, his opposite number in China. They represent powerful underlying currents – some of self-interest, some of group interests, and yet others of geo-graphical or historical origin. These forces are like tectonic plates, moving at their own pace – individuals, large organisations, and even most national entities cannot change them. Some of these issues will never be resolved. Yet, because they are big issues, many great minds pretend that they can be solved with big solutions. It has become a challenge that many great minds have taken up; the search for the Holy Grail of Development. But there isn't one solution. The challenges must be tackled from a different angle altogether. Few governments or international organisations can solve them. Voluntary organisations certainly cannot play any substantial role in these areas; they are too weak and irrelevant. Any attempt at intervention at this level of the Grand Opera is wasteful and unproductive. These issues are of such global significance that they should be dealt with not just as part of the concern of the aid and development lobby, but of a much wider constituency. They require better global citizenship. Long-term change can eventually be achieved through a wider effort at education of all citizens and that should be done in a consistent and continuing manner, possibly under the direction of a single body. In this way the issues can become non-partisan ones on which broad political participation can be accepted.

The number of new efforts at coordinating or starting initiatives to save the world from its ecological destruction or to provide peace tends to be an ego trip for the people involved. It would be far better and less wasteful to use the existing tools and try to improve them. Voluntary bodies in development to achieve their own aims should be able to agree – if they ever can – on a basic international agenda of priorities they wish the intergovernmental bodies to adopt. They should then advertise the resulting document widely, e-mail and fax it to anyone they think might be interested and leave it at that. The demand for reforms in these areas of human activity is almost always made only in the context of poverty reduction. Most people thus remain unaware of the effects these forces have on the economies and the lives of rich nations as well as those of poor nations. Take just one example; the enormous transfers of funds across the world have destabilised the capital markets of the North and of the South. One should welcome the suggestion that a very small tax should be levied on all such transactions (the so-called Tobin Tax[3]), proceeds from which would go toward international development. But it will never come into being because there is no mechanism to ensure that it is enforced.

From compassion to solidarity

Staggering amounts of aid have been given over the years to the poorest countries in the world, most of them in Africa. Yet we have the evidence from the most relevant study under the auspices of the World Bank, that at the macroeconomic level there has been no major change except where the recipient countries are already well governed and have sensible economic policies[4]. Why have things not changed? The immediate thoughts must be that the aid the North has given has not been of the right type or that the targets it has tried to hit have not been the right ones or that aid has been given to the wrong people. These thoughts beg questions; has the North failed because it has assumed that what works in its economic world works in other worlds as well? Are there other tools that should be used? If the answer to these questions is 'yes', then perhaps everyone should re-examine what the approach should be. There is of course a very simple quick answer to doubts about aid. Aid, particularly when it has been directed to the grassroots, has certainly had some positive effects. It has to some extent been the only force that has assuaged some of the damage that other forces attacking the poor world have caused – the forces examined in the first three chapters of this book, where we have seen how arms purchases, capital flows, debt repayment, migration, and payments under intellectual property rights cost far more than the aid the North gives. On top of that the pattern of trade has been generally anti-developmental. Aid on the whole has thus been a succession of band aids.

The general approach must be that we all need to support development from the base upwards. This does mean helping local people build their village school: help to any Ministry of Education is a secondary matter. Those who wish to support this developmental approach need to understand directly what the poor want. Where we have the poor involved in revealing their own priorities, such as in the massive 2000 World Bank study, *'Voices of the Poor from Many Lands',* referred to on page 20, we find, unsurprisingly, that they want what the rich have but are unaware of having – peace, food security, water and sanitation, shelter and energy – because they are now deeply embedded in the North's lives. International organisations, multilateral and bilateral donors also work towards these objectives, although one should not assume that their overriding motive is generosity. But – and it is a big but – it is the way in which those objectives are being pursued that we need to address.

Voluntary agencies should concentrate on working at the grass-roots with their partners in the poor world. Here they can make a significant impact; at present there are too many very small projects, in too many countries. These ultimately are self-defeating; to make a serious impact, but there needs to be a smaller number of larger projects, requiring a greater effort of cooperation, but with greater results and also with much greater visibility. The activists must make it clear to governments and voluntary organisations from the North and the international organisations to which they subscribe that their focus must be to address poverty at its most actual level. A trickle-down approach not will achieve baseline development – it has to be bottom-up. Policy-makers should encourage the delivery of services at the village level. Similarly everyone should encourage popular participation in the village, the district, the region, by working through elected leaders as the contact point. Currently all systems are geared to contacts with the centralised powers, the ministers, the government officials, the politicians based, generally, in the metropolitan cities. This is not to say that a decent Ministry of Education or Ministry of Health are not highly desireable. They are – but it will take a long time for these bodies to become truly effective.

Voluntary agencies, the most important intermediaries in the relationship between the North and the South, both because of their high visibility, but also because of their flexibility and adaptability, must change the tenor of their appeals for support from the general public. Their current presentation encourages people in the North to view the peoples of the South as objects of compassion rather than individuals seeking to achieve the same things as them. Northern societies were not well off as recently as 50 years ago, but the North has resolved the problems and challenges for the majority of its peoples through political leadership, cohesion, investment, education and slow consolidation of progress. In *Angela's Ashes*, an autobiography describing great poverty in Ireland in the 1930's, the author describes scenes of poverty reminiscent of today's South[5]. Those who care need to offer engagement and solidarity and not just compassion.

The international agencies and even the largest donors (including the Global Fund to Fight AIDS, Tuberculosis and Malaria) want to attack particular illnesses, for example, but they aim to do this by improving the systems that deliver services to meet those needs, not by addressing the needs themselves. They thus automatically become prisoners of that system: inevitably they attack problems from the top down. This is true for any of the major objectives in development, including health, education, and other elements of improvement to daily life. But there are serious limitations in using doctors to decide the best way to deliver medical services. Nurses or barefoot doctors might be more relevant, but they are not part of this system of inter-mediaries because they do not have the power. Such improvements should not be left to the intermediaries, the professionals, to decide upon. Intermediaries are like every other group in society; the strongest and the most vocal make the running.

Host countries and international donors should be encouraged, for example, to change their tactics in order that they strengthen medical services at the base and holistically, not attack a disease in isolation. This is yet more evidence that the North applies solutions that some-times work in the richer societies to problems they meet in other societies, thinking that the results will be the same. Northern societies rely on centralisation of decision-making: all decisions need to be made at the national level for the sake often of non-existent or unnec-essary coherence, but most of the time they have the human resources to make coherence work or the financial resources to absorb the waste. By not cooperating more effectively at the international level in the field of aid, the bilateral donors add to the problems not to the solution of the problems in the South; they burden weak central struc-tures in the South.

The North relies overwhelmingly on governments as the main instruments of change and implementation. In the South that approach goes pear shaped. Inevitably the North works through the richest and not through the poor, in fact most of the time through the extremely rich in the poorest countries. Consequently, the top people are the first beneficiaries of a top-down approach. This cannot always work; in dealing with ill-health the international community should encourage prevention and to that end education is vital. Donors should be developing clinics and train local personnel to become better barefoot doctors and better birth attendants, not setting up national committees that will entice good doctors away from their existing workloads because of better pay or conditions. Doctors have a vested interested in the existing system; they created it.

Some home truths
Let us debunk some commonly held beliefs:

The poorest are becoming less poor. There are insufficiently reliable data (even if we wanted to be guided by them) to define how many people are poor, but we know more people are getting poorer because there are more of them and the cake available to divide among them is not growing. Everyone gets a bit less, ever less, on average, with the richer among the poor getting a bit more. Poverty is growing in the world at large; in percentage terms there might be fewer of the very poor people, but in absolute terms the number is growing. The sum total of human misery is not diminishing.

The present crisis will pass. That may be true for the North; within perhaps five years the North might have recovered some of the millions of lost jobs. But the increase in food prices in 2007 and 2008 and the global economic recession from late 2008 onwards will increase the number of people on the verge of starvation to around two billion. An additional 200,000 to 400,000 children will die because of the worsening economic conditions[6] and an additional 40 million children will become malnourished. The effects on their health and mental abilities[7] will have consequences across generations. In July 2009 OXFAM UK estimated that Africa would loose around $245 billon during 2009 because of the worsening world economic conditions[8].

Globalisation helps the poor. Global trade policies have little positive effect on the lives of the poorest across the globe; they help certain groups among the poor. They help the better-off people in the poorest countries disproportionately more. Few poor countries have benefitted. In a period of economic retrenchment across the world, the poor will be abandoned to their own fate more than ever before. Solutions need to be localised because problems are local. The whole world will no longer be able to rely on the ever increasing consumption of the North.

Growth is economic development. This is a classic error; the more activities there are, the greater the appearance of growth. More surgical operations do not mean that people are healthier – it means that surgeons are busier. More car crashes translate into an increase in the GDP of a country. That is hardly a meaningful form of development.

Improving central governments is the best tool for development. Northern governments are mesmerised by this mirage. If only Southern governments were better, they think, everything else would be better too. Citizens in the North believe that Southern governments represent the wants and needs of their people, as opposed to the needs of Northern governments to have someone to talk to or negotiate with. The only level of governance at which change will occur is local government. Even traditional forms of governance might be a better vehicle to achieve change than existing national structures – which are fundamentally, in most countries, a Northern imposition.

International private corporations will solve the problems of the poor world. FDI could be a key in those countries that have assets that attract foreign companies, but these have no natural inclination to work for local development – their role is to maximise returns to their shareholders back home. They often cause the 'resource curse'. Corporate social responsibility for most companies is an after-thought. It cannot work unless the culture of organisations changes. The key role must be played by private entities operating at local level under forms of local control, meeting the needs of local people, not multinational companies competing on world markets.

The North/West dominates the world. That is rapidly becoming a self-evident fallacy; economic power in the world has already shifted to the G20 and economic dynamism to the BRIC countries. Any hold that the North might have had in the past is slipping away. In November 2008 the IMF and the World Bank were asking Russia and China to lend them money (but not offering them directorships in either institution!).

Northern values are universal. The North believes that it has adopted universal standards of fairness, equality, accountability, democracy widely accross all of its societies. Unfortunately it has not. Rich societies are grossly unequal, unjust, often undemocratic. Most of those who care have no power. Most of those who have power do not care. We are all creatures of our societies and trapped in our own histories and other people are similarly creatures of theirs. Not everyone believes in noblesse oblige, even in rich societies, and in other societies the very idea would be seen as patent nonsense. One starts with helping one's family, and possibly one's clan. A more complex society will demand greater inputs and more refinement.

The aid the international community gives is beneficial. Aid in emergencies must remain a priority, but long-term aid is probably causing a continuing dependence, thus delaying the challenge for people to solve their own problems. Second-hand clothing and donated bicycles retard the development of home industries. They are, of course, easier to give than creating the relevant workshops in poor countries. Aid can and must be made more beneficial.

Establishing human rights should be the first priority. The North places too much emphasis on meeting the needs for free speech and free political participation for the individual; the poorest want more bread and more physical security. The best way to achieve these aims is to work through collective social organisms. The poor will fight for their own rights once they have acquired more individual wealth and greater security.

'It's economics, stupid!'

Establishing good financial governance is high on the agenda of the international financial institutions (IFIs). The hope is that this will reduce poverty, but the problems of poverty should be tackled from another angle altogether: generating economic prosperity for poor people. Until this basic target is addressed, the battle against world poverty will fail. Through economic activities they might achieve a modicum of prosperity that will allow change, but economic development will not happen of its own accord. The global market and the rules that the North has established based around its interests, including the rules that facilitate globalisation, are making national/local economic progress less possible. The IFIs try to operate through governments of the South, which are no more capable of directly generating economic prosperity than those of the North, and through financial instruments that in most parts of the South do not work or do not exist. No government has the tools to translate goals into economic realities. National goals need to be set, and within these there needs to be a framework that local institutions will translate into local economic development.

The MDGs set out at the General Assembly of the UN in 2000 are indeed a mix of desirable political and social goals for mankind, but policy-makers in New York missed out entirely the means for the realisation of those goals. For example, how are we going to make development sustainable so that every child in the world can carry on learning, not just go to school perhaps for a few years? This problem was exacerbated by the avoidance in the MDGs of two key global issues; limiting population growth (the need for family planning) and migration. Setting goals and even initiating a discussion on either of these two topics would not have been politically acceptable to the governments that met in New York in 2000 and both had therefore to be dropped. But these two missing goals are actually of fundamental importance for achieving prosperity for the poorest.

Inspite of their obvious limitations, the MDGs are nevertheless an amazing achievement and all aid efforts should support their implementation.

Determining long-term priorities

Understanding and implementing the priorities of the poor need to be achieved through a process much more participatory than the systems of democracy the North has developed. The North is going through a different economic and therefore political cycle, meeting different needs in different times and different circumstances. In Northern societies the basic priorities of everyone are largely met after an election no matter the party they supported. Elections are not about the vital issues that determine survival – they are not about water and roads and personal security. But in more divided societies support for different political parties in a context of winner-takes-all leads to continuing discontent[9]. In conditions in which there is a low level of literacy and little social cohesion, for example, local communities and non-state actors have a vital role to play. The South needs dynamic social civil society and effective accountable government. Decisions on how to tackle basic priorities need a technocratic approach; creating food security, supplying water, creating jobs for unskilled people, generating power supply, and reducing the rate of population growth are goals that cannot be achieved by having more elections contested by more political parties. There must be different vehicles for the exchange of practical ideas and opinions. South-South cooperation is likely to be more productive than North-South cooperation in this respect because of having had to confront the same issues.

The economic crisis engulfing the North is offering governments, communities and non-state actors (including private companies), in both North and South opportunities to be more audacious and innovative. It is the time to set up ambitious new partnerships and define new goals. But governments will not be capable of doing that; governments in the North will be more and more obsessed with their own crises, and governments of the South do not seem yet to be aware that their people will be hit even more severely than the people in the North – they will suffer far more in both relative and absolute terms. The challenges confronting the poorest – and those who wish to support them – are huge. The structures of society need to be challenged to meet the gravity of the challenges; local institutions need to be strengthened so that they can be used to tackle the obstacles to development. It is a complex set of interrelated issues. Isolation in both the physical and planning senses is no longer a viable survival technique. Schools should be used to educate entire communities on issues affecting their own development. New vehicles to deliver economic development must be used; they could include direct partnerships and deals between different countries; private partnerships that use the discipline of private enterprise and the measurement of returns, using cost/benefit analysis with a wider scope. These requirements indicate three overriding development goals that must be tackled simultaneously. Governments in the North and in the South, as well as voluntary organisations and individuals, all have a role to play in ensuring their attainment. The goals are:

- to develop societies and communities

- to stop welfare aid and replace it with 'smart aid', namely targeted development

- to meet the basic needs of the poor through the work of the poor.

CHAPTER EIGHTEEN

Developing societies and communities

Many dispassionate readers who have sympathy with the poor world will be appalled at the thought that someone who cares about the South should advocate a push to modernity at the cost of local traditions. After all, the North has defined modernity and in the process destroyed other societies. But it cannot be ignored just because it sounds offensive; to achieve any degree of progress profound changes must occur in Southern societies. Modernity and economic progress, demand that societies be stable, that people should have ways to sustain and govern themselves, control their populations, become more economically active, and have governments able to govern and preside over efficient bureaucracies. To achieve these goals you need education and equality, to enhance the status and role of women in society (not just for the sake of equality, but because the woman is the most stable and reliable member of the community), and to enable everyone to benefit from economic enrichment. For these to happen there needs to be some degree of capital accumulation which in turn requires efficient tools such as decent physical infrastructure, schools, financial instruments, and efficient transport systems[10]. We might not like it, but pastoral societies cannot now remain self-sufficient and are unlikely even to survive. Romantic attachment to survival in the desert helps no one. Development will require more radical change than we have hitherto been willing to contemplate.

The need for reforms of the most fundamental nature is nowhere more sharply manifested than in the Arab world. The 2009 UN Arab

Development Report highlighted what the lack of challenges to the status quo can lead to. Real GDP per capita in the 21 countries that form the Arab world (they include countries like Sudan, Chad and Mauritania that are also part of sub-Saharan Africa) grew by 6.4 per cent between 1980 and 2004, just 0.5 per cent per year. The right to vote outside traditional religious or ethnic structures is highly restricted. Unemployment is up to 45 per cent. Employment opportunities to even highly qualified people are restricted. Everyone wants to escape. There has been more emphasis on security of the state than on the security of the individual. People in no way 'own' their countries[11]. The study is all the more telling because the analysts are almost all Arab in origin.

Education, education, education

Education is without doubt the key to unlock economic and social development for the very good reason that it unlocks personal potential. It could be implemented within a relatively short period of time and would have lasting repercussions across all fields of human activity – from human rights to property rights, from democracy to agricultural improvements. The World Bank realised as far back as the mid 1960s that educating women farmers improved overall agricultural production. More education would empower women to change their status in society and give them greater control over their fertility. Educating men through relevant physical skills would be, for example, a first step towards the construction of better housing.

This is not a call for a uniform or even a formal approach to education. Certain issues can be better communicated through, for example, theatrical shows, or story telling, or by training children to teach other children[12]. All such initiatives have been tried somewhere in the world and should be encouraged; there are some very interesting initiatives developed by groups of people within the poor world itself and these can be replicated. But the key point is that it must be done through the simplest tools possible. Chalk and blackboards and radio and television are used very successfully in many parts of the world, not only for general didactic purposes but also to encourage better farming or health techniques. But teaching at the most elementary level through projects such as the one laptop per child are still a luxury and the more basic systems should be given greater priority.

The school at the centre of the community

In many parts of Kenya and Uganda the humble local school has shown it can be the key to the development of an entire local community. Schoolchildren are fed a decent meal at lunchtime; this improves both their health and their learning capacity. Parents are keener to send their children to school if they are fed at the same time as they are learning (and if the school is free!). Schools should be able to grow their own food and through such work transmit farming understanding and technique. Schools where girls who have reached puberty can use separate toilets show greater retention of girls than those with shared toilets. Such local adaptation and flexibility cannot be implemented at national or international level. Schools need good heads and good parental and community support to achieve that level of flexibility. Schools can be the most important transformational force within each village; the school council can be the centre of the community and the school the physical centre of village life.

The school can become the place where farmers are taught farming techniques, where the nurse can explain basic hygiene to would-be mothers, or where HIV/AIDS education can be imparted to different groups. It can be the location of the local library and the local computer centre. It can have a television set powered by solar energy for educational purposes (as is currently the case in Mali, Burkina Faso, Niger and probably elsewhere). In Botswana, Swaneng School (and similar schools in other parts of the country) encouraged entire villages very successfully to develop a school curriculum to meet the need of the community for more farmers, carpenters, bricklayers, electricians and plumbers. They followed the pioneering work of Paolo Frère, the Brazilian educationalist who championed the need to make education relevant to society. He also talked about the need for literacy and education as essential tools for liberation: nothing has changed[13]. This has been copied in countries such as Malawi, where the government has taken the lead role in the fight against HIV/AIDS by using the school as the vehicle for education. It is the first step towards modernity.

Societal cohesion

One of the most important elements in creating an environment in which economic development can take hold is the invisible element of societal cohesion. At the base of democracy there must be a sense of acceptance of rules and that in turn needs mutual trust and respect. In any setting, if it is impossible to trust your neighbours and those who rule over you, a feeling of mistrust will influence all actions of the community. A society in which services are provided for everyone, irrespective of their status or connections to those in power – that is, neutral service – requires a sense of mutual obligation founded on trust. A wide range of facilities in all societies – schools, universities, hospitals, sports centres, social services, clinics – aim to serve the community as a whole. Rich people take all of that for granted. Where societies have to face economic and social change to meet the challenge of economic development, they also face a transition in the nature of the mutual bonds of trust between their members. In traditional societies neutral service to everyone runs against ethnic and neo-patrimonial rules[14]. It took generations for this ethic of neutral service to grow and take root in Northern societies. The two World Wars have probably been among the most important forces in creating that feeling of mutual dependence and cohesion as well as a shared fate within European nations. Even the EEC was born out of a sense that the traditional enmities in Europe could not be allowed to continue and had to be tackled through strong new institutions. By contrast, in societies in which there is continuous strife, such as Rwanda or Burundi, there cannot be any lasting development of society as a whole due to the continuing mutual hatred between Hutus and Tutsis[15]. The mutual distrust breeds despair: it is a vicious circle.

The modern form of citizenship generates many unquantifiable benefits; from the feeling that everybody is in the same boat to the creation of an officer class to bring ideas of leadership and management from the army back into civilian life. The army and the police force have always been among the most powerful unifying forces in Britain. In most Northern societies the management of large-scale enterprises benefitted from the training of an officer class in the armed forces, long before business schools discovered and further refined (sometimes to the point of absurdity) the same ideas of management and strategic objectives.

It will be difficult to create that sense of cohesion between small communities or ethnic groups that have managed to survive by isolating themselves from the rest of the world, for example, because they have always been nomadic or because of traditional rivalries. Traditional hierarchies have similarly had an interest in emphasising differences and opposing wider community allegiances. People who work in the former Yugoslav republics and Albania comment that it will take the best part of this century for traditional feelings of hatred to change. Schools will be one of the unifying forces; we have in the US the example of a mosaic of societies emerging through a common school system and service in the armed forces to form a common powerful community. Each component of the mosaic is united with others in many ways and yet remains identifiable through its own rites and internal rules. This is another argument for using schools as the main tool for creating local communities.

National civilian service

Lack of ethnic homogeneity in most African countries is one of the key elements that militates against national cohesion and is one of the key barriers to building nationhood and mutual obligations. It works against the creation of an overarching structure in society, because loyalties and obligations are ethnically defined. Democracy cannot emerge from ethnic loyalty, and neither can it be created without some feeling of common allegiance. There is a range of specific initiatives that nations should support to build that allegiance to the common good. For example, in the early days of independence many African countries had national civilian corps – something between a civilian military service and a more grown-up version of the Boy Scouts or Girl Guides. In Ethiopia in the 1960s and early 1970s every university student was sent to teach or work in another part of the country for a year. Zambia and Uganda had similar schemes. Young people should be encouraged to spend some time, perhaps up to a year, working with others, from other parts of their own country on projects that benefit their communities. They should be paid a modest allowance, perhaps by outside donors, to take part in such service. Completion of such service would be compensated with further education. In the last few years similar schemes have been reinstated in several countries across the world.

A national service which is totally civilian in its approach could be a powerful tool of development as well as an aid to raising consciousness. Young men and women who arrive illiterate can be taught to read and write in such an environment by others who are already literate. There was such a service in the armed forces in Britain until the abolition of national conscription. Other skills could also be developed through military service: in Argentina the Government used the army (long before the military dictatorship) to improve agriculture in various areas of the country. The army became the mechanism through which young men and women were trained in the techniques of agriculture. They were introduced to the use of tractors and other sophisticated machinery. The army also became the tool through which the Government brought elements of sanitation into rural areas and in some places built the first stage of physical infrastructure. Service in civilian corps could also be the tool to impart basic elements of organisation and management – vital skills at all stages of change. Service of young people together will have other benefits; building a sense of common purpose, a sense of obligation to other members of the community, a sense of equality, and escape from very restricted mental and physical confines. It can be abused of course, but so are most current tools of development, including the armed services or public works contracts or international aid or medical services.

There is a long tradition of groups undertaking voluntary work within local communities in the South. Voluntary workcamp associations, for example, have been doing this sort of work for at least 60 years. There are examples of such groups across all of Africa and they are genuine local initiatives. The work of Christian Aid and CAFOD (the Catholic Agency for Overseas Development), both UK-based organisations, done through sister organisations in the South, has always been one of the most effective forms of development at the grassroots. Churches across Africa have always managed to support small local initiatives. Other organisations in the UK that work in agriculture, such as Farm Africa, have discovered more local projects than they could possibly partner with. The development of large new organisations in the 1960s and 1970s that had no grassroots partnerships swamped such local groups instead of allowing them time to grow and develop. It took until the mid 1990s for international aid agencies to rediscover the need for genuine local partners [page 158].

Women at the centre of development

In the poor world, particularly in Africa, women are the engine of development. They enjoy few rights in law and have low status in society, but they are the key to development. Women are much less mobile than men and their roles as mothers and homemakers make them the linchpin of the family and of the community. Women reinvest up to 90 per cent of their incomes in their families and their communities, as against men who reinvest only 30 to 40 per cent[16]. Those who set the agenda need to bear this in mind and ensure that in all developmental activities women are given the same advantages as men in terms of schooling, education, and finance for example, and when in doubt, greater benefits. But helping women must be done initially by helping cooperative bodies of women; within such structures they will develop their own roles and strengthen their position. It is probably impossible for a woman to advance and acquire rights on her own; it has to be done through social networks and institutions. The resulting economic and social empowerment of women will eventually lead to changes in society. In the deeply traditional Muslim societies of coastal West Africa women have far fewer legal rights than men, but socially they are more important because they command the petty trading along the entire coast. Legal changes will come about eventually because of this empowerment. We need to build on this sort of economic success to achieve legal empowerment, not use the law to achieve empowerment.

Cooperatives and social structures

The cooperative movement is moribund in most parts of the North. There are cooperative societies in certain parts of the UK, but they mainly own retail shops, sometimes well-run, but as a social movement cooperativism is dead. Even the Cooperative Bank in the UK, which in the last few years has trumpeted an interest in ethical investment, probably developed that approach because its public relations advisers and market research people have told them that there is a niche market to be reached. On the other hand, the cooperative movement in other societies – such as Sweden and Norway – has remained very active and its long-term aims have remained consistent. They remained faithful to the fight against apartheid for over 25 years and played a key role in its dismemberment. Mutual societies, building societies, savings banks, friendly societies, credit unions, and other social structures have virtually withered away in the UK – a sign that these sorts of institutions that enabled Britain to achieve economic progress have become less relevant as people have grown richer. However, in early 2009 the British Government was floating the idea of establishing a non-profit social bank using the network of post offices across the UK.

The older forms of social structures described above should be encouraged in new and poorer societies. In the developing world, microcredit institutions are a similar type of local initiative which needs to be backed. By themselves they will not be sufficient to provide the full range of financial services that the poor need; these will have to emerge slowly in response to the needs of the poorest. They will be different from modern-day banks of the North and more like the old style banks that Mr Barclay and Mr Lloyd set up to serve the Quaker communities in the 17th and 18th centuries. Other existing examples include the many associations of women in the South who are fighting against lack of status and, by exposing sexual abuses or discrimination and engaging the whole community, make it more difficult for men to continue their abuses. Only civil society organisations can provide such support: it will take many years, if ever, for many governments to fight against exploitation of women. Farmers' groups can organise themselves to export organic produce. One such body, for example, set up in Malawi and backed by VSO, is enabling farmers to develop their internal structures and press for more democracy in their communities.

The spillovers from such efforts are evident all around. It is probably impossible in the short run to envisage the establishment of a comprehensive land ownership system – although it must remain a vital objective – but adapting traditional structures through pressure from cooperative efforts is a useful first step in such a direction. Traditional leaders will not abandon their traditional powers without a lot of opposition. Turkeys do not vote for Christmas. The social structures mentioned above would be one way of challenging traditional power structures. Once farmers have become more prosperous they will be more willing and able to challenge the traditional structures that oppress them.

Settling nomadic communities

In several African countries national governments need to address one of the most intractable issues of all – the resettlement of nomadic people. The challenges of dealing with nomadic people are that they do not appear on the radar in any society and that their way of life is doomed. In chapters two and three [pages 24-46] we have seen how the relentless advance of the desert, the increase in population and the reduction in the availability of water force nomadic people to move elsewhere and in so doing encroach on the land and livelihoods of sedentary people. This gives rise to conflicts that will get worse; the phenomenon is at the root of the inability of several African governments, ranging from Kenya in the east to Senegal in the west, to create systematic land tenure. There are courageous attempts to resettle Maasai in various parts of East Africa and such attempts should be supported.

Empowering local democracy

By definition local democracy can be effective and real only if small numbers of people are involved. Once we have large national states, there has to be less democratic control over locally sensitive issues. There are still vibrant local democracies in Europe. The best example is probably Switzerland with its 23 cantons, but the Scandinavian countries are also good examples – all are very small states where there is a determination and ability to make democracy work and where local institutions respond to local wants. No less than 20 of the 50 States of the US have a population of fewer than three million people. There can be genuine democracy at that level. A balance must be struck between serving the interests of local groups – which might be purely ethnically based – and the wider interests of the community, but it is certainly more likely that local structures will be more responsive to local needs and situations.

One of the nine components of the Federation of Ethiopia is the Southern Nations, Nationalities, and People's Region, and covers the South West of the country. In the 2007 census it had an estimated 15 million people split into 45 indigenous ethnic groups. Six languages were spoken by 24 per cent of the population and 22 languages by less than 15,000 people each[17]. A Federation, where the powers of the state are at a level closer to the people, certainly makes more sense here than a central power in a country that covers the size of German and France combined, with less than 45 per cent of the population literate and poor communications. The appropriate structures will not emerge overnight; those who have been oppressed for centuries will have it deeply implanted in their minds that they have no right to make their own decisions. But it needs to be done and it is easier to engage the most humble farmer in decisions about specific needs – such as about the location of a school or a clinic – than in the more abstract ideas of better governance. It is another aspect of aiming for specific goals.

Building at the base

The problems of poor communities are multifaceted; they need water and food reserves and clinics and schools and so on. It is almost inevitable that, when aid is given from the outside, each of these challenges is seen and dealt with in isolation. Yet dealing with each of these challenges in a poor society in isolation is unlikely to succeed in the long term. For example, foreign voluntary organisations have always been attracted to projects in health and education. They try to meet the challenge of 'their' individual project without connecting with other elements in the fight against poverty. A clinic in a village cannot survive unless there is a school, a water well, and a community that has been enabled to provide for their continuing maintenance. Although there are plenty of examples of successful initiatives supported by both foreign donors and civil society, including good schools and clinics, many more have either disappeared or have to be continuously supported from the outside because the community does not have the tools to support them; it is a greater problem than just 'owning' the project. A series of one-off interventions to overcome endemic shortcomings in poor societies cannot succeed in overcoming the poverty of the mass of people. Poor schools cannot be improved unless a donor is committed to remaining engaged for many years. It is a continuing drip feed that avoids improving fundamentally the health of the patient. The pump cannot be maintained if there is no operative to maintain it. The clinic cannot survive if the nurse goes to a job in the UK or the community has not been trained.

The planning capacity in most poor countries is weak and the implementation capacity possibly non-existent, which means that foreign donors have more say than host governments, and also at the wrong level. There is no doubt that many decisions about the needs of a country as a whole must be undertaken within a wide geographical or regional structure. If not, one ends up with too many primary schools and no secondary school or too few teacher training establishments. Every district would be working in isolation. To that extent there must be a clear hierarchy of planning from national to local levels and all levels in between. Everyone, especially potentially interventionist donors, should be clear as to where these lines of demarcation are. Policy-makers should encourage countries to reserve national planning for key strategic elements, such as external defence and therefore armed forces, tertiary education, major roads, airports, ports, scientific research, import policies. Other issues should be left to a lower level of planning and decision-making. Non-state actors need to become far more involved at the most local level of economic decision-making in the poor parts of the world and leave the IFIs and other grand institutions to make their choices in their own spheres.

Too many decisions that should be made in-country are not made locally but at the head offices of international agencies or foreign donors. Decisions regarding the development of Togo or Malawi should be made by people who work on the ground in those countries and who are representative of a plurality of interests – national governments, local governments, international organisations, regional organisations, local civil society, and non-governmental organisations. During the 1980s and 1990s most key decisions in international development were taken in Washington – where the World Bank, the IMF, and the US Treasury are based. The 'Washington consensus' is the most egregious example of elite capture of all, something that the North always condemns when it occurs in the South. More devolution of decision-making to local levels by locally based bodies will also enable more transparency. Local decision-making would also enable groups of people (e.g. women, the physically handicapped and members of minorities) who are not members of any elite, networks or systems to join in the decision-making process. It would lead to more grassroots democracy.

There are thus some clear policy options that one has to choose from. The present system of external intervention tends to be one of vertical insertion leading to vertical segregation; schools are established in this district and that village and then remain isolated, in the sense that they are managed from sources that do not respond to local control. Each component of need then requires a long-term commitment by either the state or a foreign donor – keeping the drip feed going. Alternatively one can try to develop a national structure in which clinics and schools and water wells all received the same degree of support and can then develop harmoniously across the whole front. That entails strengthening the institutions of the state to enable them to cope with the challenges. Yet, we have seen in a previous section how difficult it is to impose structural improvements from the top and how impossible it might prove to be in the long term. But the most promising approach must be to enable local people to sustain their own schools and that means developing their economies. Even in some of the most powerful and repressive societies, including China, increasing prosperity and education make more people question authority. More people in China are putting pressure on the authorities because of the continuing abuses that take place in planning regulations or in the inspectorate of medicine or in the failure of banks. People will demand more accountability. China will eventually change internally and will have to cope with the increasing demands at the base (this is certainly Will Hutton's thesis in his book *The Writing on the Wall*). It should be a lesson for voluntary organisations; state structures per se should not be a particularly important target for the outsider to aim at. What matters in development is a good school not a good Ministry of Education; you can have good schools with an incompetent Ministry. The next step after a good local school is one level up, the district school system, not regional offices of the Ministry of Education.

National governments and their bureaucracies, except in a few small homogeneous countries, for many more decades will remain weak and incapable to deliver the services for which they were set up. Donor need to understand and accept that they need to switch to much more local channels and work through good planning and administrative structures. The challenge is much clearer on the economic front. There cannot be many more challenging conditions anywhere in the world than in the Zinder or Maradi regions of Niger, where local farmers have been developing their agriculture and forestry. Villages of extremely poor farmers in 2002 were producing more food and were able to take care of trees within areas which they considered their own than 20 years earlier. Better water management and a feeling of ownership – although not legally entrenched in any way and thus fragile at best – enable people to feed themselves and care for their forest as a tool of economic advancement[18]. Economic prosperity will enable people to create appropriate structures of their own choosing. That will lead to more fundamental and more widely-spread change in their social and political environment.

CHAPTER NINETEEN

Replace welfare aid with targeted development

We have seen in the first part of this book the magnitude and complexity of some of the forces that impact on the South more than the North. What are the changes needed to attack world poverty and give the South the chance to develop?

There cannot be one single solution to what is a long list of different problems that affect various countries across the South. Above all the answers to underdevelopment and poverty require great flexibility, because the poor are not a homogeneous group and the different groups of poor people need different targeted approaches. The first set of obstacles to the poor is the very system within which the North lives, and which has improved the lives of most of the people there, but is actually causing damage to the South. The North should take steps to remedy or at least assuage some of the ongoing damage it causes. Accepting more goods that have been processed and thus value-added in the South would be one way to achieve this aim. Compensating poor countries for the loss of their ablest people would be another. But few of the most basic measures will ever be implemented – they require a spirit of global altruism that is beyond the terms of international relations. As Lord Palmerston put it: 'Nations do not have permanent friends; they have only permanent interests'. It would require a seismic intervention to change things and by definition the poorest do not have the power to cause change. The 'Make Poverty History' campaign, waged in the rich world in 2005, was great at the time and within four years every major nation on the planet was reneging on their promises.

The second set of obstacles has been the nation state itself, and the series of highly dubious priorities and demands that the North places on the mechanisms of the state of the South. Northern policy-makers have an imperfect understanding of the role, power, function, but particularly limited implementation capacity of the state in most of the South, because by and large they operate in response to very different physical and historical environments. Most international initiatives, including the work of the World Bank, IMF, and WTO, seem to weaken the states of the South. Within that context, government-to-government aid initiatives, aimed at improving the mechanisms of delivery of services in the South, are destined to fail.

If we wish to pursue activities that will permanently improve lives and above all create an environment in which the poor can become less poor, there are remedies that can be applied, but they involve being more active on behalf of the poor and more determined to find out what they need and to support their initiatives. Economic development will not happen of its own accord; it needs to be kick-started and nurtured. There must be more interventions aimed directly at the poor, not at their rulers or even those who speak now on their behalf, unless they have been freely elected to represent them.

There should be clear rules of engagement of the North with the South and of Southern societies with their own people if they wish to implement 'development'. Such engagement is also Goal 8 of the Millennium Development Goals, global partnerships for development. The rules of engagement should include above all an urgent determination to produce more food to prevent the massive starvation that the world is facing. But there are other priorities on both sides; in order to achieve sustained long term development, the North must commit itself to long-term commitment – not succumb to the temptation of short-term aid interventions. Both North and South must agree to common policies of implementation, including effective and detailed local planning, massive educational inputs, building the physical infrastructural, applying appropriate technology, mitigating the losses to the poor arising from migration, accepting the priorities of the poor world not of the rich world, introducing more protection for infant industries, working towards more equality of opportunity, improving grassroot democracy and making serious efforts at introducing transparency, eliminating corruption and generally improving governance.

The first human right

The international community, particularly civil society, has been focusing in the last few years on the issue of human rights (interpreted as individual rights). Voting rights, equality of all men and women before the law, the right of women to have control over their own bodies (and thus the right to abortion) and others have become shibboleths. It is being forgotten that these rights were realised in Northern societies as a result of other achievements in the system, for example the education and economic empowerment of women. In a very poor society, to emphasize the right to vote is to put the cart before the horse. In the short term the world needs to produce more food just to prevent starvation[19]. If you are starving, satisfying your basic need for food is all you care about. Nor can there be personal independence without some financial independence. If we want equality, let us ensure improvements on the economic front. To readjust rights in a static society will only encourage the different groups in power to protect their positions and entrench their views – not to open up. Too often Northern voluntary organisations are among the worst offenders of the top down approach by pushing their own agenda. The first human right is that of the right to life. That means a person should have access to food and water. It also means being given the tools with which to determine a future of their own choosing. In political terms this means the strengthening of social organisations through which the poorest can organise themselves and through them change their social and economic environment.

Economic development is possible if such measures are allowed to occur at the base, not come down from the top. Neither will it come as a result of amorphous outside influences. Changes at various levels are required; institutions need to be strengthened, government bureaucracies to be improved, planning to be clarified, clear policies established on development, local democracy reinforced, commercial initiatives facilitated. The commercial and industrial sectors, which in most poor societies remain minuscule and often operate illegally, must be encouraged to flourish. The problem has been that education, welfare, health often require a sophistication of management that few poor countries can afford. The microenterprises of the poor should have received some of the support that international bodies have given to the institutions of governments and the social sectors.

The world needs massive agricultural development

Agriculture is the battleground of the attack on world starvation; the long-term development of local agriculture must be the top priority. The world will need between 50 and 70 per cent more food by 2030, depending on whom you believe. This scale of increase will be required to counter the combined pressures of population growth, rising demand for food in the form of animal proteins, biofuels, growing water scarcity, loss of land due to desertification and increasing urbanisation[20]. There is simply not enough remaining arable land available in the world to achieve the target of food for all under present conditions; the amount of arable land is actually decreasing. In the short term there will be a sharp increase in the number of people who will be suffering from shortages, because of decreasing food stocks, higher prices and reducing production[21]. The answer is to increase production yields; the key element here is more intensive farming by small-scale farmers on their existing land, with suitable backup. But substantial additional food production will require bringing additional land under cultivation, and that requires serious investment. At present cereal yields in Africa are about one tonne per hectare, whilst in Europe and some of the more prosperous parts of Asia they are three to four tonnes per hectare[22].

It is a myth that there are large tracts of land in Africa or Latin America ripe for cultivation. The land needs to be irrigated and nurtured – there are severe limits to what can be achieved simply by reliance on rainfed agriculture. This means investment in reservoirs, canals, wells, seed nurseries, storage facilities, energy production. Within the weak administrative structures of most of the South, it is difficult to envisage Governments having the resources, financial and administrative, to implement the investment required. What is needed is better public planning, combined with private implementation. Private investment is likely to be more successful because it involves direct 'ownership' and thus direct involvement. The first step in this process must be clear forms of land ownership – the problem that the governments of both the rich and the poor worlds have avoided, and for which the poorest suffer the consequences. No government, private agency or international donor can really hope to be able to tackle the issue of growing more food without finding some way round long term management of water and land planning. All impinges on clarity of land tenure.

Immediate measures

A key problem for the small farmer is the lack of means to get produce from the farm to the market. In the short term it should be possible to make many ad hoc arrangements under which produce can be gathered, stored and distributed. The best way to kick-start this process would be to use the mechanism of a guarantee to purchase from farmers all they produce at a set price for perhaps five to ten harvests ahead. As part of this process, more farmers should be offered common warehousing and transport facilities, credit facilities, energy (preferably solar powered), facilities to draw water, good quality implements, access to fertilisers and better seeds (including seeds that are more resistant to increased salinity or drought) without forcing farmers to buy these at unreasonable prices from rich private companies.

Voluntary agencies from the North should use the tool of private ownership to acquire land tracts on long-term leases in key countries in the South where currently there are estates that can be leased, such as Malawi and Ethiopia. They could become model landlords, form partnerships with local groups, and in the long term enable local families to own land either individually or communally. The cooperative model could be a useful first step in the move from traditional and unreliable land tenure systems to more modern systems. However, cooperative land ownership need not mean cooperative production and marketing, which could dampen personal entrepreneurship. Voluntary organisations, working through local partners, could introduce modern farming techniques, with adequate investment in water, irrigation, energy and storage facilities. These organisations would have a vital power of initiative in modernising agriculture, which others would copy. In the long-term commercial investors (particularly domestic ones) would be encouraged to invest.

The challenge of land tenure

Traditional village structures have never guaranteed land holding to individual families, but this arbitrary process has been of little consequence until the advent of population pressure and land shortages[23]. The need to grow more food has changed this casual approach to land distribution. The status of women in this process is essential; the woman is the de facto breadwinner, farmer and head of the family in most households in rural Africa. Her status, however, is so low that she does not have a say in traditional land distribution and inheritance rights. Education will be the start of her journey of liberation.

The North and the international aid community must accept that the transformation of land ownership is an enormously difficult undertaking for democratic governments in the South, although perhaps easier in those countries that are less democratically governed. The process will mean negotiating with the traditional chiefs. Of course there will be problems, but if safari parks can be created for the enjoyment of foreign tourists (in other words, so that they are enticed to visit Kenya and Tanzania and spend), solutions can be found for ownership systems that will ensure the provision of food for local people. Any reader familiar with the problems of the South will throw their hands up in horror at the thought of the bureaucratic nightmares that will occur in the process of land registration, but it is an issue that needs to be tackled by all policy-makers. The establishment of that right will be a clear manifestation of the willingness of the more privileged classes, in both the North and the South, to help the poor. Vested interests in this area are so deeply entrenched and control over land so closely connected with traditional patronage that no one wants to tackle this particular hornet's nest. The vagueness of the discussion about land tenure rights is part of the problem at all levels of discussion over 'development'. Within the aid forums, such as the

Paris Declaration on Aid and the Accra Forum on Aid Effectiveness, all governments stress the need for 'ownership' by the poor countries of their 'own' development. However, like so many other things in this field, that concept is somewhat nullified by the vagueness of the wording. Does it mean 'owned' by democratically elected governments of the South? Or does it mean local communities? Or perhaps their representatives? What matters is not the discussion in the capital cities of the world; the only 'ownership' that really matters is that the farmer tilling a bit of land the size of a back garden in the suburbs of London should really 'own' that bit of land.

There is no unique model that all can follow, but some clear principles need to be introduced. There should be a public land registry, clearly able to demonstrate ownership. Many countries in Africa have land ownership of different types. In some, the land in the cities is clearly deemed to be owned by the family that lives on that land[24]. They have acquired residential or squatters' rights. In others, there has been traditional, or customary, land which has been primarily the right of traditional rulers or chiefs or elders to allocate. Kenya and Malawi at independence had large estates, often managed by foreign individuals and companies that were paying rent to the state for the privilege of farming that land for fixed periods of time. More recently Zimbabwe and Namibia found ways to create land leases for white farmers as a way to ensure food security. The British Government set up the Commonwealth Development Corporation (CDC) in 1948 to do the same work on a cost covering basis. It developed agriculture and forestry and related industries in the countries in which it operated, generating income for those countries and developing skills for thousands of workers. However, in more recent years the CDC has unfortunately moved away from agriculture and primarily into mining, and it has thus become another vehicle for speculative investment by the North in the South. The fact that it is a publicly owned body makes the situation even sadder. Its original remit would have been the model for many other institutions to follow.

Long-term commitment to development

The Northern world has been very fickle in its relations with the

South. There are obvious reasons for this; one American president might be keener on overseas aid than another. In the UK a Labour Government tends to be more generous, but cannot commit a conservative government that might possibly follow it. Voluntary organisations, whose income most of the time depends on irregular donations, are not able to plan for the long term. Northern governments should be willing to support projects over a long period, through their entire development cycle, not just for a year or two, before expecting them to stand on their own. This is again an area in which the commercial world shows us that, as long as mutually beneficial interests have been developed, the relationship will continue. IKEA [page 115] will remain committed to its plant in Bangladesh over a long period as otherwise it will not recoup its initial investment.

Coherence in development support

In trying to tackle each challenge individually one issue is inevitably set against the other. Northern bodies – both official and private – are all supporting a range of disjointed initiatives that are all researched and initiated separately – of waste of both effort and money. This is inevitable when the eventual beneficiaries are not making the choices and someone else is making them on their behalf: 'we' decide what 'they' want. But if 'we' were to allow more local participation, 'they' would be able to make more of their own choices and those choices would be far more consistent and long-lasting. The very existence of so many different players in the world of aid and development makes consistency virtually impossible. There are over 80 official (that is, government-backed and funded) bilateral aid organisations around the world; they will never speak the same language. Only when Southern countries are well governed and strong can they force donors to tow the line. This applies to aid from both official donors and private voluntary agencies. The only way to create coherence is to start from the needs on the ground and build up development inputs from there, not relaying on an incoherent, multi-headed top-down process.

Building the physical infrastructure

There is a desperate need for better physical facilities in all poor countries. There are however two basic associated requirements: there has to be a bias towards rural areas, where poverty is greatest, and such physical facilities need to be implemented at the right level of technology. This would create millions of jobs and again help to generate the crucial momentum in economic development. The great advantage of building physical infrastructure is that it would create jobs at the lowest level of skills. It does not take long to learn how to use a pick and shovel or to carry stones from a quarry to the construction site. Workers on such projects will eventually be able to move on to higher skills in house building or road building. Water and sanitation require reservoirs and cesspits, as well as simple water conduits (which can be built with clay or made with local materials) and farmers need canals for irrigation. Feeder roads to link villages to larger centres of population, schools, public buildings (ranging from local markets to offices for local councils, prisons, police offices and health clinics) are also required. All such activities require not so much a massive injections of funds, as a focused determination that this is where development must start. The transport map of the UK was transformed by the network of canals built through the 18th and early 19th centuries. The transport map of some parts of inland Africa could be transformed through the development of canals. There are lakes in many parts of East Africa that could support a network of canals that would provide water for irrigation. Malawi is currently studying plans to use the water from Lake Malawi to feed such a network of canals. The actual construction work could be done following examples of the work done currently by some relief agencies through 'food for work' programmes: people are paid partly in cash and partly in kind. Strategic plans for local water management across wide areas (possibly at national level), with detailed implementation to be carried out at local level are the starting requirements.

Health

In the field of health, the North is sold on issues of cure, not of prevention. This is an excellent example of how its priorities differ from those of the South and are possibly in conflict with them. If there were more clean water, there would be far fewer deaths caused by inadequate or non-existent levels of sanitation. Tackling health before improving water is the wrong way round, but, as we have seen, the medical profession from the North dictates the terms of the debate and imposes its own solutions on the South. Training more doctors in the poor world who will migrate to the rich world is of no benefit to the poorest. For years the key health worker in China was the barefoot doctor, a general nurse who would move from village to village, giving sensible precautionary advice – such as boiling water before drinking it and washing hands after defecating. This is the sort of approach to health issues that the North should accept as a priority in the South instead of pushing its own.

In many countries there are traditional birth attendants. They could be trained to upgrade their skills, even if they do not have access to upgraded facilities. This is being done successfully in Indonesia: traditional birth attendants take government-certified courses and in return receive a small financial reward. The ability to control the size of your family is of fundamental importance to both the individual family and to nations that are chronically short of food; women with just a few years of education demonstrate a better understanding of how to avoid unwanted pregnancies than those with none[25]. It is essential that maternal health be improved, and again, there are prac-tices that are operating in some parts of the world that can be fol-lowed. In villages in Indonesia in the 1980s and 1990s people who agreed to enter family planning programmes where they could learn how to control the size of their families were helped to benefit from microcredit schemes. It worked and there was no compulsion.

Appropriate technology and technology transfer

Governments of the North are pressurising governments of the South to invest in large-scale infrastructure projects, but they tend to be prestigious projects (such as major city roads, airports, power stations and big dams). China is doing the same and prefers to encourage recipient countries to think about airports before meeting the local needs for better rural roads. It also wants to be awarded the associat-ed construction contracts. Such policy worsens the imbalance of eco-nomic opportunities between the rich and poor within poor countries, between the urban and the rural areas. This is not say that there is no need for better main roads to connect, for example, centres where food is grown to the markets where food might be sold. Large projects might well have to be put out to international tender, but the key measure for determining who gets the contract should be the element of appropriate technology transfer, not the price, and therefore the challenge of the low level of initial skills. These projects need to be adapted to enable local enterprises to participate preferentially in their construction. In this alternative method of tendering one could develop ways to create tripartite partnerships involving international companies tendering for the work, international aid donors to fund the training and other non-investment aspects of the work, and local communities through their local entrepreneurs earning an income. This is another area in which voluntary organisations have a freedom to experiment in a way that governments or international agencies cannot. Most of them have shied away from any intervention out of a genuine fear of becoming involved in what does not concern them or in areas where they do not have any expertise. Where the latter is concerned, the simple answer is that they should acquire it.

Commercial and industrial partnering

In all countries of the South there is a need for a range of basic products that is rarely satisfied locally. They would include, for example, the construction of local water pumps, wheelbarrows, carts, agricultural tools and the production of dairy products to satisfy, in the first instance, the food needs of infants and young children. Simple furniture, footwear, clothing and other products could be produced locally and there should be a determined policy to twin small- and medium- scale enterprises in the North with their counterparts in the South. Such partnerships should also be developed to train personnel in similar, but nascent, enterprises in the South. Purchases in the South by foreign embassies and offices of international agencies and voluntary bodies should be directed towards local items.

Direct links

On the whole, the peoples of the North at a personal level are often generous in their attempts to help the South. They misunderstand, however, the nature of the challenge. Individuals in the North often find it difficult to relate to the South because they see the peoples of the South, particularly those of Africa, as living on a different planet. So long as this continues it is inevitable that the only approach people from the North will consider is one of charity: 'They are poor and we are rich, therefore we should help'. This huge gulf can be mitigated through more people-to-people contacts. A village in Somerset that 'adopts' a village in Africa may well discover parallel interests in preserving the local primary school or the local woodland. Links that are being established by schools in the North with schools in the South are also to be welcomed.

Sending books or help in any other form to a school that is integrated into the community, whose council plays an active community role, whose head informs the parents of the money given to the school from all sources, and whose pupils can maintain the village water pump and grow their own food, is to contribute to the development chain. Helping a family without an adult breadwinner or an elderly or handicapped person is all very laudable, but it is not a contribution to development. It is part of the relief effort.

Many outsiders might doubt that there are enough local groups in the South on which to build a base for the sort of grassroots development that has been advocated throughout this book, but there are literally hundreds of such groups. We need to go no further than the links that Christian churches or Moslem groups in the UK have developed with sister organisations in the South. Tools for Self-reliance, a small British voluntary organisation supplying refurbished tools to projects in Africa and Latin America, has come across hundreds of self-help groups, far more than they could ever assist[26]. These are the grassroots where support should be given. But the same agencies should be conscious that diluting their support is one of the key problems. Many international voluntary agencies have intervened in the South to carry out their own agenda, and have assumed they were members of local civil society, when clearly they had no legitimacy to such claim. They should aim to work together in a more concerted manner to identify those problems that outsiders can help to solve and would be more successful if they had more clearly defined targets. In a context in which hunger and poverty are likely to increase dramatically, this challenge is all the more urgent. The international community and concerned individuals simply have to be much more pro-active in their approach if they wish to tackle world poverty effectively.

The challenge of implementation

We have repeatedly seen in this book that in the poorest countries there are not only problems of a magnitude that by and the large the North does not have to face, as well as a dearth of tools to implement the required changes. The present system most of the time cannot deliver what the poorest need: it is not fit for purpose.

Why do things go wrong? Apart from the innumerable examples of blatant corruption and inefficiency, and we have referred to some of them, the management of public funds in any country is a huge challenge. In Britain it is often claimed in Parliament and in the press that the scale of errors in both defence and computer contracts is almost equivalent each year to half of the total aid budget[27]. But most of the time both investment and aid projects go wrong in the South because the working environment in a poor and undeveloped country is so weak. It is impossible for change and controls to be imposed from the top with the realistic hope that all will work well. Even the best run schemes of medicine distribution or village development fall foul of geography, local inefficiency, mismanagement and outright greed and corruption. At the time of writing this chapter (mid 2009) the press reported that an estimated $450 million of EU and Global Fund money had been embezzled in Uganda and in Tanzania drugs worth $819,000 to combat malaria were missing in a recent audit. Large quantities of drugs had expired after being left in unrefrigerated warehouses because there was no means to distribute them[28]. Warehouses that should be refrigerated cannot be, because there is no electricity. The generator has broken down because a spare part is missing. There might be one good maintenance engineer but he has had to go up-country because his mother has died. The lorries that should be bringing the new drugs from the airport to the clinic in the distant village have ran out of fuel and the convoy is stuck somewhere along the road.

So, even without corruption, the system is just so weak that ordinary activities cannot be carried out successfully. This is why a farm needs to build its own reservoir and silos, purchase its own trucks, have its own fuel tanks, run its own electricity generator, sometimes build its own road to access the main road to the airport or the main city, develop its own seed nurseries, and so on. None of these activities can be done on a small scale and none can be done in isolation. In a sophisticated economy the road is provided by the state or is supported by a toll on universal usage. The banking system earns income from all sorts of commercial activities, not just from the farmer. The electricity is generated for universal use and paid for by everyone – the city dweller, the local industrial unit, the school, the government office, not just the farmer. On the other hand, everything in the weak environment of the South can become economically distorted and most projects unviable. So, the entire environment needs to be improved and that means the dozens and dozens of different physical, economic and social activities that go to make up a well functioning country.

Where the international donors are involved in trying to overcome the challenges, one must be realistic. It will never be possible to coordinate the activities of several aid donors and international bodies at the level of their respective head offices. The very cacophony of multilateral, bilateral, regional and private donors results in overlap and confusion, and leads inevitably to groups, ministries, politicians vying with each other for influence and power. The effectiveness of grandest international initiatives and bodies can only be judged by the actual delivery of their mandate at the coalface, and that requires the strengthening of local offices which is where coordination can be implemented. For example, decisions as to where to open the new schools, how to recruit the teachers, set the curricula must be taken at local level, through a joint operation of the host government and a local office representing the external donors. At the moment too many decisions are taken at a point too far removed from the grassroots and do not take account of very mundane local needs.

Reforms at the international level

One of the major problems is that the multiplicity of activities in countries of the South involving international organisations and donors leads to contradictory demands on weak administrations. The main international bodies cannot be substantially reformed to become better agents for poverty reduction. The UN is the place where, for example, the US makes a deal with France over its intervention in Haiti and the US agrees that it will not interfere with French activities in Polynesia. That is realpolitik, but at least in theory at the UN everyone is on an equal footing and every country has one vote. What needs to change is for planning and decisions on specific programmes and projects to be carried out not in New York, Geneva or Nairobi, but at the level where it makes functional change, that is, as close as possible to site of the problems. We need also to separate clearly political decision-making from the practical implementation of such decisions. This already happens, in the political sphere for example in the separation and the implementation decisions regarding peacekeeping operations approved by the UN Security Council. It calls on Member States to offer troops, but then should leave it to the local commanders to take day-to-day decisions. In the development sphere should the UN decide that education is the first priority, it would be right for it to raise the necessary funds internationally, but the implementation of individual projects has to be left to the appropriate bodies in the different countries, at the coal face. We need to localise, not centralise. That means not adding to the central power of international bodies, but if anything, reducing it by narrowing the focus of their activities. Localising such actions could also lead to removing the layer of political interference because the challenges become more technocratic.

Reforms at the national level

Each country is governed by parallel sets of priorities: some will be dictated by the personal interests of ruling elites, some by ethnic considerations, some by physical challenges, most by their history. Every country has an ongoing agenda of activities that it must cope with. This would include the usual tasks of paying the salaries of its civil servants, maintaining existing schools, relations with neighbouring nations, ensuring sufficient energy supplies, keeping the army and the police happy. It is enough to stretch the weak administrative structures of most states. Many of the priorities translate into actions that one would not necessarily sympathise with, but short of physical conquest, the outsider has only a limited role to play in the determination of national priorities. In addition to this, poor countries have to invest to achieve this mythical 'development' under pressure both from their own people (or sections of their own people) and the international community. It represents a series of challenges that are extremely difficult to achieve. What we do have now, however, is the fact that all countries in the world, particularly the poorest and smallest ones, have accepted the MDGs and this offers an ideal framework within which changes can be encouraged.

Country-to-country management support

How can we get out of the crucial weakness in the body public, the impasse of lack of management ability in the public sector in most poor countries, lack of purchasing power, unsatisfactory approaches to tendering, inefficient delivery of services to the poor, nepotism, corruption, lack of transparency and some of the other problems that we have looked at in previous chapters? As we have seen, more aid at improving governments has not achieved its purpose.

I would like to propose that a radical new approach should be considered. Country-to-country deals should be struck between the North and the South where both wish to commit themselves to development. Every poor country should form a partnership with a developed country. Such partnership could include, for example, the US with Liberia, the UK with Sierra Leone, France with Ivory Coast, Switzerland with Rwanda, Norway with Mozambique, Sweden with Senegal, Ireland with Zambia. The direct deal between the Northern and the Southern countries should be for a defined period and transparent in its aim; it would result in stronger commitment on both sides. It would have to spell out in great details the objectives and targets that would have to be reached by given dates. This would be along the lines of what Britain did with Sierra Leone in 2000. The British Government sent small army detachments to support the reinstatement of the President who had been overthrown by rebels. In exchange, the British Government received assurances that basic issues of concern to all habitants of Sierra Leone, including the provision of water, health clinics, education, and local voting rights, would be re-instated. Britain then withdrew in 2002. With the benefit of hindsight, it is clear that the benefits were short lived because Britain withdrew too soon and the local structures in Sierra Leone proved too weak to carry out its part of the deal. They would have to last much longer than two years – possibly 20 to 25 years. The main advantage would be that aid and development would be delivered within a framework that would be made much more robust because of the presence of a major foreign partner able to offer the key missing element – efficient management.

Apart from the host government and the principal foreign partner, there would be a third party involved in the operation of the deal, namely, the international aid community represented by the UN Development Programme. The work of the international NGO community could be integrated in these national partnerships. This sort of bilateral deal would make individual efforts at aid giving and development much more coherent and effective. China, as we have seen, is much more deeply involved – and will be far more effective – in so many African countries because it offers a wide set of interventions, including long and short term investment, commercial and trading initiatives all under the one umbrella of state backing. The lack of coherence of Northern aid giving is doing no one any service, least of all the intended beneficiaries. In addition, the UK, the US, France, and the other major donors are each currently engaged in too many poor countries, and the result is that the level of aid given is too thin and too superficial.

The framework within which the two partners would work would be the priorities set out in the MDGs, priorities to which all forward-looking African governments are already subscribing. The partners should sign a legal agreement to remain engaged for a given number of years, detail into that contract the support that the Northern partner would offer in terms of skilled administrators, teachers, university staff, civil servants, police and army personnel over the life of the project. In other words, the help offered would be holistic and coherent and would spread over a range of sectors, not just the most glamorous. The agreements and operational progress would be subject to regular joint monitoring and public reporting under the supervision of an independent agency and a regional body such as the African Union.

Some countries simply would not find any such partners because they have not reached a stage at which this sort of partnership could work. This would be true for Nigeria and DR Congo, for example, because neither is at an institutional level of government where this sort of partnership with an OECD country could work. On the other hand, China might be a more powerful and organised foreign partner for either country simply because, as we have seen, it is able to coordinate public and commercial intervention in a manner that the West is not. This is not to advocate that all ties between the UK and Nigeria should be cut: there might well be viable long term links that should be pursued- perhaps a church in Britain or a school in France with their homologous bodies in Nigeria. At the wider level though, any bilateral or multilateral official aid to Nigeria must be seen as being ineffective in the general miasma of corruption and venality of the governing classes.

The proposal of a joint partnership for development between a rich and a poor country will be viewed in some quarters as re-establishing colonialism. Yet one could strongly argue that well-planned deals, with contracts to deliver certain specific items of aid and development – so many kilometres of main road or railways, so many water reservoirs, so many houses – with detailed provisos on local involvement and participation, would be a much better way to monitor whether the MDGs are being achieved and to ensure their final fulfilment. It is estimated that for some of the poorest countries the amount of aid they receive is equivalent to about half of government spending[29]. More effective administration would make that input much more productive and the partnership would lead to more inputs. The size of the economies of so many countries in Africa is very small; the budget of the London Borough of Southwark is about the same as that of Malawi or Eritrea[30] and the total economy of sub-Saharan Africa is about the same as that of greater London.

Consequently, the UK could start with perhaps two or three countries in Africa that are willing to join in this experiment. Other countries will be more than keen to follow suit if they see that it can work, and there would appear to be some countries with which such a partnership could work easily; Ghana, Tanzania, Uganda, Malawi for example would be some of the candidate countries for the UK to link with that come to mind. The comprehensive involvement of a developed country would also lead to more private businesses from the rich partner. Only a radical departure such as this can break the impasse in which most of the poorest countries, particularly those in sub-Saharan Africa, find themselves: that which arises from competing demands on limited budgets and conflicting international pressures.

Local development offices

The first step in the implementation of such a partnership would be the establishment of a joint office in the Southern partner country to deal with planning and execution. It would be part of the contract that all external aid would be channelled through such an office. A strong local office would be able to resist corruption and institute transparency because of the staff that would have to be recruited from both partners. Over time, such offices would become more sophisticated at dealing with local problems, through institutional memory and experienced staff. If the international community agrees to give what it gives to, say, Malawi entirely through the one coordinating office in Lilongwe, Malawi will start to see real benefits in a short space of time. In addition, if the Government of Malawi has agreed to a proposal with UNESCO that a new university will be built within its territory, what matters is that it should be established quickly within the Malawian rules and regulations, not those of the head office of UNESCO in Paris. The local joint development office would have the task to implement the projects and ensure that they are integrated into national priorities. Strengthening local planning and development offices will make it much more possible for the economic priorities of weaker partner to be pursued and protected from the day to day vagaries of political decisions and even of political interference. This is where coordination could achieve an even more important role; committed support from international agencies would offer a viable alternative to weak national and local government planning infrastructure.

Setting up a longer term commitment would also be a way to enable a deeper involvement; if a country has decided to provide universal education over a 10-year period, the task needs to be broken down, say, into 500 primary schools, 50 secondary schools, 10 teacher training colleges, and so on. That could mean that many more teachers, some young and inexperienced, and others more experienced, could be brought in from the richer partner. As we have seen in a previous section, it is cheaper to build one road of 1,000 kilometres than 50 roads of 20 kilometres each, but a developing society will usually gain far more from the latter than the former. Those specific targets can then be subcontracted to national or international development organisations with a clear target that they will be out of the country within 20 or 25 years. It could also be a way to ensure that more people in the donor partner who might originate from the Southern partner become involved; this would mean that a Ghanaian living in Britain would be keener to go back to Ghana under this sort of umbrella partnership than attempt to go back on his/her own. It would enable the integration of a Northern national health service with the health services of a Southern partner, rather than removing its ablest personnel. This sort of initiative would be easier when a capable Northern partner provides the umbrella for a comprehensive development partnership.

CHAPTER TWENTY

Meeting the basic needs of the poor

There are governments in some of the poorest countries in the world that have shown a determination to tackle the issues of poverty head on; Rwanda, Malawi, Ethiopia are certainly in this group. There are others where clearly there is no such intention: North Korea and Burma spring to mind. A partnership for development should start with those countries where there is a determined approach to engage in development. Even if the country-to-country partnerships proposed in the previous chapter are difficult to realise, the larger international voluntary agencies should enter into partnership with national governments or local authorities to carry out an agenda for development. To transform themselves from agents of relief to agents of development might force them to restrict the number of countries in which they operate. They would also have to integrate much more closely their operations with those of other voluntary bodies and with those of the host nations. Both measures, however, should be welcome.

There are three key areas round which a sound development policy can be built. They should become the urgent targets of governments and non-state actors. The first step must be to grow much more food to avoid massive famines. The second must be education: it is the base on which all long term development can be built. The third must be job creation to ensure longer term survival. In each case there are several measures that non-state actors, in spite or perhaps because they are smaller and thus more supple, could lead the way. Once they have started their operation, the wider and more expensive measures could be introduced by governments.

Ensuring food security

If the international community, through bodies such as the World Food Programme (WFP), ceased to purchase grains and other food from the rich countries that have been encouraged to accumulate surpluses, and instead were to place orders for the same items of foodstuff from producers in the South, within a few years they would help kick-start development on the land. The WFP until recently was making it impossible for small-scale local producers in the South to compete against imported food. In the last few years the Gates Foundation has made funds available to the WFP to purchase food locally. This is an example that other international private voluntary organisations should and could copy. At a later stage governments of the North in conjunction with governments of the South should replicate such initiatives by providing the funds with which to create a virtuous circle leading to food independence in each of the countries that are traditionally short of food – and that means most of Africa. But Southern governments alone will not in the short term have the funds or the capacity to intervene to kick-start this cycle of activity. Very few local investment vehicles are strong enough to invest in agriculture to a substantial extent. Foreign enterprises that might be interested in investing in the South are not sufficiently attracted to supply a purely domestic market, where the profits will by definition be very low and the risks very high. The greater the degree of political and economic uncertainty, the less likely it is that the investor will be willing to risk capital. (Interestingly, daring venture investors who have been putting money into Africa seem to be doing very well and were getting better returns in 2007 and 2008 than by investing elsewhere[31].) Intergovernmental agencies do not have funds or the jurisdiction – they can only provide advice. Therefore, in the immediate future food security for the poorest will be dependent on bilateral government-funded schemes and external non-profit agents. Both need to find ways to boost the productivity of the small farmer.

There are two different but complementary approaches that development agencies could take. The first is to lobby locally and internationally so as to ensure that in normal circumstances food should never be donated from outside any given area, but procured within it. Farmers in most cases would grow more food, climate permitting, if they only had an assured market. The traditional working of the open international market would kill off, and has killed off, the development of any such attempt at food security; dumping surplus food on the markets of the poor, as the EU has done for years, is adding to the numbers of those who will be poor. But the lesson is clear: in the short and medium term, local farmers must be assured of purchases. In other words a guarantee is required that if contracted quantities of food are supplied at contracted times, a pre-agreed price will be paid. Although difficult, this process would be effective in enabling the small local farmer to scale up. This practice could be followed by the many bodies that work in agricultural development on the ground. The approach requires planning on a long-term basis and the willingness to support the price shortfall. In the early part of 2008 farmers in Kenya were not prepared to plant more food, in spite of the offers of the WFP to buy it, because they were not sure that the price would hold. This outgrower mode of operation is common in many countries in Africa and is the way by which most of the produce Europe receives from Africa are grown. The middleman provides the common services of storing, packing, transporting the produce. Development agencies could for a determined time become the middleman or contract someone to do it on their behalf.

The second approach should be for the NGOs themselves to invest in land through specifically established investment vehicles, and develop agriculture on a major scale. They should use the techniques of private enterprise, and, even more importantly, harness its discipline of contractual obligations. Private enterprises tend to be far more efficient than governmental bodies and charities, their planning is clearer and their aims are more specific. One could envisage such an investment body working backwards from receiving a guaranteed order from a major customer – a body such as the host government, the WFP, the EU or a bilateral aid donor – to leasing so many thousands of acres of land. The investor/NGO should be thus able to borrow internationally the funds required for investment against such firm guaranteed purchases. They would then take the responsibility to invest in water and other infrastructure, as well as the more direct food production tools (nurseries, organic manure supplies, warehouses).

To implement the policy outlined above, NGOs would have to negotiate with host governments to obtain rights of tenure on those lands for at least 25 years. There are countries where there is land available for leasing, including Mozambique, Malawi and Ethiopia, and the first projects could start in these or other countries where governments are able to offer long-term leases. Each such investment should be between, say, 15,000 and 25,000 hectares to ensure economically viable units of operation. A large tract of land, say, in Malawi would have a contract to produce perhaps 20,000 tons of maize, 10,000 tons of sorghum, 3,000 tons of potatoes and so on, contracted to be purchased at each harvest over the following five years. There would thus be four parties to each such deal; the host national government, the local or regional government, the investor, and the donor/purchaser. Such deals should be undertaken in the full glare of the media. A body such as AGRA [page 176] could draw up a model agreement and statesmen of international stature, including Kofi Annan (who is Chairman of AGRA) with his iconic status in Africa, should be brought into the picture as a court of arbitration in case of disputes. There are now bodies such as the Council of World Elders, established in July 2007 by Nelson Mandela, or the Ibrahim Foundation who could play a similar role, enabling elder statesmen from African countries and elsewhere to ensure that Southern governments do not feel colonised by Northern corporations.

Once the investors have acquired the land, they would in effect become powerful players in the areas under their control. Apart from ensuring long term food supplies, such investment would inject cash into the local economy. The employer would pay a weekly wage for the work rendered and villagers would become more independent. The managers could do all the things that are needed, such as better water management, building of local roads and transport facilities, silos for storing food, appliances powered by solar energy because these are all inputs required for producing food more effectively. They could become model employers: train their workers and enable them to gain a financial stake in their projects, introduce organic manure projects to transform waste vegetable materials into fertilisers, devise a range of microfinance schemes among their workers. By having to follow the discipline of the market, the investors would have to ensure that funds are not wasted and would have to calculate how to deliver those services in the most effective manner. The discipline of the private sector can achieve these where the public realm cannot. If the operation is on a sufficiently large scale, hand-tool making could be developed locally. Through the shareholding scheme, the workers would in effect buy back the lease from the investor.

There are interesting precedents for all these proposals in projects all over the world. Rather than endless investigation, what is required is wider application of farming techniques that are already known to work, and more efficiency in delivery. The propagation of such techniques would be more rapidly and successfully achieved by encouraging the development of local social organisations, from cooperatives to women's groups, from trade unions to school committees. If workers were paid for their work in part through vouchers to be redeemed for food purchases or other locally made items, this would boost local demand and redistribute local purchasing power. Such schemes are again being reintroduced in some cities across Europe, particularly Germany and the UK, but also in other parts of the world under different names. In many parts of the world they are known as community exchange networks, and in the UK as 'lets'; vouchers are redeemed with local shops and local service providers and the spend thus remains within the local economy.

Within the estates that have been described above, there would be groups of villagers who would need support, because they would not be able to compete for work with able bodied workers. They would include the physically handicapped, the older and younger members of the communities. But within a wider operation, jobs for the less mobile members of the community could be found and the social protection schemes that have been mentioned in an earlier chapter could be applied; partner NGOs could be brought in. The commercial discipline of paying a good wage for good work would thus be complemented by some other partner with relief help. Strengthening such vehicles would ensure that the poorest are not forgotten and would improve the delivery mechanism of relief.

Education

Education has been neglected by the international aid community and must be given the highest such priority by development organisations. A massive injection of funds into education is urgently required throughout the poor world and could be deployed in a relatively short time. Most countries have plans to expand education, but are desperately short of teachers. Foreign donors should meet the costs of employing local teachers and of seconding more of their own staff once a detailed jointly worked detailed education plan. Widely spread education at the primary and secondary levels will transform the aspirations, skills and job opportunities of millions of people in a matter of a few years. It will improve agriculture, education, health, planning, but also governance and democracy. It will reduce the rate of population growth. A better coordinated effort would enable a Northern partner, for example the UK, to join the secondary education system in Ghana with its counterpart in the UK. It was estimated that some 53,000 young Britons (aged 18 to 24) were on short or medium term secondments in the South in mid 2009[32]. Too many of them are like paratroopers who descend from the sky and eventually return to the sky or wherever they came from. As part of a well-thought out comprehensive development plan voluntary organisations from the UK could offer more computers to more schools and more villages and such initiative would then become a genuine development project and not a one-off donation.

It is sad that so few people from ethnic minorities who have left their countries are financially able to volunteer to work abroad, simply because too few of them can afford to work without a paid reward. One of the most interesting initiatives in the aid field is a programme undertaken by the UNDP called TOKTEN[33]. Under this scheme, nationals from poor countries who have migrated to rich countries are seconded to work in their countries of origin for defined periods on a local allowance without losing benefits back in their new country.

This is the sort of programme that voluntary agencies should be supporting; it would be one immediate way by which the South could be compensated in some way by the loss of qualified people. The Ghanaian doctors in our society should be encouraged to spend time back in Ghana. Ghana gives Britain more aid through the skilled medical personnel it loses to Britain than Britain gives in aid to Ghana [see page 44]. A capable person of Ghanaian origin who might be working in the UK could be a more effective teacher within a shorter period of time in Ghana than the ablest non-Ghanaian. Eventually, a national service corps would be able to deliver teachers and nurses to villages year after year, provide operatives who would keep the water pumps functioning, introduce the most basic health prevention measures.

Jobs

Amartya Sen showed quite clearly that in times of famine it is not that food becomes scarcer – although it might; it is that access to food for the poorest becomes much more difficult. If you have no money, you starve. Economic independence is the basis of personal independence, not the other way round. The challenge therefore is to enable poor people to acquire the means to earn an income; in other words, millions of jobs must be created across the poor world[34]. There is an exact alignment, on the one side, between the need to ensure food security, provide shelter, meet the demand for water and sanitation – all the basic needs of the poorest – and, on the other side, the opportunity to kick-start the cycle of local economic development by using local manpower to provide the powerless with an income. An ambitious programme of investment in food security would feed people and at the same time absorb into employment millions of people who cannot be sustained by traditional farming alone. There is generally a long way to go before any form of major industrialisation as the North understands it (that is to say, processing and manufacturing) can be attained. There are some exceptions of course, and what Lesotho is doing now is evidence of this: thousands of jobs have been created there through direct links with companies in the North. The real conundrum, of course, is that those jobs depend on the demand in remote parts of the world, the very parts of the world that will be hit in the recession that started in 2008. Many of those jobs will simply disappear forever.

The largest number of jobs within the poor countries must be created in activities closely linked with the land. Public works to serve local communities – road building, water projects, schools, clinics and silos could be initiated. About 40 per cent of Asian agriculture is irrigated, compared with four per cent in Africa; here is the first challenge[35]. Plant nurseries would satisfy farming needs. Organic composting of waste from vegetation or animal sources could provide cheap fertilisers. Forestry would contribute to the development of timber-based industries of furniture making and house building. Animal husbandry would form the basis of meat and leather industries. A thriving brick-making facility would enable the erection of better houses. Even if in the worst cases such income generation were not sustained, it would have demonstrated the potential of an income-based economy and would have injected some cash into the economic system, together with examples of what could be achieved. It would create markets; for example, people working on road building need to purchase food. It would enable people to start to specialise, even if at the lowest level of skills – road building, stone crushing, well drilling, and so on. It would also, and this is no mean achievement, revalue the status of rural areas against that of the city.

Generating local purchasing power

Until about mid 2008, when Keynesian economics became acceptable again, the doctrine of market infallibility had dominated both national and international agenda for a good quarter of a century. The main reason why economies in the poorest countries in the South have not developed is that the key lesson of Keynesian economics has not been applied by the international community and Southern governments do not have the resources to implement it – even if they wished to. In line with Keynes, demand must be stimulated to produce what is wanted or needed, but particularly food. Economic development in the South must start from the demand side. Keynes famously said that in situations of persistent unemployment, people should be paid to dig holes in the street and others to fill them in. The same principle should be applied in the South. But efforts at job creation imply good development planning. In poor countries overall decisions, as we have seen, need to remain in the hands of central government, but this needs to be accompanied by detailed local economic capacity. Boosting supply-side in the context of the South – producing items for a non-existent local market or for a distant market – is seldom a choice. The private sector in most small economies cannot start the ball rolling because it tends to be too small and too weak, and medium-size private enterprises that could respond to local needs and local opportunities do not exist or are not under local control. A market for some of even the more basic needs – say, simple clothing or sandals – cannot develop in the absence of any purchasing power. The banking sector that in the more sophisticated environment is often the midwife of economic development is not appropriate because it is not responsive to local demands. As we have seen in chapter 8, the distant market is not an option to small producers, especially where, for a variety of reasons, their cost basis is too high, as is the case for most of inland Africa.

In the previous chapter we have looked at the enormous obstacle of land tenure. It is vital that a land ownership system be introduced as soon as possible at national level. If the foreign donor is required to pay for the entire operation, so be it. It is the only way in which the longer-term measures of environmental protection for everyone, but particularly the weakest, can be introduced. This includes the building of dams, reservoirs and canals, roads, forests, seed nurseries, and local power stations. So long as there remains uncertainty over land tenure, none of these long term measures can be accomplished and therefore one of the major vehicles for creating millions of jobs cannot be implemented.

A concluding comment

The sort of deal advocated in the previous chapter, under which a developed country would form a partnership with a poor country, would enable a more holistic approach to the challenge of development than anything being done at present. It would enable many of the measures that at present are treated in isolation to be brought back together. It would be most fundamental challenge to existing hierarchies and the feudal conditions of many Southern societies because it would offer alternative approaches. There would be radical improvements in the delivery of services and in the approach to solving the needs of the poorest, not because the people of the North are integrally more honest or efficient than those of the South, but because they have developed more efficient tools for delivery and more checks and balances into the system. I have no doubt that it would enable a greater cross-section of people from the North to become personally engaged with people in the South. The continuing engagement of teacher with teacher, pupil with pupil would lead to profound changes on both sides. The army from the Northern partner would be able to undertake join training exercises with the Southern partners, the police of one with the police of the other.

It is unlikely that the dramatic changes require will be implemented any day soon. I would hope however that non-state actors from the North, particularly some of the larger voluntary agencies in the EU and in the USA, could sharpen their targets and genuinely attack some of the key bottlenecks that are preventing millions of people in the South from achieving any form of development and thus of liberation.

REFERENCES

PART ONE

1 According to UNESCO, the cost of educating all of the world's children at primary level by 2015 will require between $8 billion and $15 billion extra spending per year. UNESCO, December 2007. US consumers spend about $30 billion per year and Europeans about $11 billion on ice cream, Worldwatch Institute, 2004

2 Amartya Sen; Development as Freedom, OUP 1999

3 The World Bank, 25 August 2008

4 Professor Townsend, London School of Economics, Discussion Paper 18 in the series of Issues in social protection; Lessons from OECD experience in low-income countries, 2006

5 FAO paper submitted to the World Food Summit, Treviso, Italy, April 2009

6 The figure comes from a report by CAFOD entitled 'Dumping on the Poor', 2002. In the EU the average dairy cow received $2.20 per day. The figure is the total value of support, including price support, cash subsidy to farmers, other subsidies. OECD and Commission of the European Communities, 2001

7 Chronic Poverty Research Centre, July 2008

8 World Health Organization, October 2008

9 Quoted in New York Times, 20 January 2008

10 Womankind Worldwide; Afghan Women and Girls seven years on, February 2008

11 Dr Teshale Tiberu; The Making of Modern Ethiopia, 1896-1974 – Red Sea Press, 1995 – makes the same point very well in accepting that as a member of one privileged ethnic group, he is writing from the vantage view of that ethnic group and will not even be able to attempt to pay justice to the other ethnic groups of his country

12 The World Bank; Voices of the Poor from Many Lands, February 2002

13 Joseph O'Hanlon and Teresa Smart; Do bicycles equal development in Mozambique? James Currey, August 2008

14 Annual Meeting of the American Geophysical Union, San Francisco, December 2008

15 Dr James Lovelock; The Revenge of Gaia, Allen Lane, 2006

16 United Nations Development Programme; Human Development Report 2006

17 HM Government; The Stern review of the economics of climate change, 30 October 2006

18 UNICEF UK, briefing, February 2009

19 The feeding of the Nine Billion. Global food security for the 21st century. A Chatham House report. Alex Evans, January 2009

20 Land Grab or Development Opportunity? Agricultural Investments and International Land Deals in Africa, IIED, May 2009

21 The Economic Observer on line, June 2008

22 The Independent Supplement, December 2008

23 Joint report by WHO and UNICEF, Geneva, July 2008

24 IIED Briefing, March 2009

25 Water supply, water demand and agricultural water scarcity in China, International Water Management Institute, New Delhi, December 2005

26 Ditto as per reference 25

27 HMG; Commission for Africa; report, April 2005

28 Razia Khan, Africa Analyst, Standard & Chartered Bank, February 2009

29 British Government Chief Scientist, Prospect Magazine, November 2008

30 National Geographic Magazine, October 2007

31 Return of the Population Growth factor, Report of the Hearings by the all Party Parliamentary Group on Population, Development and Reproductive Health, January 2007

32 Peter Popham, The Independent, May 2007

33 African Development Bank; Annual Report 2008

34 Estimated deaths attributable to selected environmental risk factors, by WHO Member States, 2002

35 Booz, Allen, Hamilton; Light! Water! Motion!, April 2007

36 David Molyneux and Alan Fenwick, Public Library of Science and Medicine, October 2005

37 Rachel Carson, Silent Spring, Fawcett Crest 1964

38 UNAIDS, December 2008

39 Camilla Toulmin, Director of the IIED, Beyond any Drought, July 2007

40 MEDACT; The International Migration of Health Workers, a Human Rights Analysis, February 2005

41 WHO Regional Office for Africa; Migration of Health Professionals in 6 countries; a synthesis report, April 2006

42 Soros Foundation network Annual Report, 2006

43 Daniel Kaufmann, The Brookings Institution, June 2009 (quoted in the New York Times, 21 June 2009)

44 IANSA, OXFAM, Saferworld; Africa's missing billions, 2007

45 Alastair Darling, Chancellor of the Exchequer, speaking in Brussels May 2008, referring to figures for 2006. Daily Telegraph, May 2008

46 Figures from the OECD Monitor. It is difficult to be precise about the amounts, as there are indirect subsidies that do not figure in the totals of subsidies on their own, such as is support for agricultural research and food inspectorates.

47 Joseph Stiglitz, Globalisation and its discontents, W. Norton, W. W. & company, 2002

48 Ha-Joon Chang; Bad Samaritans, Random House, 2007. See also; Professor Robert H. Wade;

REFERENCES

Governing the Market, Princeton University Press, 2006

49 Raj Patel; Stuffed and Starved, Portobello 2007 gives much evidence of this exploitation

50 I was then working at the Economist Intelligence Unit – part of the Economist group – and we were forever looking at project proposals in Africa and Asia

51 Susan George; A Fate Worse Than Debt, Penguin 1988 and The Debt Boomerang, Pluto Press, 1992

52 OECD Secretariat; paper prepared for the G8 meeting in L'Aquila, July 2009

53 World Bank paper in preparation for the Monterrey Conference on Finance for Development, 26 February 2002

54 Raymond W. Baker; Capitalism's Achilles Heel; Dirty Money and How to Renew the Free-market System, John Wiley and Sons, 2005

55 Global Integrity Annual Report, 2008

56 Craig Murray; Murder in Samarkand, Mainstream, 2006

57 UNODC; World Drug Report 2009

58 David Batstone; Not for Sale: The return of the global slave trade and how we can fight it, Harper's, San Francisco, 2007

59 Misha Glenny; McMafia; Crime without frontiers. The Bodley Head, February 2008

60 Home Office report on illegal drugs, 21 November 2007

61 Professor Bob Picciotto, formerly Vice-president of the World Bank, Evidence to the House of Commons, December 2004

62 Christian Aid: False profits; robbing the poor to keep the rich tax-free, March 2009

63 An interesting study of the rise of the middle classes in India undertaken by Chakravarthi Ram-Prasad appears in the September 2007 issue of Prospect magazine. The novel 'Q&A' (on which the film 'Slumdog Millionaire' was loosely based) is another examination of the contempt of the rich classes v. the poor of India

64 Survival International, annual report 2006

65 Richard Wilkinson and Kate Pickett's, The Spirit Level, Allen Lane, 2009

66 The Ibrahim Index of African Governance, the Mo Ibrahim Foundation, September 2008

67 Chatham House; International Affairs quarterly, volume 72, No 3, 1996

68 UNDP: Human Development Report 2004

69 Graham Robb: The discovery of France, Picador, 2007

70 David Woodward and Andrew Simms: Growth isn't working: the unbalanced distribution of costs and benefits from economic growth, New Economics Foundation, January 2006

71 Jon Maguire; The Justi Plan, cru, 2002 is a novel that takes this issue to its logical end

72 Robert Cassen and Associates; Does Foreign Aid Help? Report undertaken for the IMF 1986

73 Roger Riddell; Does Foreign Aid Really Work? OUP 2007

74 I must declare an interest as I was a director of War on Want at the time when it exposed the scandal, in the mid 1970s

75 Report of the Panel of Experts on the Illegal exploitation of natural resources and other forms

of wealth of the Democratic Republic of Congo, April 2001 (the report has been amended and added to frequently over the years)

76 OXFAM America, January 2009

77 Organic Consumers Association; Cotton subsidies and Cotton Problems, February 2004

PART TWO

1 Professor Christopher Dyer; Making a living in the Middle Ages, Yale University Press, 2002

2 Gregory Clark: A Farewell to Alms, Princeton University Press, 2007

3 Lawrence E. Harrison; The central liberal truth; how politics can change a culture and save it from itself, OUP USA, 2006

4 Gregory Clark, op. cit.

5 The World Bank, Human Development Report 2008 is all about agriculture. It is a vital document and should be read by anyone who is interested in development at the grass-roots

6 Joseph Stiglitz and Andrew Charlton; Fair trade for all. How Trade can promote Development. OUP USA, November 2005

7 George Soros; The New Paradigm for Financial Markets: The Credit Crisis of 2008 and What It Means. Public Affairs, October 2008

8 Mange Tout, Director: Mark Brozel, Dispatches, 1997

9 Dr Alexander Phiri, Agricultural University of Malawi, in a report for Africa Invest, June 2007. I worked for Africa Invest, a fund investing in agriculture in Africa, from June 2007 to October 2008

10 Muhammad Yunus; Banker to the poor: Micro-lending and the battle against World Poverty, Perseus Publishing, 2009

11 One of the bodies studying these issues is the Gatsby Foundation, the largest British philanthropic funds investing in agriculture in Africa

12 Some extremely poor people in the slums of Lagos (which is as poor as you can get) have formed self-help groups to employ teachers to teach their children

13 This joke was told to me by Michael Kapessa, but I understand that it has existed for sometime in international circles

14 The Observer, 28 October 2007

15 Joseph Stiglitz; Globalisation and its discontent, New York, Norton, 2002

16 Land tenure; Changes in 'Customary' Land Tenure Systems in Africa, edited by Lorenzo Cotula, IIED, 2007

17 International Poverty Centre; 'The unresolved land reform debate' Research Brief no 2, November 2006

18 See House of Commons Select Committee on International development, Report on Water and Sanitation, July 2007

19 See the Forum Europe-Latin America organised by FRIDE, Madrid, for a full exploration of these issues, February 2008

20 Hernando de Soto; The mystery of capitalism; why capitalism triumphs in the North and fails everywhere else. New York: Basic Books, 2000

REFERENCES

21 Op. cit.

22 Paul Collier; 'The Bottom Billion', OUP, 2007

23 It is not just an Anglo-Saxon challenge; Armand Rioust de Largentaye from the Agence Française de Développement highlighted it as one of the challenges faced by the French government at a seminar at ODI, 15 January 2009

24 The highly descriptive term was coined by the International Crisis Group

25 I am indebted to Professor Lord Desai of the London School of Economics for a tutorial on this issue during our shopping at East Dulwich Sainsbury's

26 Dambisa Moyo; Dead Aid, Allen Lane, February 2009

27 Vince Cable, MP; Annual meeting of the UN Association of the UK, 2004

28 Richard Dowden: Altered States, Ordinary Miracles, Portobello, September 2008

29 Linda Melvern; the Ultimate Crime. Wilson & Day Ltd, 1995

30 Cabinet Office information, February 2009

31 WHO estimated in early 2009 that one quarter of all medicines in poor countries were fake

32 Sonya Maldar; Rest in Pieces – police torture and deaths in custody in Nigeria. Human Rights Watch, July 2002, describes a horrifying system that is clearly out of control

33 For corruption in Africa, see the excellent book by Matthew Lockwood; The State they are in, Practical Action, 2007

34 Nick Mathiason, the Observer, January 2009

35 The issue has been well examined by George Soros' Open Society in its annual report for 2007

36 See the Report of the Africa Commission, April 2005

37 See Dr Ha-Joon Chan: Kicking Away the ladder, Development Strategy in Historical Perspective, Anthem Press, June 2002, for the arguments for protectionism in the early stages of development

38 I am greatly indebted to Dr Adotey Bing for making this crucial point

39 Dambisa Moyo op. cit.

40 Teddy Brett, London School of Economics on the BBC World Service series on Doing Business in Africa, February 2007

41 The World Bank; Business Environment Survey 2007, Private Sector Views

42 Mr Mervyn King, Governor of the Bank of England, April 2008 was one of the first influential voices to pronounce against the banking fraternity

43 Martin Wolf; The man who owns the news; inside the secret world of Rupert Murdoch, Random House, October 2008

44 Roger Riddell; Does Foreign Aid Really Work? OUP 2007

45 Ian Linden; Global Catholicism, C Hurst & Co, January 2009

46 The Economist, Annual report, 2007

47 The classic study was undertaken by David Dollar and Craig Burnside in 1997. 'Aid, policies and growth', Policy Research Working Paper series 1777, The World Bank

48 Stephen Browne; Aid and Influence: Do Donors Help or Hinder? Earthscan, 2006

49 Jo Ritzen, former Vice-President of the World Bank; A chance for the World Bank, 2005

50 Manuel Sanchez-Montaro; the Political Dimensions of hunger, FRIDE (Fundación para las Relaciones Internacionales y el Diálogo Exterior), Madrid, February 2009

51 World Bank's evaluation unit, Update 58

52 Linda Melvern, op. cit.

53 The matter has been very well analysed by Vidal Martin in a paper called 'African mistrust of Northern Justice' for FRIDE, Madrid, January 2009

54 US Congressional investigation, 2006

55 The Observer Food Supplement, May 2007 'How America is betraying the hungry children of Africa' paints a devastating picture of the consequences of donated food on Malawian farmers.

56 CARE: 16 August 2007

57 In June 2008 the US Congress rejected for the third time a proposal by the President to allow just 25% of US food aid funds to be used to purchase food abroad, Los Angeles Times, 16 June 2008

58 Chicago Council on Global Affairs, 25 February 1009

59 Ashraf Ghani and Clare Lockhart; Fixing Failed States, OUP, 2007

60 The UN Humanitarian Aid Co-ordinator, Jan Egeland, said a record 90 countries – many of them poor – contributed to the relief effort along with militaries from 36 nations and 500 non-governmental organizations from around the world. John Cosgrave estimates that there were closer to 180 international NGOs

61 AIMS (Afghanistan Information Management Services), February 2003

62 See for example: Yash Tandon; ending aid dependence. Fashamu Books, November 2008

63 Social protection in Africa, Frank Ellis et al, Edward Elgar Publishing Ltd, February 2009

64 Devereux & Call-Black: Effectiveness and Impact of Social transfer Schemes, DfID, June 2008

65 Information from Dr Saad Al-Harran, senior lecturer in Islamic Microfinance Project at the Centre for Islamic Banking, Finance and Management, Universiti Brunei Darussalam (UBD), July 2008

66 Indira Campos; The World To-day, Chatham House, June 2008

67 The Times, Leader, September 1983

PART THREE

1 Gunnar Myrdal, Asian Drama: An inquiry into the Poverty of Nations, New York: Twentieth Century Fund, 1968

2 Nassim Nicholas Taleb; The black swan: the impact of the highly improbable, Allen, June 2007

3 Gawdat Bahgat; Sovereign Wealth Funds, Journal of International Affairs, November 2008, and UNCTAD Investment Report 2008 (using 2007 figures)

4 James Kynge; China shakes the world, the rise of a hungry nation, Weidenfeld & Nicholson, 2006, gives many example of how this operates in China

5 Simon Caulkin in the Observer has written considerably on these issues and has been consistently brilliant

6 See for example; David Pryce-Jones, Middle East Quarterly, Spring 2004

7 New Economics Foundation; Migration and the remittances euphoria: development or dependency, London, 2006

8 World Bank, Migration and Remittances Factbook, 2007

9 The Economist, 7 November 2008

10 J.D. Fage, A History of Africa, Routledge, 4th edition, 2001

11 The American University in Cairo. Trasnational Broadcasting Studies. Civil Society in the Arab World, issue 4, Spring 2000

12 Will Hutton, the Observer, 25 January 2009

13 Martin Jacques: When China Rules the World: the Rise of the Middle Kingdom and the End of the Western World. Allen Lane, July 2009

14 Will Hutton, The writing on the Wall; China and the West in the 21st Century. Little Brown, January 2007

15 Jung Chang & Jon Halliday. Mao the unknown story. 'China was not only the poorest country in the world to provide aid, but its aid was the highest ever as a percentage of the donor country's per capita income' page 481. The bibliography quotes Copper Jon F., China's Foreign Aid, Heath, Lexington 1976 page 125, 3

16 The Economist, 11 July 2009

17 Pieter Bottelier; China's economic downturn. What lies ahead? The John Hopkins University, February 2009

18 Vince Cable: the Storm: The World Economic Crisis and What it Means. Atlantic Books, London, 2009

PART FOUR

1 Jean Francois Rischard: High Noon – 20 Global Problems, 20 years to solve. 2002, Perseus Books Group

2 US congressional investigation, July 2008

3 The Tobin Tax is named after the American Nobel Economics Laureate who first proposed it in the early 1970s as a way to reduce currency volatility in international capital movements. Tobin never associated himself with the proposals that the income thus generated would be devoted to the cause of the South

4 Aid, policies and growth, David Dollar and Craig Burnside, the World Bank, 1997

5 Frank McArthur; Angela's Ashes, Scribbner, 1996

6 Robert Zoellick, President of the World Bank, March 2009

7 Ms Josette Sheeran, Executive Director of the World Food Programme, Chatham House, March 2009

8 Oxfam, July 2009, based on World Bank information

9 Richard Dowden; Africa, Altered States Ordinary Miracles, September 2008, Portobello

10 John Darwin; After Tamerlane, The global history of Empires, Allen Lane, 2007

11 UN Arab Human Development Report, 21 July 2009

12 Panos; Missing the message, November 2003. The document explored a wide varieties of ways in which everyone could be taught about HIV/AIDS and ways to promote protection. It was the most widely read document ever produced by PANOS

13 Paolo Frere; Pedagogy of the Oppressed, 1968

14 Professor Patrick Chabal, Professor of Lusophone studies in the University of London, has written extensively on this subject. See for example his 'Reflections on African Politics. Disorder as a Political Instrument', in Encyclopaedia of African History, Routledge, 2004

15 Nigel Watt; Burundi; op. cit. and Richard Wilson; Titanic Express, Continuum, 2006, both describe the sense of continuing hatred and fear that pervade the peoples of both countries

16 Mrs Ngozi Okonjo-Iweala, Managing Director of the World Bank at the World Economic Forum in Davos, January 2009

17 Website of the Federal Government of Ethiopia

18 IIED; Promoting the re-greening of the Sahel, November 2007

19 WFP, July 2009

20 Alex Evans, Centre for International Cooperation, June 2009

21 FAO, 30 June 2009

22 AGRA, 2009

23 International Poverty Centre, Research brief no 2 November 2006; The unresolved land reform debate

24 I was involved in a World Bank project in Djibouti City in 1983 enabling local families to become owners of their plots in exchange for a payment that could be made over several years and would be used to bring modern water supply and sewerage to the city

25 Amartya Sen; Development as Freedom, OUP 1999

26 Glyn Roberts and Mark Smith; Keeping something alive, Tools for self-Reliance, September 2008

27 Report by Bernard Gray into the Ministry of defence procurement decisions, quoted in a Parliamentary debate, 6 August 2009

28 The Observer, 23 and 30 August 2009

29 Professor Adrian Wood, University of Oxford, Financial Times, 4 September 2008

30 The budgets of Malawi and Southwark for 2009-2010 are on page 189

31 Scipio African Investment, London, January 2009

32 The Independent, 2 August 2009

33 TOKTEN: Transfer of Knowledge Through Expatriate Nationals. It is run out of the United Nations Volunteers office in Bonn

34 International Poverty Centre; Jobs, jobs, jobs, the policy challenge, November 2008

35 Mohamed Bouvogui, IFAD, May 2008

INDEX